Question&Answer
EMPLOYMENT LAW

Develop your legal skills with Longman

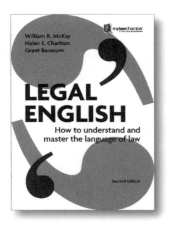

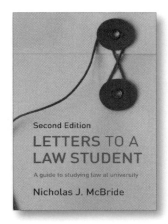

Law Express
Q&A

Question&Answer
EMPLOYMENT LAW

Jessica Guth
University of Bradford

Charanjit Singh-Landa
Ealing Law School

Longman
is an imprint of

PEARSON

Harlow, England • London • New York • Boston • San Francisco • Toronto • Sydney • Singapore • Hong Kong
Tokyo • Seoul • Taipei • New Delhi • Cape Town • Madrid • Mexico City • Amsterdam • Munich • Paris • Milan

Pearson Education Limited
Edinburgh Gate
Harlow
Essex CM20 2JE
England

and Associated Companies throughout the world

Visit us on the World Wide Web at:
www.pearsoned.co.uk

First published 2012

ISBN: 978-1-4082-4992-5

British Library Cataloguing-in-Publication Data
A catalogue record for this book is available from the British Library

Library of Congress Cataloging-in-Publication Data
A catalog entry for this book is available from the Library of Congress

10 9 8 7 6 5 4 3 2 1
15 14 13 12 11

Typeset in 9/12pt Helvetica Neue by 3
Printed and bound in Malaysia, CTP-KHL

Contents

Acknowledgements vii
What you need to do for every question in Employment Law viii
Guided tour x
Guided tour of the companion website xii
Table of cases and statutes xiv

Chapter 1: The sources and machinery of employment law 1

Chapter 2: The employment relationship 11

Chapter 3: The contract of employment 31

Chapter 4: Statutory employment rights 49

Chapter 5: Equality law 83

Chapter 6: Equal pay 111

Chapter 7: Wrongful dismissal 131

Chapter 8: Unfair dismissal 141

Chapter 9: Redundancy 167

Chapter 10: Transfer of undertakings 187

Chapter 11: Trade unions and their members 207

Chapter 12: Industrial action 227

Bibliography 245
Index 247

Supporting resources

Visit the **Law Express Question&Answer** series companion website at **www.pearsoned.co.uk/lawexpressqa** to find valuable student learning material including:

■ Additional **essay and problem questions** arranged by topic for each chapter give you more opportunity to practise and hone your exam skills.

■ **Diagram plans** for all additional questions assist you in structuring and writing your answers.

■ **You be the marker** questions allow you to see through the eyes of the examiner by marking essay and problem questions on every topic covered in the book.

■ Download and print all **Attack the question** diagrams and **Diagram plans** from the book.

Also: The companion website provides the following features:

■ Search tool to help locate specific items of content.

■ E-mail results and profile tools to send answers to friends and tutors.

■ Online help and support to assist with website usage and troubleshooting.

For more information please contact your local Pearson sales representative or visit **www.pearsoned.co.uk/lawexpressqa**

Acknowledgements

The authors would like to thank their friends and families for their patience and support throughout this project. Jessica would particularly like to thank Ann Blair for sharing tried and tested questions and for her expertise and guidance which started my employment law journey. Charanjit would particularly like to thank his parents, his niece Sheetal, Surinder and all those who are forever an inspiration to him and his writing. Thanks must also go to the reviewers who no doubt helped to improve this book and to Zoë Botterill and her team at Pearson for their invaluable efforts.

Publisher's acknowledgements

Our thanks go to all reviewers who contributed to the development of this text, including students who participated in research and focus groups which helped to shape the series format.

What you need to do for every question in Employment Law

Employment law is a popular subject and something that most of us can relate to. This is both a great advantage and disadvantage. Most of us have some basic knowledge of employment law and what our rights as employees are. Some of us also have experience of being employers and the vast amount of regulation that must be complied with. All of us can somehow relate to the world of work and this can make it easier to remember the relevant legal provisions.

However, the employment law field is also fast moving and complex so there is a great amount of confusion about some areas and knowledge can quickly become out of date. You must therefore keep up to date with the legal provisions and ensure you use recent case examples and recent academic commentary as discussed throughout your course to back up any points you make.

Problem questions are popular in employment law. Don't be tempted to base your answer on what the media thinks the law is or on what you have experienced in your own life; make sure you really do learn the legal provisions and apply them. Many of the basic employment law principles come from common law and you should be aware of the common law and contractual underpinnings of employment law. You must also recognise, though, that there has been a huge expansion of statutory employment law in recent years.

Essay questions often focus on the effectiveness of the law in a particular area and here you can really show off your wider reading and knowledge of the context. You can use your general knowledge and experience to highlight areas where practice perhaps differs from the law as it is presented in textbooks. You should also acknowledge the contribution that other academic disciplines such as Human Resource Management and Business Studies can make to your understanding of employment law. Finally, remember that standpoints and backgrounds are important in shaping views. Employers, employees, ministers and trade union officials may view the same piece of legislation or the same case very differently. If you acknowledge this and explore these issues, you will demonstrate a wide and detailed knowledge of this area of law.

Good luck!

Guided tour

What you need to do for every question in employment law

Employment law is a popular subject and something that most of us can relate to. This is both a great advantage and disadvantage. Most of us have some basic knowledge of employment law and what our rights as employees are. Some of us also have experience of being employers and the vast amount of regulation that must be complied with. All of us can somehow relate to the world of work and this can make it easier to remember the relevant legal provisions.

However, the employment law field is also fast moving and complex so there is a great amount of confusion about some areas and knowledge can quickly become out of date. You must therefore keep up to date with the legal provisions and ensure you use recent case examples and recent academic commentary as discussed throughout your course to back up any points you make.

Problem questions are popular in employment law. Don't be tempted to base your answer on what the media thinks the law is or on what you have experienced in your own life; make sure you really do learn the legal provisions and apply them. Many of the basic employment law principles came from common law and you should be aware of the common law and contractual underpinnings of employment law. You must also recognise, though, that there has been a huge expansion of statutory employment law in recent years.

Essay questions often focus on the effectiveness of the law in a particular area and here you can really show off your wider reading and knowledge of the context. You can use your general knowledge and experience to highlight areas where practice perhaps differs from the law as it is presented in textbooks. You should also acknowledge the contribution that other academic disciplines such as Human Resource Management and Business Studies can make to your understanding of employment law. Finally, remember that standpoints and backgrounds are important in shaping views. Employers, employees, ministers and trade union officials may view the same piece of legislation or the same case very differently. ■

What to do for every question – Find out the key things you should do and look for in any question and answer on the subject in order to give every one of your answers a great chance from the start.

1

The sources and machinery of employment law

How this topic may come up in exams

The first topic to be covered in employment law courses is often an examination of the sources of employment law and the machinery and institutions most relevant in this area. However, this topic does not appear in exams all that often. Rather, it is treated as background information. Where it is examined, you will usually have to evaluate the current system, comment on past reforms and suggest improvements or alternatives to the current system. Problem questions in this area are very rare.

How this topic might come up in exams – Learn how to tackle any question on this topic by using the handy tips and advice relevant to both essay and problem questions. In-text symbols clearly identify each question type as it occurs.

 Essay Question   **Problem Question**

Attack the question – Attack attack attack! Use these diagrams as a step by step guide to help you confidently identify the main points covered in any question asked.

Answer plans and Diagram plans – Clear and concise answer plans and diagram plans support the planning and structuring of your answers whatever your preferred learning style.

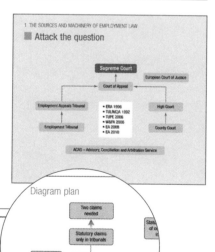

1 THE SOURCES AND MACHINERY OF EMPLOYMENT LAW

■ Attack the question

Diagram plan

Answer plan

→ Briefly consider tribunal jurisdiction before Trade Union Reform and Employment Act 1993 (TURERA).

→ What were the problems with the limits placed on tribunals?

→ Evaluate changes brought about by TURERA and subsequent reforms.

→ Do those changes address the problems indentified earlier?

→ What issues remain?

Answer with accompanying guidance – Make the most out of every question by using the guidance to recognise what makes a good answer and why. Answers are the length you could realistically hope to produce in an exam to show you how to gain marks quickly when under pressure.

Case names clearly highlighted – Easy to spot bold text makes those all important case names stand out from the rest of the answer, ensuring they are much easier to remember in revision and in the exam.

Make your answer stand out – Really impress your examiners by including these additional points and further reading to illustrate your deeper knowledge of the subject, fully maximising your marks.

Don't be tempted to … – Avoid common mistakes and losing easy marks by understanding where students most often trip up in exams.

Bibliography – Use this list of further reading to really explore areas in more depth, enabling you to excel in exams.

---

2 THE EMPLOYMENT RELATIONSHIP

Answer

Although many employment rights depend on being able to establish employee status, there is no useful statutory definition of 'employee'. The definition in the Employment Rights Act 1996 (ERA 1996), s 230(1) is circular and thus of little help. Definition of this important concept has therefore been left to the courts. A number of tests have been developed over time but application of the tests is not always easy. This essay briefly considers the situation before the case of **Carmichael v National Power [1999] HL** before examining the case itself and the case law following it in more detail to ascertain whether it is now easier to decide whether someone is an employee or not.

Historically the tests for employee status have developed from one of control (**Yewens v Noakes [1880] HC**) to one of integration (**Cassidy v Ministry of Health [1951] CA**) or economic reality (**Market Investigations Ltd. v Minister of Social Security [1969] HC**), culminating in the modern multi-factor test established

been of particular importance when considering cases of atypical work, agency and temporary work (see **Motorola Ltd v Davidson and Melville Craig Group Ltd [2001] EAT, McMeechan v Secretary of State for Employment [1997] CA, Montgomery v Johnson Underwood Ltd [2001] CA** and **Daces v Brook Street Bureau [2004] EAT, Cable & Wireless v Muscat [2006] CA, James v Greenwich LBC [2008] EAT**).

The second test that developed was the integration test (**Cassidy v Ministry of Health [1951] CA, Stevenson, Jordan and Harrison Ltd v MacDonald and Evans [1952]**). This test considers whether the work carried out is done as an integral part of the business. It seems straightforward but raises questions of definition. So, for example, it may not always be clear what is integral to the business

✓ Make your answer stand out

- Consider other factors such as attendance, performance, etc, in more detail, perhaps with more examples from case law you have discussed in your lectures.
- Expand your criticism of LIFO. Might this be age discrimination? Why do you think it is so durable as a concept?
- You could discuss discrimination in selection with reference to the Equality Act 2010 and the protected characteristics in more detail to really show how these areas of law interlink.
- Offer advice as to what you think would make a fair selection procedure. Consider what sort of selection grid or score card you could use and how that might operate.
- Make clearer the difference between having an established procedure which should be followed and situations where there is no procedure, where there is just an overall requirement of reasonableness. This would show a deeper understanding of the law.

Don't be tempted to...

- Outline what redundancy is or what the criteria for it are. The question is just about selection so that is where you have to focus your answer.
- Ignore LIFO (as some students do) because you think it is unfair, and focus on discussing what you think would be fairer. Given that LIFO is so often used, you really do need to engage with it fully.
- Go overboard with case examples. Some examples liven things up and illustrate your points, showing that you know the area of law well. If you give too many examples you risk running out of time and being too descriptive.

Bibliography

Brodie, D. (2004) 'Reflecting the Dynamics of Employment Relations: Terms Implied from Custom or Practice and the Albion Case', 33 ILJ 159
Brodie, D. (2008) 'Mutual Trust and Confidence: Catalysts, Constraints and Commonality', 37 ILJ 329
Cabrelli, D. (2007) 'Discretion, Power and the Rationalisation of Implied Terms', 36 ILJ 194
Davies, P. and Freedland, M. (1993) Labour Legislation and Public Policy (Oxford: OUP)
Deakin, S. and Morris, G. (2009) Labour Law, 5th edn (Oxford: Hart Publishing)
Department of Trade and Industry (1998) Fairness at Work (Cm 3968)
Dex, S. and Sheibl, F. (1998) 'Should We Have More Family Friendly Policies?' 16(5)

Guided tour of the companion website

 Book resources are available to download. Print your own **Attack the question** and **Diagram plans**

 Additional **Essay and Problem questions** with **Diagram plans** arranged by topic for each chapter give you more opportunity to practise and hone your exam skills. Print and email your answers.

 You be the marker gives you a chance to evaluate sample exam answers for different question types for each topic and understand how and why an examiner awards marks. Use the accompanying guidance to get the most out of every question and recognise what makes a good answer.

All of this and more can be found when you visit **www.pearsoned.co.uk/lawexpressqa**

Table of cases and statutes

■ Table of Cases

Abadeh *v* British Telecommunications plc [2000] All ER (D) 1456, EAT **97**

Abernethy *v* Mott, Hay and Anderson [1974] ICR 323, CA **149, 162**

Albion Case (2004) 33 ILJ 159 **36**

Alexander *v* Bridgen Enterprises Ltd [2006] ICR 1277, EAT **146**

Ali *v* Christian Salvesen Food Services Ltd [1997] 1 All ER 721, CA **216**

Allonby *v* Accrington and Rossendale College [2004] ECR I–873, ECJ **116, 119, 127**

American Cyanamid Co *v* Ethicon Ltd [1975] 1 All ER 504, HL **240**

Anderson *v* Pringle of Scotland Ltd [1998] IRLR 64, OH **185**

Anglian Homes Ltd *v* Kelly [2004] EWCA Civ 901, CA **146**

Attridge Law (A Firm0) *v* Coleman (2007) *The Times*, 12 January **103**

BBC *v* Hearn (1977) *The Times*, 20 May **234**

Barber *v* Guardian Royal Exchange Assurance Group (Case C–262/88) [1990] ICR 616 **116, 117**

Barton *v* Investec Henderson Crossthwaite Securities Ltd [2003] ICR 1205, EAT **120**

Bass Leisure Ltd *v* Thomas [1994] IRLR 104, EAT **180**

Bell *v* Lever Brothers [1932] AC 161, HL **39**

Berriman *v* Delabole Slate Ltd [1985] IRLR 305, CA **200, 203**

Best *v* Taylor Woodrow Construction [1975] IRLR 177, Ind Trib **184**

Betts *v* Brintel Helicopter Ltd [1997] 2 All ER 840, CA **192**

Bilka-Kaufhaus GmbH *v* Karin Weber von Hartz [1986] ECR 1607, ECJ **125**

Bloxham *v* Freshfields Bruckhaus Deringer (2006) 9 October, 2205086/2006, EAT **107**

Blue Circle Staff Association *v* Certification Officer [1977] 2 All ER 145 **210, 220, 223**

Blundell *v* The Governing Body of St Andrew's Catholic Primary School [2007] ICR 1451, EAT **53, 57, 62**

Boston Deep Sea Fishing *v* Ansell (1888) 39 Ch D 339, CA **37, 39, 164**

British Airways *v* Starmer [2005] IRLR 862, EAT **69**

British Airways plc *v* Unite the Union [2009] EWHC 3541 (QB) **240**

British Coal Corporation *v* Secretary of State for Trade and Industry, *ex parte* Price and Others [1994] IRLR 72, DC **180**

British Home Stores Ltd *v* Burchell [1980] ICR 303n, EAT **149, 154, 163**

British Labour Pump Ltd *v* Byrne [1979] IRLR 94, EAT **145, 146**

British Leyland (UK) Ltd *v* McQuilken [1978] IRLR 245, EAT **216**

British Telecommunications *v* Ticehurst, *see* Ticehurst *v* British Telecommunications

Brook and Others *v* London Borough of Haringey [1992] IRLR 478, EAT **185**

Bromley *v* Quick [1988] ICR 47, EAT **115, 124**

Brown *v* Welsh Refugee Council [2002] All ER (D) 21 (Jun), EAT **80**

Brunnhofer *v* Bank der Österreichischen Postsparkasse (Case C–381/99) [2001] ECR I-4961, ECJ **116, 120, 124**

Bunce *v* Postworth Ltd, t/a Skyblue [2005] EWCA Civ 490, CA **15**

Cable & Wireless v Muscat [2006] EWCA Civ 220, CA 28

Camelot Group plc v Centaur Communications Ltd [1998] 1 All ER 251, CA 78

Canniffe v East Riding of Yorkshire Council [2000] IRLR 555, EAT 94

Capper Pass v Lawton [1976] IRLR 366, EAT 114, 123

Carlin v St Cuthbert's Co-operative Association Ltd [1974] IRLR 188, NIRC 151

Carmichael and Leese v National Power plc [1999] 4 All ER 897, [2000] IRLR 43, HL 13–17, 20, 24, 25, 29

Cassidy v Minister of Health [1951] 2 KB 343, CA 14, 19, 24, 28

Chessington World of Adventure v Reed [1997] IRLR 556, EAT 87

Christel Schmidt v Spar-und Leihkasse der fruheren Amter Bordesholm, Kiel und Cronshagen (Case C–392/92) (1994) The Times, 25 May, ECJ 191, 192

Clark v BET plc [1997] IRLR 348, HC 139

Clark v Nomura International plc [2000] IRLR 766, CA 139

Clarke v Eley (IMI) Kynoch Ltd [1982] IRLR 482, EAT 185

Coleman v Attridge Law and Another (Case C–303/06) [2008] All ER (D) 245 (Jul), ECJ 61, 64, 102, 104

Commission v United Kingdom (Case 61/81) [1982] ECR 2601, ECJ 115

Commission of the European Communities v United Kingdom (Case 165/82) [1984] 1 All ER 353, ECJ 87

Cornwall CC v Prater [2006] EWCA Civ 102, CA 15–17, 29

Cotswold Developments Construction Ltd v Williams [2006] IRLR 181, EAT 16, 17

Courtaulds Northern Textiles v Andrew [1979] IRLR 84, EAT 35, 38, 43

Cox v Wildt Mellor Bromley Ltd [1978] IRLR 157, EAT 170, 175, 180, 183

Croft v Consignia plc [2002] IRLR 851, EAT 37, 39

Dacas v Brook Street Bureau [2004] EWCA Civ 217, EAT 15, 28

Danfoss Case, see Handels-og Kontorfunktionaerernes Forbund i Danmark v Dansk Arbejdsgiverforening, acting on behalf of Danfoss

De Souza v Automobile Associations [1986] IRLR 103, CA 94

Delaney v Staples [1992] 1 All ER 944, HL 4, 5

Devis (W) & Sons Ltd v Atkins [1997] 2 All ER 321, CA 159

Dines v Initial Health Care Services and Pall Mall Services [1994] IRLR 336, CA 191, 192

Dr Sophie Redmond Stichting v Bartol (Case C–29/91) [1992] ECR I-3189, ECJ 190

Dryden v Greater Glasgow Health Board [1992] IRLR 469, EAT 135

Dugdale v Kraft Foods [1977] 1 All ER 454, EAT 114, 123

Duffy v Yeomans and Partners [1995] ICR 1, CA 145, 146

Ealing London Borough Council v Race Relations Board (CRE) [1972] 1 All ER 105, HL 88, 89

Eaton v Nuttall Ltd [1977] 3 All ER 1131, EAT 114, 123

Edmund Nuttall Ltd v Butterfield [2005] IRLR 751, EAT 37, 40

Edwards v Chesterfield Royal Hospital NHS Foundation Trust [2009] EWHC 2011 (QB), HC 138

Edwards v Skyways [1964] 1 All ER 494, HC 215

Electrolux v Hutchinson [1976] IRLR 410, EAT 114, 123

English v Thomas Sanderson Blinds Ltd [2008] EWCA Civ 1421, CA 102

Environment Agency v Rowan [2008] IRLR 20, EAT 98

Express and Echo Publications Ltd v Tanton [1999] IRLR 367, CA 20, 29

Faccenda Chicken v Fowler [1986] 1 All ER 617, CA 36, 40

Fairfield Ltd v Skinner [1992] ICR 836, EAT 76, 77

Falconer v ASLEF and NUR [1986] IRLR 331, Cty Ct 232, 235

Farthing v Midland House Stores [1974] IRLR 354, Ind Trib 185

Fellowes v Fisher [1976] QB 122, CA 47

Ferguson v John Dawson and Partners (Contractors) Ltd [1976] 3 All ER 817, CA 21

Fisher v Hoopoe Finance Ltd [2005] All ER (D) 51 (Jun), EAT 171

Foley v Post Office [2000] All ER (D) 1137, CA 149, 154, 164

Foreningen af Arbejdsledere i Danmark v Daddy's Dance Hall A/S (Case 324/86) [1988] ECR 739, ECJ 194, 195, 205

Gallagher v Alpha Catering Services [2004] All ER (D) 262 (May), EAT 73

Gascol Conversions Ltd v Mercer [1974] IRLR 155, CA 216

Ghaidan v Godin-Mendoza [2004] UKHL 30, HL 103

Goodwin v The Patent Office [1999] IRLR 4, EAT 97

Grant v South West Trains Ltd (Case C–249/96) [1998] ECR I-621, ECJ 87

Greenhof v Barnsley MBC [2005] All ER (D) 347 (Oct), EAT 38

Greenwood v British Airways plc [1999] IRLR 600 97

Grundy v British Airways plc [2007] EWCA Civ 1020, CA 116, 120

HIVAC v Park Royal [1946] 1 All ER 350, CA 37, 40

HM Prison Service v Dolby [2003] IRLR 694, EAT 9

Hampton v Lord Chancellor and Another [2008] IRLR 258, ET 103, 106, 107

Handels-og Kontorfunktionaerernes Forbund i Danmark v Dansk Arbejdsgiverforening, acting on behalf of Danfoss (Case 109/88) [1989] ECR 3199, ECJ 115, 120, 124

Hardwick v Leeds AHA [1975] IRLR 319, Ind Trib 34

Hardy v Tourism South East [2005] IRLR 242, EAT 171

Harris v Richard Lawson Autologistics Ltd [2002] EWCA Civ 442, CA 215

Hewlett Packard Ltd v O'Murphy [2001] All ER (D) 91 (Sep), EAT 15

Hobson v Park Brothers (1973) (Unreported) 171, 184

Horkulak v Cantor Fitzgerald International [2004] EWCA Civ 1287, CA 139

Hunt v Storm Communications Ltd and Others (2006) Case No 2702546/2006, 27 March 2007, Reading Tribunal 2007 203

Hynd v Armstrong and Others [2007] IRLR 338, IH 195, 200, 204

ISTC v MFI – formerly Hygena (Scunthorpe) (TUR1/29/00) (2001) 2 February 2 212

Iceland Frozen Foods Ltd v Jones [1982] IRLR 439, [1983] ICR 17, EAT 143, 144, 147, 149, 152–154, 160, 163, 164

James v London Borough of Greenwich [2008] EWCA Civ 35, EAT 13, 16, 26, 28, 30

Jenkins v Kingsgate (Clothing Productions) Ltd (Case 96/80) [1981] ECR 911, ECJ 86

Johns v Solent SD Ltd [2008] EWCA Civ 790, CA 107

Johnson & Bloy (Holdings) Ltd v Wolstenholme Rink plc and Fallon [1987] IRLR 499, CA 46

Johnstone v Bloomsbury Health Authority [1992] QB 333, CA 35, 37, 39, 67

Jones v Associated Tunnelling Co Ltd [1981] IRLR 477, EAT 42

Kapadia v London Borough of Lambeth [2000] IRLR 14, EAT 98

Keeley v Fosroc International Ltd [2006] All ER (D) 65 (Oct), CA 135

Kent Management Services v Butterfield [1992] IRLR 394, EAT 5

Kirker v British Sugar plc [1998] IRLR 624, HL 98

Kraus v Penna [2004] IRLR 260, EAT 79

Lawrence and Others v Regent Office Care Ltd and Others (Case C–320/00) [2002] All ER (D) 84 (Sep) 116, 119, 127

Levez v TH Jennings (Harlow Pools) Ltd (No 2) [2000] ICR 58, EAT 116

Lionel Leventhal Ltd v North [2005] All ER (D) 82 (Jan), EAT 171, 184

Lister v Hesley Hall Ltd [2001] UKHL 22, HL 92

London Metropolitan University v Sackur [2006] UKEAT 0286 06 1708 (17 August 2006) 200, 203

London Underground v National Union of Railwaymen [1989] IRLR 341, QBD 238

Lumley v Gye (1853) 2 E & B 216, QBD 231

MSF v Refuge Assurance plc and Another [2002] IRLR 324, EAT 172

McClintock v Department of Constitutional Affairs [2008] IRLR 29, EAT 101

MacFarlane and Another v Glasgow City Council [2001] IRLR 7, EAT 18, 20, 29

McMeechan v Secretary of State for Employment [1997] IRLR 353, CA 28

Malik v BCCI SA (in liquidation) [1997] 3 All ER 1, HL 35, 37, 38, 40

Mandla v Dowell Lee [1983] 1 All ER 1062, HL 93–95

Market Investigations Ltd v Minister of Social Security [1969] 2 QB 173, QBD 14, 19, 22, 24, 28

Marks and Spencer plc v Martins [1998] IRLR 326, CA 94

Mason v Ward End Primary School Governing Body [2006] IRLR 432, EAT 145, 146

Massey v Crown Life Assurance Co [1978] 2 All ER 576, CA 21

Melia v Magna Kansaei [2005] EWCA Civ 1547, CA 81

Metrobus Ltd v Unite the Union [2009] EWCA Civ 829 240

Middlesborough Council v TGWU [2002] IRLR 332 171, 172

Miklaszewicz v Stolt Offshore Ltd [2002] IRLR 344, IH 80

Miles v Wakefield MDC [1987] 1 All ER 1089, HL 230

Montgomery v Johnson Underwood Ltd [2001] EWCA Civ 318, CA 13, 15, 20, 21, 24, 28

Morrow v Safeway Stores plc [2002] IRLR 9, EAT 44

Morton Sundour Fabrics Ltd v Shaw (1966) 2 ITR 84, CA 175

Motorola Ltd v Davidson and Melville Craig Group Ltd [2000] All ER (D) 1353 (May), EAT 28

Murray and Another v Foyle Meats Ltd [1999] 3 All ER 769, HL 175

Muscat v Cable & Wireless plc [2006] EWCA Civ 220, CA 15

National Coal Board v Galley [1958] 1 All ER 91, CA 215

National Coal Board v Sherwin [1978] IRLR 122, EAT 123

National Union of Teachers v Mrs L Watson [2006] All ER (D) 84 (Aug), EAT 63

North Riding Garages v Butterwick [1967] 2 QB 56, CA 176

Norton Tool Co Ltd v Tewson [1973] 1 All ER 183, NIRC 150, 155, 164

OBG v Allan [2005] EWCA Civ 106, CA 232

OCS Group UK Ltd v Jones and Another [2009] All ER (D) 138 (Sep), EAT 192

O'Brien v Associated Fire Alarms Ltd [1968] 1 WLR 1916, CA 34

O'Kelly v Trusthouse Forte [1984] QB 90, [1983] 3 All ER 456, CA 14, 29

Office Angels Ltd v Rainer-Thomas [1991] IRLR 214, CA 48

P v S and Cornwall County Council [1996] All ER (EC) 397, ECJ 87, 92

Palacios de la Villa v Cortefiel Servicios SA (Case C–411/05) [2007] ECR I-8531, ECJ 107

Parkins v Sodexho Ltd [2002] IRLR 109, EAT 79

Paton Calvert & Co v Westerside [1979] IRLR 109, EAT 176

Pickstone v Freemans plc [1988] 2 All ER 803, HL 115, 128

Polkey v AE Dayton Services Ltd [1988] AC 344, HL 143, 145–147, 149, 152, 154, 155, 158–160, 163–165

Porcelli v Strathclyde RC [1986] IRLR 134, Ct of Sess 89, 102

Power v Regent Security Services Ltd [2008] 2 All ER 977, CA 200

Preston and Others v Wolverhampton Healthcare NHS Trust and Others (No 2) [2001] 3 All ER 947, HL 116

Protective Services (Contracts) Ltd v Livingstone (1992) (unreported) 183

Provident Financial Group etc. v Hayward [1989] 3 All ER 298, CA 47

Qua v John Ford Morrison Solicitors [2003] IRLR 184, EAT 53, 58

RJB Mining v NUM [1997] IRLR 621, QBD 239, 243

Rask and Christensen v ISS Kantineservice A/S (Case C-209/91) [1992] ECR I-5755, ECJ 190, 191

Ready Mixed Concrete (South East) Ltd v Minister of Pensions and National Insurance [1968] 1 All ER 433, HC 14, 18–21, 24, 28

Reda v Flag Ltd [2002] IRLR 474, PC 35, 39

Redrow Homes (Yorkshire) Ltd v Wright, Roberts and Others [2004] EWCA Civ 469, CA 71

Robertson and Jackson v British Gas Corp [1983] , CA 215

Robertson and Others v Department for Environment, Food and Rural Affairs [2005] EWCA Civ 138, CA 116, 119

Robinson v Crompton Parkinson Ltd [1978] IRLR 61, EAT 35, 38

Rodway v New Southern Railways Ltd [2005] EWCA Civ 443, CA 53, 57

Roger Bullivant Ltd v Ellis [1987] IRLR 491, CA 46

Rolls Royce v Unite (Trade Union) [2008] All ER (D) 174 (Oct), HC 181

Roofdec Ltd v O'Keefe [2008] All ER (D) 195 (Dec), EAT 139, 140

Royle v Trafford BC [1984] IRLR 184, QBD 230

SG&R Valuation Service Co v Boudrais [2008] All ER (D) 141 (May), HA 47, 48

Sagar v Ridehalgh and Sons Ltd [1931] 1 Ch 310, CA 34

Scally v Southern Health and Social Services Board [1991] 4 All ER 563, HL 35

Secretary of State for Employment v Associated Society of Locomotive Engineers and Firemen (No 2) [1972] 2 QB 455, CA 135

Simmons v Hoover Ltd [1976] 3 WLR 901, EAT 242

Sinclair v Neighbour [1967] 2 QB 279, CA 153

Singh v British Steel Corp [1974] IRLR 131, Ind Trib 215

Solectron Scotland Ltd v Roper [2004] IRLR 4, EAT 34

South East Sheffield Citizens' Advice Bureaux v Grayson [2004] IRLR 353, EAT 15

Southampton City College v Randall [2006] IRLR 18, EAT 98

Spijkers (JMA) v Gebroeders Benedik Abattoir CV and Alfred Benedik en Zonen BV (Case 24/85) [1986] , ECJ 190, 191, 194, 198, 199

Squibb UK Staff Association v Certification Officer [1979] 2 All ER 452, CA 210, 220, 223

Stevenson, Jordan and Harrison Ltd v MacDonald and Evans [1952] 1 TLR 101, CA 28

Strathclyde Regional Council v Wallace and Others [1998] 1 All ER 394, HL 123

Superclean Support Services plc v (1) Lansana (2) Wetton Cleaning Services Ltd (1997) Unreported, 20 May, EAT 192

Süzen v Zehnacker Gebäudereinigung GmbH Krankenhausservice (Case C–13/95) [1997] ECR I–1259, ECJ 189–193, 197

Swain v West (Butchers) Ltd [1936] 3 All ER 261, CA 39

Sybron v Rochem [1983] 2 All ER 707, CA 40

Taff Vale Railway v Amalgamated Society of Railway Servants [1901] AC 426, HL 231, 234

Taylor v Kent County Council [1969] 2 All ER 1080, QBD 176

Thomas v Farr plc [2007] EWCA Civ 118, CA 47

Thomas and Betts Manufacturing Co v Harding [1980] IRLR 255, CA, [1978] IRLR 213, EAT 171, 176, 184

Ticehurst v British Telecommunications Ltd [1992] IRLR 219, CA 229–231, 243

Tadd v Eastwood and Daily Telegraph Ltd [1983] IRLR 320 216

Tower Boot Co Ltd v Jones [1997] 2 All ER 406, CA 92

Transport and General Workers Union v Gala Casinos Ltd t/a Maxims Casino Club TUR1/119/2001 (2001) 1 November 211

Treganowen v Robert Knee Ltd [1975] IRLR 247, HC 4, 5

United Bank Ltd v Akhtar [1989] IRLR 507 , EAT 35

Walker v Josiah Wedgwood & Sons Ltd [1978] IRLR 105, EAT 151

Webb v EMO Air Cargo (UK) Ltd (Case C–32/93) [1994] QB 718, ECJ 89

Webb and Others v Sandaw Products Ltd and Hall Foundries Ltd (EAT/477/79) 240

Weber von Hartz v Bilka-Kaufhaus [1986] IRLR 317, ECJ 104

Western Excavating v Sharp [1978] 1 All ER 713, CA 44, 143, 144, 146

Wheeler v Patel [1987] IRLR 211, EAT 195

Whiffen v Milham Ford Girls' School [2001] All ER (D) 256 (Mar), CA 170, 185

White v British Sugar Corporation [1977] IRLR 121, Ind Trib 87

Whitehouse v Blatchford and Sons Ltd [1999] IRLR 492, CA 200, 204

Wilkinson v Springwell Engineering Ltd (2007) ET/2507420/07 103

Wilson v Circular Distributors Ltd [2006] IRLR 38, EAT 16, 17

Wooding (GW) v Stoves Ltd [1975] IRLR 198, Ind Trib 184

Woods v WM Car Services (Peterborough) Ltd [1981] IRLR 413, CA 38–40, 42, 44

Yewens v Noakes (1880) 6 QBD 530, CA 14, 19, 24, 28

Young v Canadian Northern Pacific Railway [1931] AC 83, PC 214

Young and Woods Ltd v West [1980] IRLR 201, CA 21

Young, James and Webster v United Kingdom (Applications 7601/76, 7806/77) (1981) 4 EHRR 38, [1981] IRLR 408, ECtHR 219

▪ Statutes

American Civil Rights Act 1964 87

Contracts of Employment Act 1963 144

Disability Discrimination Act 1995 38, 96, 97, 103
Pt II 96

Employment Act 2002 7–9, 145, 158
  s 98A(1) 145, 146, 159
  Sch 2, Pt 1, Ch 1 145
  Sch 2, Pt 1, Ch 2 145
Employment Act 2008 2, 145, 159
Employment Protection (Consolidation) Act 1978 144
Employment Relations Act 1999 210
  Sch 1 210
Employment Rights Act 1996 2, 27, 52, 57, 62, 76,
  79, 80, 148, 152, 161, 170, 202, 219, 243
  s 1 196
  s 13 74–77, 204
  ss 17–22 74, 77
  s 27 76
  Pt IVA 79
  s 43A 79, 81
  s 43B 79, 81
  s 43C 79, 81
  s 43D 79–81
  s 43E 79–81
  s 43F 79–81
  s 43G 79–81
  s 43H 79, 80
  s 43I 79
  s 43J 79, 81
  s 43K 79, 81
  s 43L 79
  s 47B(1) 81
  s 57A 64
  s 80 53
  s 80F 58, 63
  s 80G 64
  s 86(6) 162
  s 92 148
  Pt X 144
  s 94 147, 148, 152, 160, 161

  s 95 148, 152, 161
  s 95(1)(a) 149, 153, 162
  s 95(1)(c) 162
  s 98 147, 148, 152, 160–162
  s 98(2)(a) 149
  s 98(2)(c) 196
  s 98(3) 162
  s 98(4) 144, 149, 153, 154, 163, 171, 184
  s 103A 81
  s 104 202, 204
  s 105 183, 184
  s 108(1) 63
  s 111(2) 5
  s 112(3)(a) 25
  s 118 204
  s 135(1) 175
  s 139(1) 170, 174
  s 139(1)(b) 176
  s 155 175
  s 203 196
  s 213 16
  s 230(1) 12, 14, 27
  s 235(4) 240
Employment Rights Act 2004 6
Equal Pay Act 1970 86, 88, 113–118, 123, 127, 128
  s 1(2)(a) 114
  s 1(2)(b) 114
  s 1(5) 114
Equality Act 2006 159
Equality Act 2010 2, 32, 64, 85–89, 91–94, 96–99,
  101, 102, 105–108, 114, 117, 118, 120, 123,
  126–128, 186
  s 1(5) 124
  s 3 98
  s 4 90, 91, 93, 96, 97, 101, 103, 105, 106
  s 5 102, 103, 105
  s 6 96, 97
  s 7 90–92
  s 9 91, 93
  s 10 88, 91
  s 11 100
  s 12 100, 101
  s 13 92, 93, 96, 99, 100, 102, 103, 105, 106
  s 13(2) 106
  s 15 96, 98, 105
  s 19 92, 93, 96, 100, 103, 106

TABLE OF CASES AND STATUTES

ss 20–22 96
s 20 98
s 20(5) 98
s 21 98
s 26 93, 100
s 27 100
s 65 127
s 65(2) 114, 119
s 65(3) 119, 123
s 65(4) 114, 115, 119, 124
s 65(5) 125
s 65(6) 115, 119, 124, 128, 129
s 69 119
s 109 90, 94, 99
s 110 90, 94
s 123 98
s 124 90, 92, 94, 96
s 136 94
s 158 105, 106, 108
s 159 105, 106, 108
Sch 1 97
Sch 1, para 1 97
Sch 1, para 2 97
Sch 1, para 6 98
Sch 9, Pt 1, para 1 103
Sch 9, Pt 2 104, 105, 108
Sch 9, Pt 2, paras 7–16 105, 106
Sch 9, Pt 2, paras 8–9 105

Industrial Training Act 1964 3
Industrial Relations Act 1971 143

Public Interest Disclosure Act 1998 78, 79

Race Relations Act 1965 87
Race Relations Act 1968 89
Race Relations Act 1976 85–89, 92–94, 108
  s 3(1) 88
  s 37 108
  s 38 108
Redundancy Payments Act 1965 144

Sex Discrimination Act 1975 85–89, 108
  s 47 108
Sex Discrimination Act 1986 87

Trade Union and Labour Relations Act 1971 144
Trade Union and Labour Relations (Consolidation) Act
  1992 2, 171, 172, 214, 219, 223, 234, 238, 239,
  242, 243
s 5 210, 218, 220, 223
s 64 233, 235
s 64(1) 235
s 64(2)(b) 235
s 71 220
s 72 219, 220
s 146(1)(c) 219
s 152 218, 219
s 152(1)(c) 219
ss 108A–108C 220
s 168 222, 224
s 170 224
s 178(2) 224
ss 188–194 179
s 188 172
s 193 172
s 218 231, 234
s 219 237
ss 226–235 238, 243
s 226 231
ss 227–230 238
s 228 239
s 234 239
s 237 242
s 244 237, 242
s 288 235
Trade Union Reform and Employment Rights Act
  1993 3–6
Tribunals, Courts and Enforcement Act 2007 8

Wages Act 1986 4
Work and Families Act 2006 2, 52, 55, 57, 63

▮Statutory Instruments

Employment Act 2002 (Dispute Resolution) Regulations 2004 (SI 2004/752) 8

Employment Equality (Age) (Amendment No 2) Regulations 2006 (SI 2006/2931) 105, 106

Employment Equality (Age) (Consequential Amendments) Regulations 2007 (SI 2007/825) 105, 106

Employment Equality (Age) Regulations 2006 (SI 2006/2408) 105, 106, 107
reg 36 107

Employment Equality (Religion or Belief) Regulations 2003 (SI 2003/1660) 88

Employment Equality (Sexual Orientation) Regulations 2003 (SI 2003/1661) 104

Employment Tribunals (Constitution and Rules of Procedure) Regulations 2004 (SI 2004/1861) 5–7, 9, 10
Sch 1, reg 26 8

Employment Tribunals Extension of Jurisdiction (England and Wales) Order 1994 (SI 2004/1623) 156, 157

Flexible Working (Procedural Requirements) Regulations 2002 (SI 2002/3207) 64

Maternity and Parental Leave etc Regulations 1999 (SI 1999/3312) 62
reg 12A 63

Public Interest Disclosure (Prescribed Persons) (Amendment) Order 2003 (SI 2003/1993) 81

Sex Discrimination (Amendment of Legislation) Regulations 2008 (SI 2008/963) 88

Transfer of Undertakings (Protection of Employment) Regulations 1981 (SI 1981/1794) 189, 190

Transfer of Undertakings (Protection of Employment) Regulations 2006 (SI 2006/246) 2, 50, 189–198, 202, 203, 205
reg 3 193
reg 3(1) 198
reg 3(1)(a) 194, 198, 203
reg 3(1)(b) 192, 194, 203
reg 3(2) 194
reg 3(3) 203
reg 4 193, 194, 198, 200, 203
reg 4(2) 194
reg 4(4) 195, 200, 203
reg 4(5) 200, 203
reg 4(9) 195
reg 4(11) 195
reg 5 196
reg 6 196
reg 7 193, 198, 199
reg 7(1) 195, 196
reg 7(2) 196
reg 7(3)(b) 196
reg 11 196
reg 13 196
reg 14 196
reg 15 196
reg 18 196

Working Time Regulations 1998 (SI 1998/1833) 67, 71–74
reg 4(1) 67, 71
reg 4(3) 71
reg 5 67
reg 5A 72
reg 10 67
reg 11 67
reg 12 67, 71
reg 13 68, 72
reg 13A 68, 72
reg 14 76
reg 15 73
reg 15A 72
reg 30 73

■European Legislation Conventions and Treaties

EC Treaty
Art 141 114
European Convention on Human Rights and
Fundamental Freedoms
Art 11 219, 244

Treaty of Lisbon 88
Treaty of Rome 88
Treaty on the Functioning of the European Union 114
Art 157 114

■Directives

Acquired Rights Directive (2001/23/EC) 189–192,
194, 198
Agency Workers Directive (2008/104/EC) 30

Equal Pay Directive (75/117/EEC) 115
Equal Treatment Directive (76/207/EEC) 87, 92, 102
Equal Treatment in Employment and Occupation
Framework Directive (2000/78/EC) 88, 96, 103,
106, 107
Art 1 106
Art 3 106
Art 3(1) 106

Redundancy Directive (98/59/EC) 172

Sex Discrimination Directive (97/80/EC) 89

Working Time Directive (93/104/EC) 66, 67, 69, 71

1

The sources and machinery of employment law

How this topic may come up in exams

The first topic to be covered in employment law courses is often an examination of the sources of employment law and the machinery and institutions most relevant in this area. However, this topic does not appear in exams all that often. Rather, it is treated as background information. Where it is examined, you will usually have to evaluate the current system, comment on past reforms and suggest improvements or alternatives to the current system. Problem questions in this area are very rare.

■ Attack the question

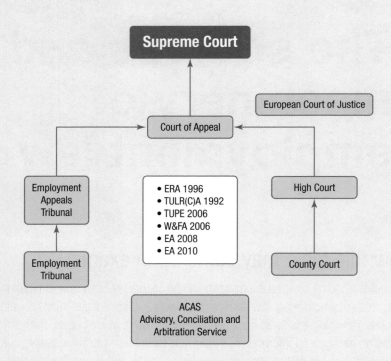

A printable version of this diagram plan is available from www.pearsoned.co.uk/lawexpressqa

📸 Question 1

Critically evaluate the extension of jurisdiction to enable tribunals to determine contract-based claims, and identify further reforms to the tribunal system which should be of benefit to claimants.

Answer plan

→ Briefly consider tribunal jurisdiction before Trade Union Reform and Employment Rights Act 1993 (TURERA).

→ What were the problems with the limits placed on tribunals?

→ Evaluate changes brought about by TURERA and subsequent reforms.

→ Do those changes address the problems indentified earlier?

→ What issues remain?

Diagram plan

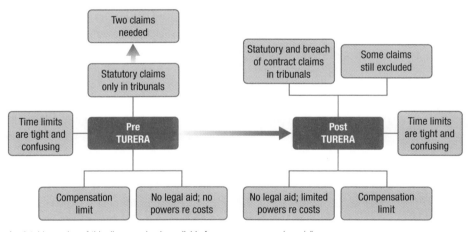

A printable version of this diagram plan is available from www.pearsoned.co.uk/lawexpressqa

Answer

Employment Tribunals (ETs) were established with a very limited jurisdiction in the 1960s (Industrial Training Act 1964) and although their jurisdiction increased over the years, in particular through the

[1] Clear introduction which indicates you understand the question.

[2] Here you have set out the key issues you will discuss and the order you will deal with them so the reader knows exactly what's coming. This really helps with marking because you do not have to search for the next point.

[3] Whenever you state a point or highlight a problem such as here it is then useful to back it up with an example. You are showing that you really understand the issue and can see how it plays out in practice.

[4] You are further backing up your point that this is a serious criticism: not just a theoretical problem but one that actually caused real issues in the courts.

Trade Union Reform and Employment Rights Act 1993 (TURERA), significant problems remained.[1] Perhaps the most obvious one was that ETs only had jurisdiction over statutory claims and any common law claims such as breach of contract must be heard through the regular court system. In addition, other criticisms can be levelled at the tribunal system such as confusing time limits and lack of availability of legal aid. This essay first discusses the ETs' jurisdictional limits before turning to other criticisms.[2]

The lack of jurisdiction over common law claims could cause problems for employees wishing to enforce their rights or seek remedies. Unfair dismissal claims, for example, also often involved a breach of contract leaving an employee in the unfortunate situation of having to bring two claims arising from the employer's action. **Treganowan v Robert Knee Ltd** [1975] IRLR 247, HC is a good example.[3] The tribunal held her to have been fairly dismissed but considered that she should have been given notice. Not doing so was a breach of contract but the ET had no jurisdiction to hear that part of her claim or award damages for the breach. The claimant thus had to pursue her claim in the County Court. The problems with this lack of jurisdiction can further be highlighted through cases arising out of what was then the Wages Act 1986. It included provisions relating to when deductions from wages could lawfully be made. If the deductions fell within the definitions listed in the Act, ETs would have jurisdiction; where they did not an employee would have to rely on the court system. While this was straightforward in relation to, for example, basic pay or even bonuses as these were defined in the Act, wages in lieu of notice caused more problems. The House of Lords held in **Delaney v Staples** [1992] 1 All ER 944, HL that such payments arose out of the termination of the employment relationship as they acted as damages for breach of contract, and thus did not fall within the Wages Act. ETs thus did not have jurisdiction to hear such claims.[4] Their Lordships in this judgment called for the extension of tribunal jurisdiction to breach of contract claims.

An extension would not only allow tribunals to act as a one-stop shop for employment claims and thus reduce complexity for employees, employers and practitioners, it would also avoid situations such as the one in **Treganowan** where two actions had to be brought. It would also avoid difficult questions of interpretation such as whether commission payments were wages for the purposes of the Wages

[5]Here you are outlining why an extension of tribunal jurisdiction would be useful and how it addresses the problems you identified above.

Act or whether complete non-payment counted as a deduction. Both these questions were answered in the affirmative by the Employment Appeals Tribunal (EAT) in **Kent Management Services v Butterfield** [1992] IRLR 394, EAT. However, both questions would have been irrelevant had the ET's jurisdiction extended to hearing breach of contract claims.[5]

[6]Clear signal that you are now moving on to consider some of the other criticisms. This helps because the reader now knows you have dealt with that point and are moving on so we can think about whether you have covered all expected points on that issue.

Further criticisms of the tribunal[6] system include the sometimes confusing time limits for bringing claims. While unfair dismissal claims must be brought within three months of dismissal, redundancy claims have a six-month time limit and, of course, the ET has a discretion to allow extensions to those time limits in certain cases (s 111(2) of the Employment Rights Act 1996). There is likely to be differing practice amongst tribunals in exercising this discretion and, as tribunal decisions are not reported, the extent of such variations in practice is not known.

The lack of legal aid is a major problem in relation to tribunals. Many claimants will at the point of bringing a claim be in a precarious financial position, often just having lost their job. Many will worry about the costs of bringing a claim. In addition, tribunals tend not to award costs. While their powers to do so were increased in 2004 and they can now award up to £10,000 in costs, they can only do so where a party or a party's representative has acted improperly (Employment Tribunals (Constitution and Rules of Procedure) Regulations 2004). It must, of course, be remembered that costs can also be awarded against the claimant. Costs can be substantial, especially given the tendency to engage legal professionals to help with the case and often also represent parties at the tribunal hearing. Employment law is increasingly complex and although the tribunal system was supposed to reduce the need for legal representation, such knowledge and skill is often seen as vital to the success of a case.[7]

[7]You have now set out what you consider to be the key issues with tribunals; now it's time to consider the changes made and the extent to which those changes address the problems identified.

[8]There is no need to repeat the points made above, you can simply refer back. You have already said that extending jurisdiction would solve some of the issues.

TURERA 1993 gave the Secretary of State the power to extend the jurisdiction of ETs and in 1994 he did so. Thus ETs now have jurisdiction to hear breach of contract claims up to a set financial limit. Certain claims such as personal injury claims and claims relating to intellectual property are still excluded but the situations outlined above in **Kent**, **Delaney** and **Treganowan** could no longer occur.[8] However, problems remain: the financial limit set means that there will be cases where the ordinary courts must be used because the

[9]Here you acknowledge the limits of the changes made – yes jurisdiction was extended but it is not universal and the limits potentially still cause problems.

financial limit is likely to be exceeded. In addition, the ETs' jurisdiction applies only at the end of the employment relationship, which means that claimants whose employment is ongoing cannot claim for breach of contract in the ET. It is also not inconceivable that a claim will involve unfair dismissal but may also cover intellectual property or personal injuries, which would still not be able to be dealt with together.[9]

[10]Here you confirm that the changes made did not address some of the other main criticisms not relating directly to jurisdiction, so those issues remain.

So while TURERA 1993 brought about some welcomed and useful changes, it has not solved all the problems and questions about legal representation, costs and legal aid[10] as well as the proper and most efficient relationship between the tribunal system and the ordinary court system remain.

 Make your answer stand out

- You could be more specific about changes brought in by the 2004 Employment Rights Act to show that some effort is still being made to improve things.
- You could add more detail about the idea that tribunals should be accessible for lay people and that this is not really the case here.
- Consider academic commentary such as that provided by P. Davies and M. Freedland (1993) in *Labour Legislation and Public Policy* (Oxford: OUP).

! Don't be tempted to…

- Simply outline the history of employment tribunals – you must focus on changes brought about by TURERA and subsequent legislation.
- Just list problems without giving examples. Case law examples help show you really understand the issue.
- Just focus on the question of jurisdiction which was solved to some extent by TURERA – there were other issues too, which still remain.

Question 2

To what exent does legislation relating to Employment Tribunal Procedure help ensure the quick and just resolution of employment related disputes? Answer this question with a particular focus on the Employment Tribunals (Constitution and Rules of Procedure) Regulations 2004.

Answer plan

→ Introduce the aim of the Employment Tribunals (Constitution and Rules of Procedure) Regulations 2004.

→ Consider the provisions relating to fairness:
  – panel make-up
  – public hearing
  – the now abolished DDP (Employment Act 2002)
  – deposits and costs.

→ Conclusion: the provisions are focused on reducing workload, perhaps at the expense of a perception of fairness.

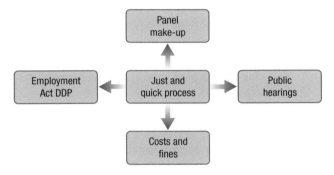

A printable version of this diagram plan is available from www.pearsoned.co.uk/lawexpressqa

Answer

[1]In your introduction try to identify what the legal issues or relevant provisions are and then set out how you are going to answer the question. This shows that you know what is being asked of you and that you have a clear structure in mind.

The Employment Tribunals (Constitution and Rules of Procedure) Regulations 2004 (ET(CRP)R 2004) govern the conduct of a wide range of procedural matters affecting the whole jurisdiction of Employment Tribunals (ETs). It therefore covers tribunal cases relating to, for example, discrimination, equal pay, unfair dismissal and breach of contract. The 'overriding objective' of ET(CRP)R 2004 is that ETs should deal with cases justly. This essay considers the extent to which the provisions achieve that aim and do so within an acceptable time frame.[1]

ET(CRP)R 2004 provide that the panel on each tribunal shall contain one representative from a panel approved by an employers'

[2]In this essay we have taken the approach of stating the provision and then going on and commenting on it. This provides a logical structure that allows you to highlight your legal knowledge and analytical skills at the same time.

[3]Show that your legal knowledge is up to date.

[4]You come back to this in the conclusion and it is a key part of the argument. Perception of fairness is as important as actual fairness. Build up your argument logically to reach your conclusion at the end.

[5]You do not have to say a lot about each point. Say what you want to say and then move on and do not feel that you have to pad out a paragraph for the sake of it. Otherwise you are likely to get drawn into irrelevance.

[6]Although these provisions are no longer in force they are worth mentioning as an example of the legislation trying to encourage early and thus speedy resolution. The attempt failed and you need to say that to show your knowledge is not out of date.

[7]This is worth mentioning because it shows that the legislation is still committed to the aim of encouraging reasonable and early resolution, it is just trying different ways of doing that. It shows contextual understanding.

organisation and one from a panel approved by an employees' organisation.[2] The Chair of the proceedings (now called an Employment Judge by virtue of changes introduced by the Tribunals, Courts and Enforcement Act 2007[3]) is a lawyer, so there is an inherent balance of interest on the panel. This ensures that the panel is constituted in such a way as to include the legal specialist knowledge required in order to apply employment law provisions accurately but also with input from both an employer's and an employee's perspective. Overall, this is likely to not only be fairer but also give the impression to those using the tribunal service that there is a fair system in place which is not biased in favour of either party.[4]

The requirement in reg 26 of Sch 1 to ET(CRP)R 2004 that ET hearings are held in public is also a means of ensuring that justice is done. Where the public can access hearings, decisions have to be made in a more transparent way to avoid being questioned by the public or the media after the event. It acts as a safeguard to ensure that law is applied appropriately and panels are not biased one way or the other.[5]

There are other provisions which try to ensure the fairness of employment law cases. The Employment Act 2002 (EA 2002) enabled the passing of the Employment Act 2002 (Dispute Resolution) Regulations 2004 (EA(DR)R 2004), which provide that an employer is almost certain to lose an unfair dismissal claim unless he has devised, published and complied with a three-step disciplinary and dismissal procedure (DDP). A DDP must include a written statement of the grounds for the disciplinary action and an invitation to the employee to attend a meeting, the meeting itself and an appeal procedure. The purpose of this provision was to encourage the employer and employee to resolve their differences before reaching the ET. However, these provisions were a failure and have since been abolished.[6] They did not lead to the earlier resolution of cases and could be seen as unfair and weighted too far in favour of employees. Employers could be penalised too easily on a technicality without a full examination of the issues. An incentive to try to resolve issues early is still in place as damages can be adjusted by up to 25% if either party does not act in a reasonable way.[7]

In order to prevent hearings which would waste an ET's time, EA 2002 gives ETs the power to strike out cases at a pre-hearing review. In **H M Prison Service v Dolby** [2003] IRLR 694, EAT, the EAT held that 'misconceived' meant that a case should be struck out if it either was 'misconceived' or had no reasonable prospect of success. This does not help further in understanding what misconceived might mean but is likely to include cases which are brought by an employee who has misunderstood an aspect of the law or how it applies. This is a sensible option as there is no point in taking a case to hearing where there is no prospect of success. It would waste time and money and ultimately also be unfair on the party who has brought the case. It is surely better to explain to the claimant that their claim is misconceived and why.[8]

[8]This returns to your point about perceptions of fairness and how the process is viewed, which is neatly building up a logical argument that can be traced all the way through your answer. This shows great analytical skills.

An ET also has the power under EA 2002 to determine cases without a hearing if the parties agree. Where cases are relatively straightforward and the ET has all the necessary documentation this can be a quicker and more cost-effective way of resolving a case. However, it does raise questions about fairness. That is not to say that panels are less likely to be transparent and fair in their decision making when the parties are not present, simply that the perception of the parties may be different where they have not had their day in court.[9]

[9]This is still building the argument but you are making the point in relation to a number of issues, so it shows that your argument makes logical sense.

To discourage employers, employees and their representatives from time-wasting, ETs can require a deposit of £500 in order that a case with no reasonable prospect of success is allowed to proceed. An ET can also disallow the costs of a legal representative who wastes the ET's time. If a party or his representative acts 'vexatiously, abusively, disruptively or otherwise unreasonably, or the bringing or conducting of the proceedings ... has been misconceived', ET(CRP)R 2004 permit an ET to impose costs of up to £10,000. This is a powerful incentive for the parties not to bring inappropriate cases to ETs.[10]

[10]This sentence is necessary here otherwise you are just describing the provisions without commenting on them and that does not really show any critical thinking skills. Just a little comment such as this one can make the difference between an analytical answer and a purely descriptive one.

The measures discussed above are all designed to reduce the workload of, and speed up proceedings in, ETs. Indeed it may be argued that the focus is on the reduction of workload and speeding up of proceedings rather than necessarily on ensuring justice and fairness. Of course, the ET maintains that the provisions aim to resolve disputes quickly while ensuring that justice is done to all parties. Yet it seems that sometimes the perception of what happens is a little different. An employee claimant who has a claim struck out because it is misconceived may feel that the tribunal is biased against employees. The party that loses after a case is decided

[11]Here you are concluding the point you have been building up to throughout, which is great. It leaves no unresolved issues, answers the question set and highlights where the issues with the legislation are.

without a hearing may feel hard done by and might feel a hearing would have produced a different outcome.[11] Overall, however, the tribunal system is working relatively well and delays are still less than in the traditional court system. The tribunal system is also perceived as more informal and easier to deal with for lay people. As such, the relevant legislation does go some way to ensure efficient and just resolution of employment disputes but there is always room for improvement.

✓ Make your answer stand out

- There is quite a lot of commentary relating to the abolition of the DDP which you could draw on.
- You could make suggestions for future amendments to procedure which you think might help fairness. This would show the examiners that you have a comprehensive understanding of how this procedural aspect operates.
- If you set out the procedure a tribunal claim goes through in more detail including the details needed on the paperwork and then the pre-hearing stage etc, you can comment on whether the process itself is set out to resolve matters justly and quickly.
- Consider the role of ACAS in resolving disputes.
- If you know them, add in some tribunal statistics of number of cases brought, struck out, settled etc to show your wider reading and contextual knowledge.

! Don't be tempted to…

- Focus only on the Employment Tribunals (Constitution and Rules of Procedure) Regulations 2004. The question is broader than that.
- Examine only one aspect such as the introduction and then abolition of the DDP. While you do not need to deal with absolutely every aspect, you do need to cover a range of issues to show you have a broad knowledge base and to answer the question fully.
- Ignore the practical implications and application of the provisions. Consider how they will be applied and seen to be applied to show a detailed understanding.

The employment relationship

2

How this topic may come up in exams

One of the most important questions in employment law is whether a person is an employee. The answer to this question determines, among other things, the extent of many of the statutory rights available to that person. Many examination papers have problem questions which involve a discussion of whether an individual is an employee or not. In many cases establishing the employment status will be relatively straightforward but there are a number of situations where things are more complicated. These relate to what some commentators call 'atypical workers' so this is where exam questions are often focused.

■ Attack the question

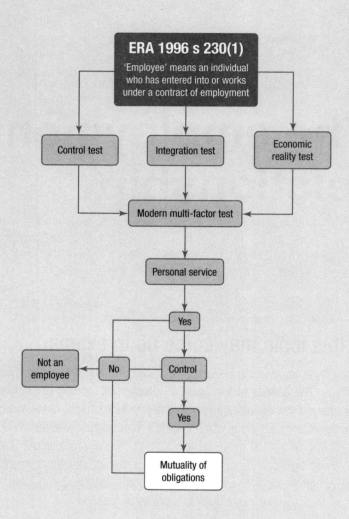

 Question 1

Consider, with reasons and a particular focus on atypical workers, whether cases since *Carmichael* v *National Power plc* [1999] have made it any easier for Employment Tribunals to determine individuals' employment status.

Answer plan

→ Briefly outline the three tests for employee status and the culmination of them in the multi-factor test.

→ Discuss *Carmichael*, highlighting that mutuality of obligations is key.

→ Discuss *Montgomery* v *Johnson Underwood Ltd* to highlight that personal service and control are the other key elements for the existence of an employment contract.

→ Outline recent developments in relation to mutuality of obligations and control/personal service as the two key elements.

→ Give a reasoned assessment of whether these cases as a whole make the decisions any easier.

Diagram plan

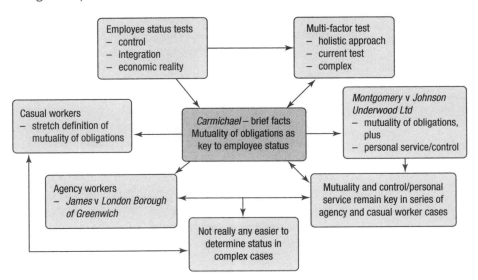

A printable version of this diagram plan is available from www.pearsoned.co.uk/lawexpressqa

Answer

Although many employment rights depend on being able to establish employee status, there is no useful statutory definition of 'employee'. The definition in the Employment Rights Act 1996 (ERA 1996), s 230(1) is circular and thus of little help. Definition of this important concept has therefore been left to the courts. A number of tests have been developed over time but application of the tests is not always easy. This essay briefly considers the situation before the case of **Carmichael v National Power** [1999] 4 All ER 897 before examining the case itself and the case law following it in more detail to ascertain whether it is now easier to decide whether someone is an employee or not.[1]

Historically the tests for employee status have developed from one of control (**Yewens v Noakes** [1880] 6 QBD 530, CA) to one of integration (**Cassidy v Ministry of Health** [1951] 2 KB 343, CA) or economic reality (**Market Investigations Ltd v Minister of Social Security** [1969] 2 QB 173, QBD), culminating in the modern multi-factor test established in **Ready Mixed Concrete v Minister of Pensions and National Insurance** [1968] 1 All ER 433, HC. The modern test requires the weighing up of all the factors for and against employee status and a holistic approach to determining the employment relationship. However, the test has been difficult to apply in particular in the context of atypical workers such as casual and agency workers.[2]

In **Carmichael** the courts considered an issue which had arisen in a number of previous cases (e.g. **O'Kelly v Trusthouse Forte** [1984] QB 90 CA): mutuality of obligations. The applicants were engaged as guides to take visitors around a power station. They regularly worked up to 25 hours a week, wore the company uniform and paid tax and National Insurance (NI) as an employed person, but they were only required to work if there was a tour booked. There were weeks where no work was carried out during which they were not paid. The Court of Appeal found mutuality of obligations on the basis that, subject to a term of reasonableness, they would be required to work if work were offered and that the employer was required to offer it to them if it was available. However, the House of Lords restated the orthodox view of mutuality of obligations. The ability of the employer to withhold work and the worker to refuse it meant that there was no such mutuality of obligation in this case.[3]

---

[1] This is a fairly short and snappy introduction which should serve you well under exam conditions. It lets the reader know that you understand what the issues raised by the question are and sets out the structure of what is to follow.

[2] This paragraph indicates that you have an understanding of the law in this area and how it operated before the case cited in the question. It is important to include a little on this otherwise it is impossible to say whether or not determining employment status is now easier. Do not be tempted to write too much here, though.

[3] A fairly brief explanation of the case is useful but stick to offering those facts which are relevant to understanding the legal principle and building up your argument.

[4] A comment here shows that you have the question in mind rather than just writing what you know about the cases – try to be analytical as you go through rather than leaving the analysis until the end.

[5] This paragraph is a quick explanation of another key case and key principle, again giving very few facts as these are not necessarily required in order to understand the principle. Quoting from a case can show you have really engaged with this area of law but do not spend ages learning quotes – paraphrasing or stating the principle is fine too.

[6] This sentence, together with the case reference, sets out the key principles required for employee status. What follows is confirmation that these principles are being applied by the courts.

[7] This paragraph shows awareness of a number of recent cases in the area and the application of the key principles identified earlier.

Carmichael itself therefore does not move the law in this area forward or clarify it in any way.[4] We must therefore look to the cases which followed. In **Montgomery v Johnson Underwood Ltd** [2001] EWCA Civ 318, CA, a case concerning an agency worker, the Court of Appeal re-emphasised the importance of the use of the multi-factor test and of finding mutuality of obligation. The case also suggests that personal service is the other key element to establishing employee status and that control is also a significant factor. Or, in the words of Lord Justice Longmore, mutuality of obligation and the requirement of control on the part of the potential employer are the irreducible minimum for the existence of a contract of employment.[5] In **Hewlett Packard Ltd v O'Murphy** [2001] All ER (D) 91 (Sep), EAT the Employment Appeals Tribunal (EAT) emphasised that first and foremost there must be a contract between the work provider and the worker and that this must give rise to mutuality of obligations if it is to be a contract of employment.[6]

This approach has been applied in a series of cases considering both mutuality of obligations and control/personal service in relation to agency workers and casual workers. In **Dacas v Brook Street Bureau** [2004] EWCA Civ 217, EAT and **Muscat v Cable & Wireless plc** [2006] EWCA Civ 220, CA the issues of control and mutuality of obligations were key in holding that agency workers were not employees of the end users. In **South East Sheffield Citizens' Advice Bureaux v Grayson** [2004] IRLR 353, EAT and **Bunce v Postworth Ltd t/a Skyblue** [2005] EWCA Civ 490, CA the lack of mutuality of obligations meant that the workers in those cases (Citizens' Advice Bureau volunteers and a casual worker completing over 140 assignments respectively) were not employees.[7]

The approach of the House of Lords in **Carmichael** must now be read subject to the decision of the Court of Appeal in **Cornwall CC v Prater** [2006] EWCA Civ 102, CA. In this case a teacher was employed between 1988 and 1998 under a succession of individual contracts to teach children who were unable to attend school. The council was under no obligation to offer any pupils to her and she was under no obligation to accept the pupils she was asked to take on. Once she had accepted a pupil, however, she was under an obligation to fulfil obligations under that contract. In a unanimous decision it was accepted that her situation could be distinguished from that in **Carmichael** as each contract contained sufficient mutuality to make her an employee and the periods where she was not an employee could then be bridged using s 213 of the Employment Rights Act 1996. A similar approach seems to have been taken in **Wilson v Circular Distributors Ltd** [2006] IRLR 38, EAT concerning a relief area manager and in **Cotswold Developments Construction Ltd v Williams** [2006] IRLR 181, EAT in which it was held that the fact that the employee has the right to refuse work, and the fact that the employer may exercise a right to withhold it, does not necessarily deprive the contract of mutuality of obligation.[8]

[8]This paragraph shows an awareness of cases which have applied the principles in an innovative or unusual way or have developed the principles further and have thus (in this case) complicated the situation somewhat.

While the law relating to casual workers still seems complex, the law relating to agency workers has recently been clarified in **James v London Borough of Greenwich** [2008] EWCA Civ 35, EAT,[9] in which the EAT gave clear guidance on determining employment status of agency workers and confirmed that rarely will there be a contract of employment between the end user and the worker because of lack of control and mutuality of obligations.

[9]This is the beginning of your conclusions showing that the case law has clarified one area (in this case that relating to agency workers).

The cases following **Carmichael** confirm that the modern multi-factor test is still the test to be applied when determining whether or not someone is an employee and in many cases the application of the test is not going to cause too many problems. However, in those situations where determining status has traditionally been problematic it seems it will remain difficult. The case law since **Carmichael** does little to clarify the test. It confirms that when applying the multi-factor test the two most important factors are mutuality of obligations and personal service/control and that without these there can be no contract of employment. However, there is little guidance in the case law on how to balance any other factors present. In addition, cases such as **Prater**, **Wilson** and **Cotswold Developments** seem to muddy the waters by stretching the concept of mutuality of obligations to new limits. In conclusion, the cases since **Carmichael** have not made it any easier for employment tribunals to determine individuals' employment status. However, while the reality of employment relationships remains as complex as it currently is, it is difficult to envisage a test which is easy to apply and does justice to the variety of contexts in which it must operate.[10]

[10]Conclusion which refers back to the question directly indicates that you really are answering the question set and are not just reciting a general answer you have learned.

✓ Make your answer stand out

- Elaborate on how cases such as *Prater*, *Wilson* and *Cotswold Developments* stretch the concept of mutuality.
- Add one or two quotes from cases if you can remember them.
- Consider in a little more detail if the cases of *Cornwall CC* and *Prater* and *Carmichael* are really that different or whether there might have been policy reasons to distinguish them.

! Don't be tempted to…

- Simply list the cases you remember without any explanation – this approach doesn't show you have understood the cases.
- Spend more than a short paragraph on the various tests – that's not what the question is about.
- Give the facts of all the cases in detail – you will run out of time and your answer will be too descriptive.

? Question 2

Tania, a mother of three young children, decides to return to work full-time. She interviews several girls for the post of nanny but decides that only Anna is suitable. Anna is a keen dancer and tells Tania that she will only be able to work until 5.00 pm as she gives salsa lessons in the evenings. As this forms a considerable part of her income she wishes to be classed as self-employed. Tania agrees that the children may sometimes spend their time out of school at Anna's house rather than hers, and that if Anna should fall ill or (very occasionally) need to give salsa lessons during the day, Anna's mother may take over her duties. Anna agrees to use her own car to take the children to and from school, but Tania pays the cost of petrol. Tania is fairly easy-going, but insists that the children do not watch TV for more than an hour a day, that Anna clears up after any meals eaten and that all toys are tidied away at the end of the day. Other than this Anna need do no housework.

Advise Tania of the benefits and detriments of Anna being classified as self-employed. Assuming that Anna's contract states that she is self-employed, assess whether an employment tribunal would be likely to regard Anna as an employee or a self-employed person.

Answer plan

→ Outline the reasons for distinguishing between employees and self-employed.

→ List the benefits and detriments to Tania including tax, NI, implied terms, statutory rights.

→ Apply the multi-factor test (*Ready Mixed Concrete (South East) Ltd* v *Minister of Pensions and National Insurance* [1968] EAT) to Anna's situation. Consider the following:
  – ability to delegate
  – children may be looked after off 'normal base'
  – control in relation to watching TV, clearing up after meals and of toys
  – significance of A's wish to be classed as self-employed.

Diagram plan

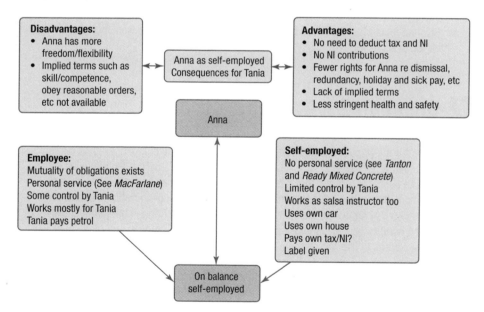

A printable version of this diagram plan is available from www.pearsoned.co.uk/lawexpressqa

Answer

[1]This first part shows that you recognise what the problem question is about and whose point of view you need to consider. This shows you have read the question fully. Many students make presumptions about what a question requires without actually reading it properly.

The answer to this scenario requires a consideration of Anna's employment status and the advantages and disadvantages associated with that status. It requires the examination of the advantages and disadvantages of self-employment from the point of view of the person hiring a worker, in this case a nanny.[1] If Anna is classed as self-employed there are a number of advantages for Tania including not having to deduct tax and National Insurance (NI) before paying Anna and not being liable for employer's NI contributions. In addition, Anna would not be able to rely on certain statutory employment rights such as unfair dismissal against Tania and Tania would not be liable for redundancy pay, sick or holiday pay, or maternity pay. She could also not be held vicariously liable for any torts committed by Anna and would have slightly less stringent health and safety obligations towards her. Both parties would not be able to rely on terms which are often implied into employment contracts as a matter of course. This can be both good and detrimental to Tania, who would not receive the benefit of duties such as the duty to obey reasonable orders, be ready and willing to work or carry out work with reasonable skill and competence. However, she would herself not be bound by the duty of mutual trust and confidence. In addition, self-employed status affords Anna more freedom and flexibility in terms of when she works and when she takes holidays and for how long. Tania therefore has less control over these matters unless they are dealt with very specifically in the contract between them. Overall, my advice to Tania would be that if agreed arrangements can be clearly set out in the contract of service, there is no reason to insist that Anna be an employee.[2]

[2]This paragraph provides a summary of the advantages and disadvantages as seen from Tania's point of view and then concludes with the advice you would give. Do not sit on the fence; you need to make up your mind if you are advising someone.

[3]This sentence shows clear recognition of what the next part of the scenario requires you to consider.

The next part of the scenario requires a consideration of the tests used by the courts to determine whether or not Anna would be classed as an employee by a tribunal.[3] A series of tests was developed over the years starting with the control test (**Yewens v Noakes** [1880] 6 QBD 530, CA) and moving onto the integration (**Cassidy v Ministry of Health** [1951] 2 KB 343, CA) and economic reality (**Market Investigations v Minister of Social Security** [1969] 2 QB 173, QBD) tests. Elements of each of these tests survive in the modern multi-factor test, which was first established in **Ready Mixed Concrete v Minister of Pensions and National Insurance** [1968] 1 All ER 433, HC. Applying this test involves a consideration of all the factors characterising the employment relationship and weighing them up against each other. Subsequent cases, in particular **Carmichael v National Power plc** [1999] 4 All ER 897 and **Montgomery v Johnson Underwood Ltd** [2001] EWCA Civ 318, CA have clarified that mutuality of obligations and personal service are the key factors without which no employment contract can exist.[4]

In the given scenario there seems to be mutuality of obligations in that Anna is obliged to accept the child care work and Tania is obliged to offer it to her.[5] This would indicate the presence of a contract of employment. However, the agreement allows for Anna's mum to take over the child care duties should Anna not be available in specific circumstances. This seems incompatible with the requirement of personal service. This approach is confirmed by **Express and Echo Publications Ltd v Tanton** [1999] IRLR 367, CA where a driver was allowed to send someone else if he was unavailable. However, in **MacFarlane and Another v Glasgow City Council** [2001] IRLR 7, EAT personal service was found to be present where a gymnastics instructor could substitute someone from an approved list when she was unable to take her classes herself. It seems this situation is comparable to Anna nominating one person who can take over her duties in specified circumstances. It seems, then, that both mutuality of obligations and personal service are present, which would indicate that Anna could be an employee.[6]

However, there are other factors to take into consideration when applying the multi-factor test.[7] Anna can take the children 'off base' and look after them at her house instead. She also uses her own car and is paid for the petrol. Parallels can be drawn here with **Ready Mixed Concrete** where the workers owned their own vehicles and maintained them at their own expense.[8] They were required to paint them in the company colours and the company could also require the owner/drivers to carry out repairs and specify where these should be done. The vehicles could not be used for work other than Ready Mixed's. The drivers were generally required to provide personal service; they could delegate to another competent driver, but the company retained the right to insist on the work being carried out in person. As far as control was concerned, they had no fixed hours of work and could choose their own routes but they had to be available if required and obey reasonable orders 'as if ... an employee'. Anna uses her own car, which she is

[4] A brief summary of the law which is relevant can be useful as it indicates your understanding of the area and sets the scene for the application of the law. It also allows you to bring in some of the key cases.

[5] This sentence is a very clear application of how mutuality of obligations works in this case.

[6] This paragraph follows on from the one above by dealing first with the two key elements of an employment contract identified above. It concludes with the advice you might give based purely on those two key factors.

[7] This paragraph recognises that there are other factors besides the two key ones indentified and examines the factors present in the scenario in light of the relevant case law.

[8] Here it is useful to explain why the facts are relevant and drawing parallels with case law shows you understand the law clearly and can apply it.

also free to use for other work and activities. She maintains the car at her own expense although Tania does pay for petrol. Anna chooses the way in which she carries out the work and can delegate that work to one other known person. While Tania has made some requests over the children's TV watching and the clearing up, she asserts very little control over the day-to-day activities Anna undertakes with the children and it is unlikely that this would be sufficient control as required in **Johnson**.

Furthermore, if Tania pays Anna direct and leaves tax and NI responsibility to her, this will be further indication of self-employed status. Anna's work as a salsa instructor may also indicate that she is self-employed as she is not wholly reliant on Tania as the sole provider of her work. Considering elements from the economic reality test as well as the integration test would further suggest that Anna is 'in business on her own account' rather than an integral part of someone else's business.[9]

[9]This paragraph highlights further factors, referring specifically to the tests developed by the courts.

Lastly, it is worth considering Anna's request to be classed as self-employed.[10] In **Ferguson v John Dawson and Partners Ltd** [1976] 3 All ER 817, CA the relationship was described as one of self-employment in spite of the fact that the individual concerned was a labour only sub-contractor. In all other respects the indications were that this was an ordinary contract of employment. The Court of Appeal held that the label could not make a relationship one of self-employment without more. In **Massey v Crown Life Assurance Co** [1978] 2 All ER 576, CA, the branch manager of an insurance office asked to have his employment status altered to take advantage of the more favourable tax regime for self-employed persons. Later he claimed that notwithstanding the label he was an employee. The Court of Appeal held that the basis of his employment had been changed and that he was indeed self-employed. In the later case of **Young and Woods Ltd v West** [1980] IRLR 201, CA the court took the opportunity to narrow the effect of **Massey** by noting that the change of status in that case was crucial. Labels are therefore not a decisive factor, but one element in the multi-factor test along with all of the other relevant indicators; and Anna's request can be taken into consideration.[11]

[10]The question specifically refers to Anna's request to be classed as self-employed, so the label the parties have given the relationship needs to be considered explicitly (which is what this paragraph does).

[11]Remember to state what the law means for the scenario. Without that, your answer is too abstract to gain many marks.

[12]The conclusion refers back to the questions and the preceding discussion and sets out the advice you would give or conclusion you would come to. Again, you should decide and the decision should be based on the considerations above.

In conclusion, following **Ready Mixed Concrete** and taking into account all the factors outlined above, it seems that there is nothing to suggest that Anna's employment relationship with Tania is inconsistent with Anna being self-employed.[12]

Make your answer stand out

- Add additional cases to illustrate the kind of duties that might be implied into an employment contract. Consult your lecture notes on implied terms.
- Set out your answer as if you were directly advising Tania – for example, in letter format.
- Expand on the factors used in the economic reality test and apply them to the situation here. Saying a little about the facts of *Market Investigations* would help illustrate this.

! Don't be tempted to…

- Simply state the law without applying it to the scenario.
- Give the facts of every case you cite; select the relevant facts that are required for your argument to make sense.
- List every case you can remember dealing with these issues; select those that are relevant to building your argument and giving your advice.
- Sit on the fence – give Anna clear advice as the question asks you to.

? Question 3

Ernest runs a small luxury cattery chain called 'Micehouse Ltd' where pet owners can leave their cats when going on holiday. Cath has been working for him for four years doing the books. She has an agreement with Micehouse Ltd that states she is to work 'when required' and in reality has worked four mornings a week ever since she started working there. Cath also works as a receptionist at a solicitor's practice down the road three afternoons a week and occasionally helps with bookkeeping in small local businesses. Cath wants to know whether she is an employee of Micehouse Ltd.

Amy was also working at the Micehouse Ltd Bradford branch grooming the cats. Her agreement states she is to work as and when required and must be available for work at short notice. She has worked between 15 and 20 hours a week for the past 13 months but has been off sick for eight weeks after one of the cats attacked her. She has been dismissed following customer complaints and wants to bring a claim for unfair dismissal.

Edward, another of the cat grooms, began working at Micehouse Ltd in Bingley through a recruitment agency on a temporary basis. The recruitment agency continued to send him to Micehouse for nine months. Ernest then realised he would need someone permanent as business showed no sign of slowing down and he advertised the job Edward was doing.

Edward got the job and was employed by Micehouse Ltd. Following a row with Ernest, Edward was dismissed four months later. He wants to claim unfair dismissal.

Advise all three (you are not required to advise on the likelihood of success of their claims)

Answer plan

→ Identify the legal issue: are the three people employees or not?

→ Set out the legal test for identifying employee status: control, integration, economic reality tests and now modern multi-factor test.

→ Apply the tests to each scenario:
   – Cath – factors both ways – what about her other work?
   – Amy – is she obliged to work?
   – Edward – agency worker, when did he become an employee of Micehouse.

Diagram plan

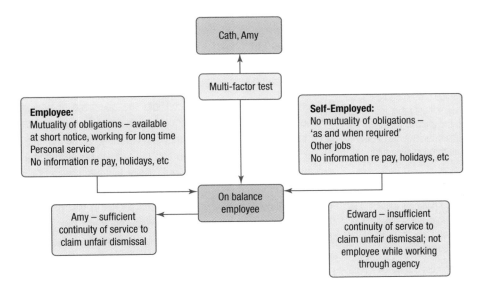

A printable version of this diagram plan is available from www.pearsoned.co.uk/lawexpressqa

Answer

[1]A brief introduction to the issues raised, which shows clearly that you have understood the scope of the question and what your task is.

[2]A brief summary of the law shows you have a grasp of the sort of considerations you will have to apply to the scenario and allows you to move on to the application fairly quickly.

[3]It usually makes sense to examine those factors classed as essential first; if they give you the answer you save yourself the trouble of having to go through everything.

[4]While the scenario does not explicitly state she must provide personal service, the facts do suggest this, so say why you think that's what the facts suggest.

[5]Remember the obligation has to be mutual.

[6]You need to make this point clear – the contract as far as we know does not suggest mutuality but the actual practice suggests otherwise.

The problem question requires an assessment of whether Cath, Edward and Amy are employees and therefore entitled to the most generous protection available in employment law. The question does not ask about the likely success of the claim; the focus is therefore on establishing whether or not the three advisees are employees or not.[1]

A series of tests was developed over the years starting with the control test (**Yewen v Noakes** [1880] 6 QBD 530, CA) and moving onto the integration (**Cassidy v Minister of Health** [1951] 2 KB 343, CA) and economic reality (**Market Investigations Ltd v Minister of Social Security** [1969] 2 QB 173, QBD) tests. Elements of each of these tests survive in the modern multi factor test which was first established in **Ready Mixed Concrete v Minister of Pensions and National Insurance** [1968] 1 All ER 433, HC. Applying this test involves a consideration of all the factors characterising the employment relationship and weighing them up against each other. Subsequent cases, in particular **Carmichael v National Power** [2000] IRLR 43, HL and **Montgomery v Johnson Underwood Ltd** [2001] EWCA Civ 318, CA have clarified that mutuality of obligations and personal service are the key factors without which no employment contract can exist.[2]

It thus makes some sense to consider the questions of personal service and mutuality of obligations in relation to Cath first.[3] There is no indication in the scenario that she can send someone else to do her work if she is unavailable and the facts suggest that she is expected to do work 'when required'. There is no indication of Cath and Ernest having contemplated anything other than personal service in this instance.[4] Mutuality of obligations seems at first glance not to be established. Cath was to work 'when required'. This suggests that Ernest does not see himself as obliged to provide her with work, although he does expect Cath to take work when he has it available.[5] However, the fact that Cath has worked four days a week on a regular basis suggests that mutuality of obligation is established after all. It suggests that Cath now has a legitimate expectation that work will be provided for her for four mornings a week.[6] In this context the case of **Carmichael** must be distinguished. While the case suggests that even a long-standing relationship between a company and someone working for that company does not necessarily give rise to an employment relationship, the arrangements in that case seemed to be more flexible. Cath appears to be working on a very regular basis that does not vary according to when work is available.

It thus seems that personal service and mutuality of service are established so the essential requirements of employee status are met. However, other factors also need consideration. For example, it would be helpful to know more about Cath's situation: whether she is responsible for her own tax payments or what the arrangements are in relation to holidays or time off sick. The fact that Cath works for two other businesses might indicate that she is in business on her own account and thus self-employed. However, this is not conclusive and it would again be useful to know more about her other activities and the basis on which she carries these out. She might be employed by the solicitors or she could be a self-employed bookkeeper. The facts given do not allow us to come to a definitive conclusion although it seems that Cath is employed by Ernest and may also be working on a self-employed basis as well.[7] The scenario does not state why Cath wants advice on her employment status and this may be worth asking first off, as it might provide an insight into what the underlying issue in this case is.

Very similar considerations must apply in Amy's case. She is clearly required to provide personal service and her contract suggests that she must be available at short notice, meaning that she is not really in a position to take any other work; the economic reality, therefore, is that she is dependent on Ernest. It also suggests that she is obliged to take the work offered to her. What is not entirely clear is whether Ernest is obliged to offer her work.[8] She has worked 15–20 hours every week for a significant period of time which might indicate he is but, following **Carmichael**, some uncertainty remains. More information on the work arrangements would be necessary to be certain. Amy requires 12 months' service to be able to claim unfair dismissal.[9] She has worked for 13 months, with 8 weeks off sick. This time off, however, will not break her continuity in service (Employment Rights Act 1996, s 112(3)(a)) so she is able to bring a claim as long as she does indeed qualify as an employee.

The situation regarding Edward is relatively straightforward. The scenario confirms that Edward is an employee and has been for

[7]It is important that you show awareness of the sort of issues you must consider in relation to working out Cath's status. It shows understanding of how this area of law operates in practice. You must decide on balance which side of the line Cath falls in this example.

[8]This is picking up the same point made above, in relation to Cath so you do not need to explain this in any detail again.

[9]You must now deal with the second legal issue arising, which is whether Amy has sufficient continuity.

[10]You should therefore not waste your time going through the tests to try to work out what the scenario clearly tells you.

[11]To be able to claim, he would have to establish that he was an employee of Micehouse when he was working there through the agency.

[12]It is useful to briefly summarise your advice at the end to conclude your answer so you can check you have covered everything you intended to.

four months.[10] In order to claim unfair dismissal, he must, however, have 12 months' service so the question arising is whether his time working through the agency counts towards his continuous service.[11] While there was some confusion in the early case law, the law relating to agency workers has recently been clarified in **James v London Borough of Greenwich** [2008] EWCA Civ 35, EAT, in which the EAT gave clear guidance on determining employment status of agency workers and confirmed that rarely will there be a contract of employment between the end user and the worker because of lack of control and mutuality of obligations. Edward was therefore not an employee of Micehouse while employed through the agency and can therefore not bring a claim.

In conclusion, it seems likely that Cath and Amy are employees and we know that Edward is. However, Edward will not be able to claim unfair dismissal because he does not have sufficient continuity. Amy can bring her claim and we are not sure why Cath seeks clarification of her status.[12]

✓ Make your answer stand out

- Integrate the legal analysis and application a little more rather than dealing with one and then the other.
- Provide a few more case examples when applying the law to the facts, particularly in relation to Cath working in more than one business.
- Set out your answer as direct advice to Cath, Amy and Edward. This will make it less abstract.

! Don't be tempted to…

- Simply state the law without applying it to the scenario.
- Give the facts of every case you cite; select the relevant facts.
- List every case you can remember dealing with these issues; select those that are relevant to building your argument and giving your advice.
- Sit on the fence – if it says 'advise' you need to do so one way or another.

🔖 Question 4

Critically examine, by reference to case law, the tests used by the courts over the years to establish employment status and briefly indicate the advantages and disadvantages of each test.

Answer plan

➡ Set out the Employment Rights Act 1996 (ERA 1996) definition.

➡ Set out each historical test in turn including advantages and disadvantages.
  – control
  – integration
  – economic reality.

➡ Set out the multi-factor test and discuss its advantages and disadvantages.

Diagram plan

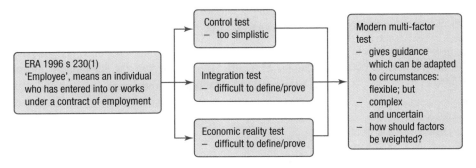

A printable version of this diagram plan is available from www.pearsoned.co.uk/lawexpressqa

Answer

The question of who is an employee is fundamental in employment law. Employees have certain important statutory rights including the right not to be unfairly dismissed which workers or the self-employed do not have. The Employment Rights Act 1996 defines an employee as 'an individual who has entered or works under … a contract of employment'. However, the definition is not particularly helpful and the courts have therefore turned to a number of 'tests' to establish who is an employee.[1]

The first test to be used by the courts in the nineteenth century was the 'control test' (**Yewens v Noakes** [1880] 6 QBD 530, CA) in which the amount of control the employer had over the employee would be determinative of employee status.[2] However, the control test was too blunt an instrument for dealing with the rising complexity of work and the labour market.[3] For example, highly skilled employees cannot be said to be under the control of their employers when carrying out their work: pilots, scientists or even lecturers provide ready examples. Although the control test is now outdated, it has not been abandoned and often features as part of the consideration.[4] It has been of particular importance when considering cases of atypical work, agency and temporary work (see **Motorola Ltd v Davidson and Melville Craig Group Ltd** [2001] All ER (D) 1353 (May) EAT, **McMeechan v Secretary of State for Employment** [1997] IRLR 353, CA, **Montgomery v Johnson Underwood Ltd** [2001] EWCA Civ 318, CA and **Dacas v Brook Street Bureau** [2004] EWCA Civ 217, EAT, **Cable & Wireless v Muscat** [2006] EWCA Civ 220, CA, **James v Greenwich LBC** [2008] EWCA Civ 35, EAT).[5]

The second test that developed was the integration test (**Cassidy v Minister of Health** [1951] 2 KB 343, CA, **Stevenson, Jordan and Harrison Ltd v MacDonald and Evans** [1952] 1 TLR 101, CA). This test considers whether the work carried out is done as an integral part of the business. It seems straightforward but raises questions of definition.[6] So, for example, it may not always be clear what is integral to the business or what exactly the business is. Integration into an organisation or business can be hard to show and thus evidential issues arise. A further test, that of economic reality (**Market Investigations v Minister of Social Security** [1969] 2 QB 173, QBD), which is in essence the reverse of the integration test and asks whether or not someone is in business on their own account, throws up similar issues.

The courts therefore gradually moved away from seeing one factor as conclusive and instead applied a more holistic test taking account of a number of factors.[7] This test was set out in **Ready Mixed Concrete (South East) Ltd v Minister of Pensions and**

---

[1] The introduction should set out why this is an important issue: it should include the ERA definition and refer to the common law tests.

[2] Each test should be explained first; this can be done quickly in one sentence, as shown here.

[3] Highlight any problems with the test and, if you can, illustrate with an example (that comes next).

[4] Here you are acknowledging that control is still an important consideration, so the test lives on as one of the factors.

[5] Giving examples shows you know your case law; if you have time you could say a little (but not too much) about these cases. You also do not necessarily need that many – one or two illustrations would suffice.

[6] Here you have explained the test and set out what the problem with it is. What follows is the illustration, or evidence, for your assertion. This is where you show you fully understand the issues.

[7] Quick explanation of the modern test, which shows you clearly understand how it works. You can then go on to illustrate it in more detail but you have quickly picked up some key marks.

National Insurance [1968] a All ER 433, HC, where it was said that a contract of service exists if these three conditions are fulfilled:

(i) The servant agrees that, in consideration of a wage or other remuneration, he will provide his own work and skill in the performance of some service for his master.

(ii) He agrees, expressly or impliedly, that in the performance of that service he will be subject to the other's control in a sufficient degree to make that other master.

(iii) The other provisions of the contract are consistent with its being a contract of service.[8]

[8]If you cannot remember the quotes, use your own words. As long as you get the meaning it does not matter at all in an exam.

This test has since been applied to cases where employment status is at issue and courts have concluded that personal service (**Express and Echo Publications Ltd v Tanton** [1999] 1 All ER 617, CA, **MacFarlane v Glasgow City Council** [2001] IRLR 7, EAT) and mutuality of obligations (**O'Kelly v Trusthouse Forte Plc** [1983] 3 All ER 456, CA, **Cornwall County Council v Prater** [2006] EWCA, Civ 102, CA, **Carmichael and Leese v National Power plc** [2000] IRLR 43, HL) must exist as a minimum for there to be an employer/employee relationship. Factors to be considered included all the elements previously considered under individual tests but each of these factors could be considered and the court's conclusion would be based on whether or not the overall picture was one of an employee or rather one of someone carrying out self-employment.

[9]You have set out the test and now move on to consider the advantages/disadvantages; this logical structure makes your answer easy to follow.

One advantage of the multi-factor test is its flexibility:[9] All relevant factors are considered, with no single factor being decisive. By looking at all the circumstances of the case, and giving appropriate weight to the relevant factors without too much reliance on one or two, the court is likely to reach a more balanced view. However,[10] there is no guidance as to what weight should be given to factors and which factors will ultimately be more important than others. Complex cases will be difficult to predict as the weight assigned to certain factors by the parties may not be the same as the weight assigned by the tribunal or court. This in turn makes it significantly more difficult for parties to know whether or not they are exposed to certain obligations, such as that relating to the employer's vicarious liability, or the right to claim unfair dismissal as an employee.

[10]If you follow an advantage with a disadvantage as done here you can deal with issues which overlap (such as flexibility being both good and bad) without having to repeat issues later.

In conclusion, it is clear that the tests had their time and place and were appropriate in relation to the cases in which they were

[11]This is a useful confirmation that you understand what the issue is and how the test provides some solutions to the issues.

set out. Application of those tests has developed into a tool which is far less blunt now than each individual test might indicate. The multi-factor test provides guidance without setting out rigid rules.[11] The guidance allows for flexibility and allows the tribunal or court to adapt the test to the case in question. However, this flexibility can also be a weakness because it provides uncertainty. Atypical employment, in particular, has caused problems in this regard and although the situation regarding agency workers is much clearer following **James**, uncertainties remain regarding the interpretation of mutuality of obligations in relation to casual and temporary workers.[12]

[12]A conclusion which summarises your points about flexibility, making clear the advantages but also the fact that there are drawbacks.

 Make your answer stand out

- Expand the discussion regarding agency workers and control by considering *James* in more detail and questioning who really has control of the agency worker.
- Refer to the Agency Workers Directive and Agency Workers Regulations.
- Expand your discussion of mutuality of obligations in relation to casual workers in particular.
- The flexibility of the approach now used is often cited as a major advantage in cases relating to directors; you could explore this.

! Don't be tempted to...

- Give lots of detail about the cases because the question asks for references to case law – only give the facts where this actually helps make or illustrate your point.
- Describe the tests in lots of detail. You need to explain them and consider their strengths and weaknesses.
- Ignore the multi-factor test and just concentrate on the historical tests. The multi-factor test is a culmination of all the tests and the one currently used, so you must consider it.

The contract of employment

3

How this topic may come up in exams

The contract of employment is central to understanding how employment law works and the topic provides great opportunities for assessment. Both essay and problem questions are common. In both cases you will be asked to demonstrate your knowledge of how employment contracts are constructed and your understanding of the different types of contractual terms. Essay questions tend to focus on the importance of implied terms, in particular that of mutual trust and confidence, a theme taken up by many problem questions too. Other questions could relate to specific issues such as protection of confidential information or the use of Section 1 statements, for example.

Attack the question

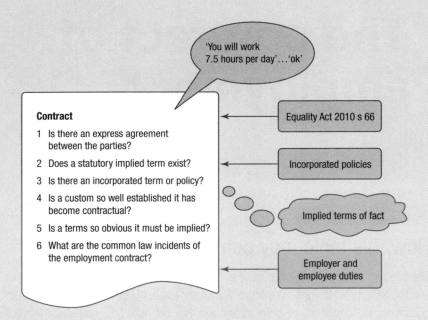

'You will work
7.5 hours per day'...'ok'

Contract

1 Is there an express agreement between the parties?

2 Does a statutory implied term exist?

3 Is there an incorporated term or policy?

4 Is a custom so well established it has become contractual?

5 Is a terms so obvious it must be implied?

6 What are the common law incidents of the employment contract?

Equality Act 2010 s 66

Incorporated policies

Implied terms of fact

Employer and employee duties

A printable version of this diagram plan is available from www.pearsoned.co.uk/lawexpressqa

📝 Question 1

Critically assess the importance of implied contractual terms in employment law.

Answer plan

→ Explain briefly the nature of the employment contract (not in writing, unlikely to expressly include all terms).

→ Consider implied terms of fact:
   – based on parties' presumed intention.
   – based on custom and practice.

→ Consider common law incidents of the employment contract – employers' and employees' duties.

→ Conclude regarding implied terms' importance.

Diagram plan

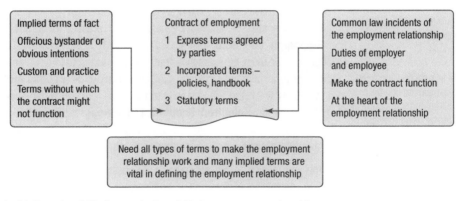

Implied terms of fact	Contract of employment	Common law incidents of the employment relationship
Officious bystander or obvious intentions	1 Express terms agreed by parties	Duties of employer and employee
Custom and practice	2 Incorporated terms – policies, handbook	Make the contract function
Terms without which the contract might not function	3 Statutory terms	At the heart of the employment relationship

Need all types of terms to make the employment relationship work and many implied terms are vital in defining the employment relationship

A printable version of this diagram plan is available from www.pearsoned.co.uk/lawexpressqa

Answer

Employment contracts, like most other contracts, do not have to be in writing and, as with other contracts, the parties are unlikely to agree all the terms and conditions which will make up the contract. While the express terms – those agreed by the parties explicitly

[1]In this introduction you set out the basic issue you are asked about and define the key terms. You have explained what express terms are, provided an overview of employment contracts and indicated the structure of your answer.

[2]By referring to normal contract law principles you are showing a broader knowledge of law and that you appreciate overlap between subjects. You are also acknowledging the common law underpinning of employment law.

[3]This section gives you the chance to highlight that you know your contract law and understand that basic contract law principles also apply in an employment context.

[4]In this section you need to explain implied terms of custom and that can best be done by using a couple of examples.

[5]The common law incidents need a little more introduction as shown here as you are now beginning to depart from the basic contract principles and are looking at something which is employment law specific.

[6]You do not have to go through all the duties in detail; a summary as shown here is fine.

– are likely to cover those items the parties consider important such as pay, working hours, place of work and leave entitlements, for example, implied terms deal with matters not explicitly considered by the contracting parties. Implied terms, in the employment context, cover implied terms of fact and implied terms of law. They will be considered in turn.[1]

Implied terms of fact are familiar from a contract law[2] context and arise out of the factual situations, either to make a contract workable or to recognise the importance of custom and practice in a particular area. As in contract law, the 'officious bystander test' also applies in employment law; and in situations where the intention of the parties appears obvious it can be implied into the employment contract.[3] An example is **O'Brien v Associated Fire Alarms Ltd** [1968] 1 WLR 1916, CA which concerned a change of workplace. The contract was silent as to the place of work but the employee had always been based in Liverpool. The court said that if a mobility clause was to be implied as a question of fact from the circumstances surrounding this situation, then its maximum extent would be the Merseyside Area.

The case that is usually cited as authority for the proposition that terms can also be implied by custom and practice is **Sagar v Ridehalgh and Sons Ltd** [1931] 1 Ch 310, CA. According to this case it must be a practice that is usual and notorious within a particular local area or industry. Further, in **Hardwick v Leeds AHA** [1975] IRLR 31, Ind Trib, it was held that such terms also had to be reasonable. In **Solectron Scotland Ltd v Roper** [2004] IRLR 4, EAT, it was doubted whether custom and practice could ever imply a term that allowed variation of other contractual rights.[4]

The law relating to the employment relationship has developed over time, originating in the master and servant relationship, and many features re-emerged in the era of contract through a process of implying the obligations arising out of employment status into virtually all contracts of employment. These 'common law incidents' of the contract of employment consist of the employer's and employee's duties.[5] They are the fundamental characteristics of the employment relationship and include the duties to provide work and be available for work, to pay wages, to obey reasonable instructions and take care and competence when carrying out work, as well as duties of loyalty and fidelity and mutual trust and confidence.[6] Some of these are vital to

[7]Remember the question: here you are partly answering it and commenting on the importance of the common law incidents – using mutual trust as an example.

[8]The first example you use should clearly set out the legal principle as done here; the examples which follow can then be read in that context.

[9]Quotes like these are easier to remember than some of the technical passages from cases and if you can remember them, they add a little context and personality to your answer.

the proper functioning of the employment relationship and mutual trust and confidence in particular has developed into a crucially important implied term.[7] For example, in **Robinson v Crompton Parkinson Ltd** [1978] IRLR 61, EAT, an electrician was unfairly and improperly accused of stealing from his employer. When he did not receive an apology he resigned and claimed constructive unfair dismissal. The Employment Appeals Tribunal (EAT) accepted the argument that there was a duty on the part of the employer to act consistently with a requirement of mutual trust. If the employer acts inconsistently with this, their conduct can amount to a repudiation of the contract.[8] In **Courtaulds Northern Textiles v Andrew** [1979] IRLR 84, EAT an assistant manager had argued with an employee and in the course of the argument said 'you can't do the bloody job anyway'.[9] It was held that the employer was under an obligation not to conduct him/herself in a manner intended to destroy or seriously damage the employment relationship. Perhaps more surprising was the more recent finding in **Malik v BCCI** [1997] All ER 1, HL that the employer was in breach of the implied duty when they conducted their business in a corrupt and dishonest manner, damaging the employee's reputation.

The centrality of mutuality is such that it has also been used to qualify apparently clear express terms. In **Johnstone v Bloomsbury Health Authority** [1992] QB 333, CA it qualified a term that seemed to allow the employer to insist on the working of excessive hours regardless of the impact on the junior doctor's health. In **Scally v Southern Health and Social Services Board** [1991] 4 All ER 563, HL it included a duty to inform employees of rights that they were entitled to exercise. In **United Bank Ltd v Akhtar** [1989] IRLR 507, EAT the EAT held that the industrial tribunal was entitled to imply into the contract a requirement that reasonable notice should be given in the exercise of the bank's power to require mobility of its employees. However, in the case of **Reda v Flag Ltd** [2002] IRLR 474, PC the Privy Council refused to allow an express term that the contract of employment could be terminated at any time to be ousted by the implied term of mutual trust and confidence.[10] It was held here that special circumstances such as mutually inconsistent express terms should be present before allowing an implied term to modify a contrary express term.[11]

[10]You have already given a number of examples which show the scope of the term; it is useful to also give one or two examples where the term has not been successfully implied.

[11]This might seem like you have gone off track and decided to focus on mutual trust but that particular implied term is vital in the employment relationship so the discussion is relevant.

The other common law incidents of the employment relationship are also important in shaping the employment relationship by, for example, ensuring that employees are under a duty not to compete with their employer or pass on confidential information to competitors. However, many of these have been deemed so important that they have been dealt with in some way by legislation. The employers' obligations relating to health and safety, as well as the whistleblower protection, serve as useful examples. Overall, however, implied terms are vital to the functioning of employment contracts. Most contracts are not written and there may be some uncertainty as to the exact detail of all terms. Implying terms of fact therefore makes sense to fill in those gaps which can be filled in without having to guess at the parties' intentions. The implied terms which relate to the common law duties of employers and employees might seem a little odd and there is an argument that contractual terms should be left to the parties and important issues should be legislated on. However, employment law develops fast and retaining this common law approach, which can develop in line with the labour market needs, also has its advantages. The centrality of implied terms can be illustrated using mutual trust and confidence as an example. This term seems to go to the heart of what the employment relationship should be about: trust and respect between the parties involved. For the reasons set out above, implied terms therefore remain of utmost importance in employment contracts.[12]

[12]Your conclusion should pull all the points together; in this case it also provides a justification for having written a fair amount about mutual trust. The conclusion also links back directly to the question, which is something many examiners look for.

✓ Make your answer stand out

- Add some academic commentary. For example, D. Brodie, 'Reflecting the Dynamics of Employment Relations: Terms Implied from Custom or Practice and the Albion Case', (2004) 33 ILJ 159; D. Cabrelli, 'Discretion, Power and the Rationalisation of Implied Terms' (2007) 36 ILJ 194.
- Expand the discussion on the other common law such as the duty of fidelity to give a more balanced picture.
- Provide examples from case law such as *Faccenda Chicken* v *Fowler* in relation to confidential information.

! Don't be tempted to...

- Simply go through all the different types of implied terms; pick and choose to highlight their importance.
- Ignore implied terms of fact and focus only on the implied duties of employer and employee.

Question 2

To what extent does the law impose on both parties to the contract of employment an implied duty of good faith?

Answer plan

→ Set out the important nature of an employment relationship.

→ Explain the implication of terms into all employment contracts.

→ Highlight the importance of mutuality of obligations and the duty of fidelity in this context and explain the duties.

→ Use examples to illustrate the extent of the duties.

→ Conclude whether the duties mean that good faith is required in the employment relationship.

Diagram plan

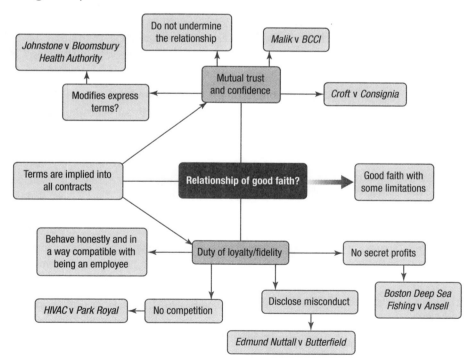

A printable version of this diagram plan is available from www.pearsoned.co.uk/lawexpressqa

Answer

The employment relationship constitutes an intimate and important contract between employer and employee. This essay considers whether or not implied duties of loyalty and fidelity and mutual trust and confidence between employer and employee now lead to a situation where the employment relationship can actually be characterised as one of good faith.[1] At common law a number of duties are implied into contracts of employment. This essay is chiefly concerned with the duty of mutual trust and confidence and the duty of loyalty and fidelity. Each will be considered in turn.

[1] This introduction restates the question and adds the focus of the essay by setting out which contractual terms you are going to consider.

The duty of mutual trust and confidence is of relatively recent origin and can best be illustrated by a series of cases identifying an obligation on the part of the employer to not act in a way so as to undermine the employment relationship.[2] In **Robinson v Crompton Parkinson Ltd** [1978] IRLR 61, EAT, an electrician was unfairly and improperly accused of stealing from his employer. When he did not receive an apology he resigned and claimed constructive unfair dismissal. The EAT accepted the argument that there was a duty on the part of the employer to act consistently with a requirement of mutual trust.

[2] First explain what mutual trust is and then illustrate your explanation with examples from case law – this shows you really do understand the law.

In **Courtaulds Northern Textiles v Andrew** [1979] IRLR 84, EAT an assistant manager had argued with an employee and in the course of the argument said 'you can't do the bloody job anyway'. It was held that the employer was under an obligation not to conduct him/herself in a manner intended to destroy or seriously damage the employment relationship. Perhaps more surprising was the more recent finding in **Malik v BCCI** [1997] 3 All ER 1, HL that the employer was in breach of the implied duty when they conducted their business in a corrupt and dishonest manner, damaging the employee's reputation.[3] Further examples might include the refusal to make reasonable adjustments under the Disability Discrimination Act **(Greenhof v Barnsley MDC** [2005] All ER (D) 347 (Oct), EAT**)**.

[3] There is a good spread of examples here, setting out the scope of the implied duty. If you had time you could expand on *Malik·v BCCI* a little because of its importance but be careful not to go off track.

By way of contrast[4], in **Woods v WM Car Services (Peterborough) Ltd** [1981] IRLR 413, CA the employee was engaged as chief secretary and accounts clerk. When the business was taken over she was first pressurised into working longer hours and to take a pay cut. When she resisted this successfully, the employer dropped

[4] It can really help clarify a point if you can bring examples falling on both sides of the line – here what might be a breach and what was held not to be.

5 You are not likely to have time to go into much detail on the cases here. Illustrate one fully as you have done in *Woods* and then briefly cite one or two more to show that you really do have a grasp of the scope of the duty.

6In this one sentence you show that you really do understand the importance of mutual trust and confidence as a term.

7You have explained and illustrated mutual trust and this section is your little conclusion for that section before moving on to the second term you want to discuss.

8Introduce the next implied term and explain it briefly. Each aspect of the term then needs a quick explanation and illustration using case law.

the word 'chief' from her job title and gave her additional duties. She left and claimed constructive unfair dismissal. It was accepted that there is an implied term of mutual trust and confidence, but there was no breach in this case. Other examples include the refusal of permission to use female toilets to a pre-operative transsexual as in **Croft v Consignia plc** [2002] IRLR 851, EAT.[5]

The centrality of mutuality is such that it has also been used to qualify apparently clear express terms.[6] In **Johnstone v Bloomsbury Health Authority** [1992] QB 333, CA it qualified a term that seemed to allow the employer to insist on the working of excessive hours regardless of the impact on the junior doctor's health. However, in the recent case of **Reda v Flag Ltd** [2002] IRLR 474, PC the Privy Council refused to allow an express term that the contract of employment could be terminated at any time to be ousted by the implied term of mutual trust and confidence. It was held here that special circumstances such as mutually inconsistent express terms should be present before allowing an implied term to modify a contrary express term.

Mutual trust and confidence is therefore of critical importance although in most cases express terms will override the implied term and parties are free to agree their terms. There is thus no suggestion that the employer must have the best interest of their employees in mind when negotiating contracts with them or that they must act in good faith toward them at that point; simply that once in an employment relationship, they must not undermine it.[7]

The duty overlaps and complements the duty of fidelity, or loyalty and honesty that an employee owes to an employer. This duty has several different aspects.[8] In **Boston Deep Sea Fishing v Ansell** [1888] 39 Ch D 339, CA, the employee had received a personal commission. This was held to be inconsistent with his duty not to make a secret profit.

There is a question whether the duty of loyalty and honesty entails a duty to disclose misconduct. Whether it does or not depends on the circumstances. In **Bell v Lever Bros** [1932] AC 161, HL the court refused to find that the duty required an employee to disclose their own misconduct. In **Swain v West (Butchers) Ltd** [1936] 3 All ER 261, CA it was held that a duty could be found to report the misconduct of other employees where the position of the employee in the company hierarchy requires this. In this case the employee was a manager carrying out the unlawful orders of the Managing Director.

It was held that because of the responsibilities carried by him as manager he was under a duty to disclose the MD's misconduct. In **Sybron v Rochem** [1983] 2 All ER 707, CA, a manager was party to a conspiracy to set up companies to compete with his employer. It was held that he was under a duty to disclose the misconduct as his co-conspirators were his subordinates. It did not matter that in disclosing their misconduct he would, inevitably, disclose his own. In **Edmund Nuttall v Butterfield** [2005] IRLR 751, EAT it was accepted by the EAT that the failure to disclose a criminal conviction on return to work had damaged the relationship of trust and confidence. These cases seem to indicate that there is a duty to act in good faith at least as far as the employee is concerned.[9]

[9]It is useful to refer back to the question using the language used in the question. It shows you are still on track and focused on answering the question. It also draws your points together nicely.

The duty of loyalty and honesty also prevents employees from competing with their employer. In **HIVAC v Park Royal** [1946] 1 All ER 350, CA an employee was prohibited from working for a competitor in his spare time. Courts have long been ready to imply a duty of non-disclosure of information about the company's business affairs (**Faccenda Chicken v Fowler** [1986] 1 All ER 617, CA) and an element of good faith is apparent in this approach.[10]

[10]While you do not have time to expand on this in any detail you are showing awareness of further issues and how they relate to the question at hand.

Cases dealing with mutual trust and confidence and the duty of fidelity have developed in such a way as to indicate a requirement of good faith in an employment relationship. Cases such as **Edmund Nuttal** suggest that there is an expectation that employees are open and honest with their employers and the case of **BCCI** highlights that this expectation can work both ways. Mutual trust and confidence cases where the doctrine was used to protect the employer rather than to protect the employee seem to have produced results which might have been harder to achieve through the application of more orthodox principles. Good faith thus seems to be part and parcel of the modern employment relationship albeit with some limitations as can perhaps be seen in **Woods**.[11]

[11]The conclusion here summarises the points made previously in a way that directly answers the question. There is no new material here but you are making as clear as possible how your earlier argument answers the question set.

✓ **Make your answer stand out**

- Add some academic commentary. For example, D. Brodie, 'Mutual Trust and Confidence: Catalysts, Constraints and Commonality' (2008) 37 ILJ 329; J. Linsday, 'The Implied Term of Trust and Confidence' (2001) 30 ILJ 1.
- Set out more clearly your understanding of good faith and whether it should or should not form the basis of an employment relationship.

! **Don't be tempted to...**

- Write only about the employer's or employee's duty; you need to consider the relationship as a whole.
- Go through all the cases you can think of. Focus on those that highlight issues of good faith.
- Ignore the fact that mutuality of obligations is a mutual duty applying to both employers and employees.

? Question 3

Since 2000, the university of west yorkshire has employed Sandra as a lecturer. In September she was asked to teach her subject to groups of part-time vocational students from 7 pm to 9.30 pm on three evenings a week. A month ago she was moved from her spacious ground floor office into a windowless basement room, which she has to share with two research students; and now she has been told that next semester she will be required to teach an extra subject. When she protests that this will leave her no time or space for her research she is told that that is irrelevant because 'it is never going to be publishable anyway'.

Advise Sandra.

Answer plan

→ Identify the issues to deal with: change in working hours, move and the comments made.

→ Identify the legal issues raised: Is there contract variation? Breach of mutual trust and confidence?

→ Consider if the change in hours might be a contractual variation and, if so, if it is lawful.

→ Consider whether events breach mutual trust and confidence.

Diagram plan

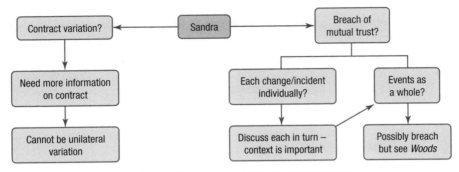

A printable version of this diagram plan is available from www.pearsoned.co.uk/lawexpressqa

Answer

[1]You've clearly set out the legal issues to be dealt with right at the start, giving the reader confidence that you know what you are doing.

This problem question raises two main issues in relation to Sandra's employment contract: first, whether or not the change in working hours is in fact a variation of her contract; and, secondly, whether recent events amount to a breach in mutual trust and confidence on the part of the employer.[1]

[2]There is a certain amount of speculation involved here; do not just presume that her contract contains a particular term unless you are specifically told that. If you do not have the information, you need to use an 'it's either this or this' sort of approach.

Sandra has been asked to teach her subject three evenings a week. We do not have any detail about her contract[2] but it would be worth asking her for a copy of it to check whether or not it makes reference to working hours. If it makes reference to working hours and does not include the possibility of working in the evenings, the university's request that Sandra teaches at these new times is a variation in her contract which cannot be enforced unilaterally by the employer. If Sandra agrees to the change, it is of course lawful. If she does not agree but has carried out her duties anyway, it is likely that she has accepted the change and it thus becomes a lawful variation (see **Jones v Associated Tunnelling Co Ltd** [1981] IRLR 477, EAT).

Similar arguments may be made in relation to her working hours and more specifically her teaching hours. We are told she is to teach three evenings a week, although we are not told whether this is in addition to or instead of her other teaching duties. In addition she is to take on another subject,which will increase her teaching hours. If her contract stipulates the teaching hours or amount of her

[3]By focusing on the fact that there is no breach of express term you are leaving the possibility open that this might be or contribute to the breach of an implied term. That's the next issue.

[4]Before you can show whether the term has been breached, you need to explain what it means.

[5]Now you can begin considering whether there has been a breach: first identify the changes/events that have taken place and consider each one in turn.

[6]Do not jump to any conclusions. Just because a change has a potentially negative effect on the employee does not mean mutual trust has been breached; context is all important.

[7]It is fine to say you need additional information in order to be able to draw a definite conclusion.

time to be spent on teaching, this may again be a variation of those contractual terms, which could not be enforced unilaterally by the university. However, if there is no specification as to teaching hours in the contract, the university's demands are not in breach of any express contractual clause.[3]

The second issue is whether or not events in relation to Sandra have amounted to a breach of mutual trust and confidence on the part of the university. The duty of mutual trust is implied into every contract of employment and obliges both parties to act in a manner that does not undermine the relationship between them (**Courtaulds Northern Textiles Ltd** *v* **Andrew** [1979] IRLR 84, EAT).[4] Considering each of the recent events in turn, it seems that the university has made a number of changes which might negatively affect Sandra at work.[5] First, she has been asked to teach in the evenings. This in itself it not a breach of trust unless specific circumstances exist: for example, Sandra having caring commitments which the university is aware of. We do not have any evidence that this is the case and, even if she does, this is unlikely to be sufficient to establish a breach of the implied term. Her move from the ground floor office to the basement also appears to be a negative move, reducing Sandra's space and privacy. However, we are not given any context in the scenario so we cannot be sure why this move took place. Again, requiring someone to move offices is not, by itself, a breach of mutual trust even if it is done for arbitrary reasons. Asking Sandra to teach an additional subject falls into the same category. It may not be ideal for Sandra but it does not seem to be a breach of trust.[6]

However, Sandra's complaint about lack of research time is met with the response that her research is not of high enough quality anyway. This seems to be a comment deliberately intended to undermine Sandra and it is difficult to see how this could be compatible with a duty to maintain trust and confidence within the employment relationship. However, much would depend on context here. We are not told whether the response was made in a heated discussion or argument or by whom it was made. Further information is required in order to be able to conclude definitively.[7]

Considering each incident in isolation, therefore, does not suggest that there has definitely been a breach of trust and confidence.

[8]If there are a number of events or changes it is always worth looking at them as a whole to see whether, taken together, events make up a breach of mutual trust.

However, looking at events together suggests that Sandra's position has been undermined by the university and that she is being singled out for treatment which might suggest a breach of the implied duty.[8] The case of **Woods v WM Car Services (Peterborough) Ltd** [1981] IRLR 413, CA suggests, however, that adding additional duties and removing the word 'chief' from the title of 'chief secretary' is not sufficient to breach mutual trust. However, in Sandra's case we have the added issue of comments about her research. Taking the conduct as a whole would suggest that the employer is behaving in a way which undermines the employment relationship. If that is established, Sandra could treat that breach as repudiatory, resign and bring a claim for unfair constructive dismissal (**Morrow v Safeway Stores plc** [2002] IRLR 9, EAT).[9] Furthermore, Sandra may have additional claims for discrimination or harassment but insufficient detail has been provided to advise on these points.

[9]Sandra will want to know what she can do about it, so briefly tell her what she can do.

✓ Make your answer stand out

- You could expand your discussion on each of the changes made by the employer, highlighting why they are not a breach when taken in isolation.
- Consider events taken as a whole in more detail. You could refer to *Western Excavating* v *Sharp* [1978] CA where the CA stated that breach must be sufficiently important to justify the employee resigning, or else it must be the last in a series of incidents that justifies his leaving.
- Consider the difference between behaving unreasonably and behaving in a way so as to undermine the employment relationship and then apply this to the situation at hand. Are the employers just being rather unreasonable or is it more serious than that?

! Don't be tempted to...

- Jump to the conclusion that there has been a breach of mutual trust because of the comments about research or because changes are being made.
- Just set out what mutual trust is – you need a detailed discussion of how that applies in the scenario.
- Ignore the issues about contract variation. It is tempting to jump straight to mutual trust but you do need to deal with all legal issues raised.

📝 Question 4

It is becoming increasingly easy for ex-employers to ensure that their ex-employees do not disclose or otherwise abuse any sensitive information belonging to the ex-employer. Critically evaluate the above statement.

Answer plan

→ Introduce the possibilities for restricting the disclosure of sensitive information: implied duty of fidelity, garden leave, restrictive covenants.

→ Consider each of these possibilities in turn, noting advantages and disadvantages.

→ Consider whether it is becoming easier for employers to restrict former employees.

Diagram plan

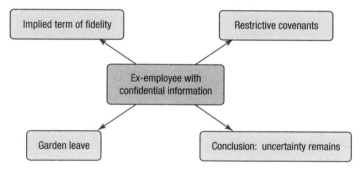

A printable version of this diagram plan is available from www.pearsoned.co.uk/lawexpressqa

Answer

[1]Set out the options open for the employer if they wish to restrict an ex-employee – it shows you know what the question is asking of you and what you will need to consider in this essay.

If an ex-employer wishes to ensure that there is no disclosure or abuse of any sensitive information by an ex-employee, the employer could either rely on a 'garden leave' clause, the implied duty of fidelity or have agreed a restrictive covenant whereby an express term in the employment contract stipulates a restraint on future activities.[1] These options require further consideration in order to answer the question set.

[2]Start by going through the options open to the employer – here we start with implied terms which seems logical but it is not the only way of doing it.

[3]Here you can highlight limitations of the approach as you are explaining it. There is no need first to explain what the law is and then to comment on it. An integrated approach like this usually reads better.

[4]You should be aware that disclosure of confidential information may sometimes be in the public interest and that protection exists for whistleblowers but you shouldn't spend too much time on this.

[5]Here you set out what the problems with the common law approach are. You then expand a little but it is really this sentence that makes your point.

[6]Here you've set out the problems with relying on an implied term; next you need to think about how those problems can be dealt with.

[7]So, having set out the issues with the common law based approach above, you can now turn to what employers have done to get round those issues.

Courts have long been ready to imply a duty of non-disclosure of information about the company's business affairs as part of the implied term of loyalty and fidelity.[2] The more confidential the information is, the more likely the courts are to grant an injunction preventing its use. For example, **Roger Bullivant Ltd v Ellis** [1987] IRLR 491, CA an ex-employee was restrained from using a card index that he had access to, which included details of all of his employer's customers. In **Johnson & Bloy v Wolstenholme** [1987] IRLR 499, CA the information was a scientific formula. The ex-employee had remembered it rather than writing it down or taking a photocopy; nevertheless, the information was protected because of its secret nature. In general, the courts are less ready to restrain information that has become part of an employee's working knowledge but it can be difficult to determine what constitutes working knowledge.[3]

In some cases an employee may wish to disclose confidential information in the public interest: to 'blow the whistle'. Problems of public policy arise when deciding whether to grant an injunction if the employee can argue that the disclosure is in the public interest. This area is now subject to statutory regulation protecting whistleblowers from unfair treatment as a result of a legitimate disclosure.[4]

It will thus sometimes be difficult for employers to know whether or not the courts will protect their confidential information and restrain competition or breach of confidence. The problem for employers is that they cannot be sure whether the implied duty will be interpreted strictly enough to protect confidential information.[5] It might be decided that it has been incorporated into the worker's general working knowledge; it might be unprotected because it was remembered rather than copied; or the public interest defence may apply. It is also worth remembering that, technically, the employers' and employees' duties end when the employment contract comes to an end and it is therefore much more difficult to apply the common law implied term to a situation where the employment relationship has ended.[6]

Employers have tried to circumvent these problems: first, through use of express terms, which can be more explicit than the implied duty may be and may also extend beyond the end of the contractual relationship itself.[7] The courts have often been wary of enforcing these so-called restrictive covenants because they offend against

8Set out the first solution
to the problem – express
restrictive covenants and
explain what they are . At
the same time you can
also highlight why they are
problematic.

9There is no real need to
explain the cases in detail.
Citing them as examples is
sufficient although, if you do
have the time, saying a few
words about each of them
would help illustrate your
argument.

10Here you are offering the
second solution and it is
useful to set out clearly
how it works and what its
purpose is.

11This explanation of garden
leave is then quickly followed
by an analysis of how well it
works.

12This is an important point
because employers need
to be aware that they might
want to use garden leave
at the beginning of the
employment relationship;
it cannot be a complete
afterthought.

13Although facts should
usually be kept to a minimum,
it is worth setting them out
here because the case goes
against the usual application
of the law and turned very
much on its facts.

public policy by acting in restraint of trade, but if certain conditions are met they may be upheld. [8] There are two basic conditions that must be satisfied if they are to be upheld: first, they must be reasonable, i.e. protect legitimate proprietary interests (in employment law this covers trade secrets and customer connections) and be reasonable between the parties; secondly, they must be in the interests of the public, i.e. not too extensive geographically or too long in duration (**see Fellowes *v* Fisher** [1976] QB 122 CA**; Thomas *v* Farr plc** [2007] EWCA Civ 118, CA).[9]

The other method used to ensure that employees cannot abuse confidential information is known as 'garden leave': employees are put on long periods of notice and paid not to work them. This is to ensure that any sensitive information has "gone off" by the time the employee is taken on by a competitor.[10] Unfortunately for the employer they are still not absolutely fool proof.[11] In **Provident Financial Group etc. *v* Hayward** [1989] 3 All ER 298, CA the plaintiff was refused an injunction restraining the employee from taking up employment towards the end of a very long period of garden leave. It was significant that there was no evidence that the employer had suffered actual detriment. There are some unresolved issues arising from the case law on garden leave. In the absence of a clause, garden leave would normally be a breach of contract as it would contradict the right to work.[12] However, the case of **SG&R Valuation Service Co *v* Boudrais** [2008] All ER (D) 141 (May), HA may give rise to some hope for employers in difficult situations. When two senior employees resigned from SG&R Valuation (SGR) Service, giving three months' notice, the company uncovered evidence of apparent wrongdoing and an intention to join a competitor company, misappropriate confidential information and damage SGR's business. The employees were put on garden leave although there was no garden leave clause in their contracts. The court determined both employees had a right to work, but that this right was not absolute. Given the evidence, the court considered it 'impossible or reasonably impracticable for the employer to provide work' and upheld the company's right to insist on garden leave being enforced until the end of the notice period.[13] However, the employers in this case had very clear evidence of wrongdoing by the employees and this is not going to be the case in most situations.

A number of avenues thus remain accessible to employers in their attempts to protect their confidential information from abuse by ex-employees. Relying simply on the implied duty of fidelity is a risky one, especially as that duty effectively comes to an end once the employment relationship ends. A better method is to use restrictive covenants that have been carefully drafted so as to protect the legitimate interests of the employer. The courts have been willing to uphold these, although they remain cautious and disproportionate restrictions on trade will not be upheld. Garden leave is therefore a popular way of ensuring that confidential and commercially sensitive information is not passed to competitors. The case of **SG&R Valuation (SGR) Service** suggests that the courts are willing to protect employers in cases of clear wrongdoing by the employee. However, making sure confidential information remains confidential is still difficult because ultimately the courts will decide what is in the public interest and thus deserves to be disclosed, what is indeed confidential information and what is a reasonable restraint on trade. In conclusion, therefore, it may have got a little easier for employers to safeguard themselves but uncertainties remain.[14]

[14]The conclusion should refer directly back to the question set and consider whether it is now easier to protect confidential information. If you can use the same language used in the question, it makes it much clearer.

✓ Make your answer stand out

- Develop your consideration of restrictive covenants by considering the matters in respect of which the employer may, in principle, seek protection: e.g. trade secrets and confidential information; trade connections; suppliers, etc. Additional cases can be cited: e.g. *Office Angels Ltd* v *Rainer-Thomas* [1991] CA.
- Take a more historical/chronological approach, focusing more on how things have changed and leading you more directly to the answer of whether it is now easier to restrict ex-employees.
- Add some discussion about whistleblower protection from the employer's point of view – how does this impact on restricting the disclosure of information?

! Don't be tempted to...

- Write much about protecting confidential information with regards to current employees; the question specifically asks about ex-employees.
- Give loads of information about the cases you cite or cite every case you can think of. Use the cases to illustrate your argument as shown in the answer.
- Write extensively about whistleblower protection – that is not what the question is about, so it should be kept to a minimum.

Statutory employment rights

4

How this topic may come up in exams

This is a very wide topic and one which can come up in a variety of ways. You need to check your syllabus carefully here because different courses have a different emphasis. Some will include detailed analysis of all provisions whereas others will place emphasis on one of those areas. Problem and essay questions are common. Problem questions tend to focus on the application of statutory rights to a specific scenario while essay questions often focus on the advantages and disadvantages of provisions or any possible problems identified in academic critique of the measures. This often includes some element of considering how the law can be improved.

■ Attack the question

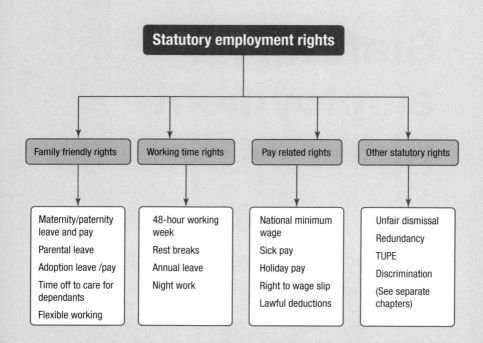

❓ Question 1

Anisah has been newly appointed as personnel manager of Furniture Fantasies, a company specialising in the production of bespoke furniture for the high end of the furniture market. The company is successful and expanding and as such wants to update its policies. It currently offers no contractual benefits in relation to family friendly rights but Anisah is keen to develop this area. She has sent you the following email – please respond to her, detailing your advice.

Email:

Dear [your name]

I am in the process of writing a new maternity, paternity and flexible working policy for Furniture Fantasies. Could you please remind me of the statutory minimum provisions and their criteria for maternity and paternity leave and pay as well as any other leave/pay parents may be entitled to. In addition I'd be grateful if you could clarify the flexible working provisions for me and give me an indication as to how you think policy and practice in this whole area is developing. I do not want to be behind the times!

Best wishes

Anisah

Answer plan

→ Briefly outline the relevant legal provisions.

→ Explain each type of family friendly leave and any corresponding pay:
  - maternity leave/pay
  - paternity leave/pay
  - parental leave
  - adoption leave/pay
  - time off to care for dependants
  - flexible working.

→ Discuss some of the issues arising from this area of law, highlighting in particular how you think it will develop.

Diagram plan

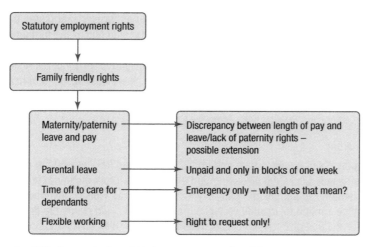

A printable version of this diagram plan is available from www.pearsoned.co.uk/lawexpressqa

Answer

Dear Anisah,

[1]Tell the client the relevant legal provisions; they can then go and look for themselves and it also shows you know where to find the law.

Family friendly rights are contained in the Employment Rights Act 1996 and Work and Families Act 2006 and are briefly outlined below.[1]

Maternity leave entitles the mother to 52 weeks leave split into 26 weeks ordinary and 26 weeks additional maternity leave. To qualify for the leave the expectant mother must inform her employer 15 weeks before the expected week of childbirth (EWC) when her due date is and when she wishes to start her maternity leave. The mother is free to choose when her leave starts: the earliest is the 11th week before EWC and the latest is the day after childbirth. The first two weeks leave are compulsory. It is then the employer's duty to notify her of her return date; when doing so, presume she will take the full leave. If she wishes to return earlier she must let you know, giving at least eight weeks notice.[2]

[2]Set out the provision clearly and succinctly.

The mother is not automatically entitled to maternity pay but if she is an employee with at least 26 weeks' continuous service before the

[3] Unless leave and pay rights go together and you automatically get both, you need to deal with them separately as we have here.

[4] Remember to check the latest figures and update this where necessary.

[5] This is an important point often missed by students so it is worth spelling out that the leave is longer than the pay entitlement.

[6] As part of giving advice on maternity leave and pay you should at least briefly consider what the law is in relation to return to work.

[7] This might seem very short but there is not all that much to explain in relation to paternity leave, so do not try to pad it out!

[8] The last three paragraphs just set out the law very briefly but clearly.

13th week before the EWC she will qualify for statutory maternity pay.[3] This pay consists of six weeks pay at 90% of the usual salary and then 33 weeks pay at the statutory rate (currently £124.88)[4] or 90% of the salary if this is lower. There is therefore no statutory right to pay for the whole duration of maternity leave.[5] If the mother does not qualify for statutory maternity pay (SMP) she may qualify for maternity allowance providing pay at the lower SMP rate for 39 weeks to those who have paid Class 2 National Insurance contributions for 26 out of the last 66 weeks.

Following ordinary maternity leave the mother has the right to return to her old job; where she has also taken additional maternity leave, she has the right to return to her old job unless this is not reasonably practicable in which case she is entitled to be given a suitable alternative position on no less favourable terms than her old one. (see **Blundell v The Governing Body of St Andrew's Catholic Primary School** [2007] ICR 1451, EAT).[6]

Fathers are entitled to two weeks paid paternity leave paid at SMP rate provided they have 26 weeks continuity of service and give notice. The leave must also be taken within the first eight weeks of the child's life. For babies born after 1 April 2011, fathers are entitled to up to 26 weeks additional paternity leave providing that the mother has not taken all her leave.[7]

Both parents are entitled to parental leave, which allows them to take off up to 13 weeks' unpaid leave to care for a child under the age of 17 (or 18 if disabled). Only four weeks may be taken in any one year and the leave can only be taken in one-week blocks (**Rodway v New Southern Railways Ltd** [2005] EWCA Civ 443, CA). To qualify, the parents must be employees with 12 months continuous service.

Finally there is a right to take time off to care for dependants that applies in situations where an emergency demands time off work. The time should be granted to allow the parent to make alternative arrangements and deal with emergencies. Longer leave and time off actually to care for a sick child, for example, would not fall under this heading (**Qua v John Ford Morrison Solicitors** [2003] IRLR 184, EAT). There is no right to be paid for this time off.[8]

In the context of family friendly rights, the right to request flexible working under s 80F of ERA 1996 must also be mentioned. This is

[9]You are specifically asked about flexible working so you must deal with it. Many students forget to mention it when considering family rights.

a right to request flexible working arrangements such as shortening hours or restructuring the work day or changing work patterns. Any request must be considered seriously by the employer but it remains a right to request only and not a right to flexible working itself. Any reasons for refusal should be set out clearly and provided to the employee. Only one application can be made in any 12-month period.[9]

[10]You should acknowledge the importance of contractual schemes. It shows that you have a wider awareness of how employment law works in practice and have done more than simply learn the statutory provisions.

While these rights provide a minimum statutory provision, many employers do provide additional contractual benefits[10] and, even where they do not, it is quite common for employers to be fairly flexible and, for example, to pay employees when they take time off to care for a dependant in an emergency even though this is not strictly required.

However, the law in this area is not without its critics and problems. Arguably, the fact that some of the maternity leave is unpaid means that it is unrealistic to think women are going to be able to take the entire 52 weeks off and the low rate of pay generally means that many simply cannot afford to take much time off at all. Fathers also seem a little forgotten in the provision of family friendly rights and

[11]This is really the start of your analysis in relation to the second part of the question asked of you. Remember you are still advising a client, though.

the two weeks leave entitlement appears rather tokenistic. There has been some discussion about tackling some of these issues by, for example, extending paid paternity leave and extending maternity pay to the full 52 weeks. However, the latter proposal in particular has however been put on hold in the current economic downturn. [11]

[12]You could expand this and add some specific academic's comments but keep in mind that you are advising a client.

Flexible working has come under particular academic scrutiny, with many commentators noting that the right to request flexible working in practice amounts to very little because employers are under no obligation to provide flexible working arrangements and indeed their obligations to justify refusal of a flexible working request are not very onerous either.[12]

[13]This shows that you are also aware of how to keep up to date. You can even be specific about the webpages or update service if you wish.

In order to ensure that you stay up to date I therefore suggest that you subscribe to an employment law update service or human resource management update service and check the government's webpages regularly.[13] When considering contractual provisions you might like to consider the potential benefits of being perceived as a progressive family friendly employer and incorporate as many flexible practices and policies as is reasonably practicable in your circumstances. Personally, I believe that the recent extension of paternity leave indicates that the provisions of maternity and paternity leave may be revised, perhaps to be more in line with the Scandinavian model of parental leave which can be shared between the parents. I do not currently foresee any changes in the other areas outlined above. If you would like me to help with the drafting or checking of any of your contractual provisions or policies, please do not hesitate to get in touch.[14]

[14]It's always nice to offer to help at the end and gives your letter a more realistic feel.

 Make your answer stand out

- Add additional academic commentary in a client friendly way by, for example, saying 'you might be interested in the following article which outlines some interesting ideas: G. James, "The Work and Families Act 2006: Legislation to Improve Choice and Flexibility?" (2006) 35ILJ 272'.
- Integrate your discussion of the provisions more with the basic legal facts given at the beginning.
- Perhaps add a little more detail on the exact legal provisions but keep in mind that you are writing to a client.

! **Don't be tempted to...**

- Just describe the provisions, your client has asked for more than that.
- Focus purely on maternity and paternity rights; the others are also of importance and must be mentioned.
- Ignore the second part of the question asking about potential future development.

 Question 2

Do you think that current employment law in the UK allows parents to achieve a suitable balance between work and family life?

Answer plan

→ Intro: outline that there are various provisions relating to family friendly rights.

→ Outline of the key legal rights/entitlements:
- maternity/paternity leave and pay
- parental leave
- leave to care for dependants
- flexible working.

→ Comment on whether these rights achieve work–life balance including:
- mothers- and maternity rights-focused
- flexible working is a weak right because it is a right to request only
- lack of adequate pay for leave
- it is often more about organisational culture.

Diagram plan

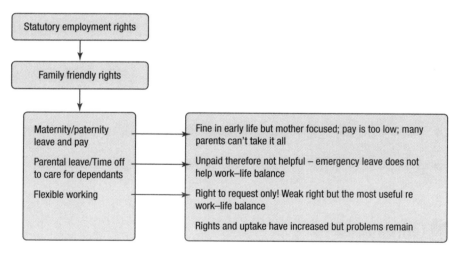

A printable version of this diagram plan is available from www.pearsoned.co.uk/lawexpressqa

Answer

Employment law in the UK makes a number of provisions to assist families in achieving an appropriate balance between work life and

[1]A clear introduction which sets out the structure of the essay.

[2]A quick summary of the provisions is enough for answering this question – you do not need to go into every detail of how the provisions work.

[3]You may need to update this figure as the rate may have changed since the time of writing.

[4]As well as setting out the law here, you are beginning to comment on how useful it is to families trying to establish a balance.

[5]Again, a brief outline of other leave rights is really all that is required but you do need to mention them.

home life. This essay briefly outlines those provisions before considering their effectiveness.[1]

Family friendly rights are contained in the Employment Rights Act 1996 and Work and Families Act 2006 and various regulations. Provisions on maternity leave ensure the mother at least can balance her responsibilities of caring for her new baby without jeopardising her employment. She will be entitled to 52 weeks leave (26 weeks ordinary and 26 weeks additional maternity leave) regardless of her length of service and requirements in terms of giving notice are minimal (15 weeks before the expected week of childbirth). Following the leave she is entitled to her old job back (after OML) or, if that is not possible, a suitable alternative with no less favourable terms (after AML, see **Blundell v The Governing Body of St Andrew's Catholic Primary School** [2007] ICR 1451, EAT).[2] However, pay for this time off is not automatic. Maternity pay will be paid to employees with 26 weeks' service and others may qualify for maternity allowance. However, both forms of pay are only available for up to 39 weeks and the statutory rate is fairly low (currently £124.88).[3]

Fathers, on the other hand, are entitled to only two weeks paid paternity leave provided they have 26 weeks continuity of service and give notice. The leave must also be taken within the first eight weeks of the child's life so this provision appears to allow the father to support the mother early on – for example, when mother and baby first return home from hospital; rather than to facilitate any real work–life balance for the family.[4] For babies born after April 2011 the father will also be entitled to additional paternity leave of up to 26 weeks as long as the mother has not used up her maternity leave entitlement.

There are then further provisions which allow for leave to be taken by parents in certain situations.[5] First, employed parents with 12 months service are entitled to unpaid parental leave of up to 13 weeks for a child under the age of six. Four weeks may be taken in one year and the leave must be taken in blocks of one week (**Rodway v New Southern Railways Ltd** [2005] EWCA Civ 443, CA).

Finally there is a right to take time off to care for dependants, which applies in situations where an emergency demands time off work. This might, for example, cover a situation where a child needs to be picked up from school urgently due to illness. Longer leave and time off actually to care for a sick child for example, would not fall under this heading (**Qua v John Ford Morrison Solicitors** [2003] IRLR 184, EAT). There is no right to be paid for this time off.

[6]Here your analysis of the rights relating to leave begins and you give a clear indication of what your core argument is, which shows confidence in your knowledge and viewpoint.

None of the leave rights discussed above particularly help in creating a work–life balance for families.[6] The maternity provisions allow mothers to stay at home and care for their child but they do not create a space for family time. Parental leave might provide some family time if parents take it at the same time or the father uses it early on in the child's life when the mother is still on maternity leave but it is unpaid and therefore it cannot be realistic to assume that many parents will be in a position to make use of this time.[7]

[7]State why you think the leave provisions are not particularly helpful – you are justifying the statement you just made.

However, in the context of family friendly rights, the right to request flexible working under s 80F of ERA must also be mentioned. Flexible working could potentially provide the answer to creating an appropriate balance between work and home life for families.[8] However, there is no right to flexible working, merely a right to request it. Flexible working might cover things like reducing hours, restructuring the working day or work patterns or allowing some sort of flexi-time arrangement. Employers must take requests seriously but they are not under a duty to grant requests; any refusal should, however, be clearly reasoned and recorded. Only one application can be made in any 12-month period.

[8]In acknowledging flexible working in this way you are indicating that the rights here are a step in the right direction towards achieving a balance.

[9] You should acknowledge the importance of contractual schemes because they are important to many employees as they can be significantly more generous than the statutory regime.

While these rights provide a minimum statutory provision, many employers do provide additional contractual benefits[9] and, even where they do not, it is quite common for employers to be fairly flexible and, for example, to pay employees when they take time off to care for a dependant in an emergency even though this is not strictly required. Surveys on family friendly rights and work–life balance indicate that the provision and take up of contractual maternity and paternity rights has increased in recent times (see, for example, Smeaton and Marsh (2006); Hayward *et al* (2007).[10] Flexible working practices have also increased with home working, reducing hours to part-time as well as term-time only contracts increasing in availability (Whithouse, 2007). While these statistics show that family friendly practices are becoming more common, it is not clear that they really allow families to achieve an appropriate balance.[11] They clearly work for some families but the Trades Union Congress (TUC) also recently reported that long hours were once again on the

[10]Here comes some of the evidence and academic discussion of the rights and their use/effectiveness. Start with the positive – rights and uptake of them have increased.

[11]This sentence then leads into the negative – what doesn't work in this area. You are keeping a really logical structure, which helps the reader understand your argument.

increase (TUC, 2008) and that there was a long hours culture in the UK which provided an obstacle to achieving work–life balance. The report *Working Families 2008*, while concluding that, overall, flexible working patterns impact positively on employee performance, also noted that some employees felt that flexible working had a negative impact on their careers. These issues have been explored further by Gatrell (2007) in the context of motherhood. Gatrell concludes that reducing hours was only available to those prepared to accept limited career opportunities or even a demotion and may therefore not be as conducive to an appropriate work–life balance as first thought. The law could do more.[12] Smith and Thomas (2009) note that women do not have the right to return to work on different terms and conditions which could increase the families' flexibility and choices. Furthermore, the low or unpaid nature of much of the leave entitlements renders them unhelpful at best to most families who can ill afford to take such time (See for example McColgan 2000). Most obvious perhaps is that fathers seem to have been forgotten about in much of the legislation and that if the UK truly wants to address questions of work–life balance for families, the role fathers play must also be at the forefront of the discussion.[13]

In conclusion, the law has moved some way towards making it possible for mothers to achieve an appropriate balance early on in a child's life. It provides for maternity leave and parental leave and, in a more limited sense, flexible working but overall the law is less important than organisational culture in achieving a supportive environment in which parents can make the best of their work life and their home life. Increasing pay for family related leave may not be an option in the current economic climate but a restructuring of leave entitlements is; and that might send a strong message that work–life balance for families is about more than generous maternity leave provisions.[14]

[12]Remember the question is about the law and the extent to which that helps, so you need to say if you think the law can do more to help.

[13]Try to give examples of where the law could be used to help and, if you have some academic evidence of this debate, add it in here. A quote, for example, could further strengthen your point if you can remember quotes easily.

[14]Conclude your essay by drawing your thoughts together and suggesting a possible legal solution.

Make your answer stand out

- Integrate the analysis and commentary with the explanation of the legal provisions – this is harder because you still have to make sure that your analysis comes together as a coherent argument.

- Highlight examples from other countries if you are familiar with them. For example, Scandinavian systems often allow the sharing of a type of parental leave rather than having set maternity and paternity leave.

- Explain what you think an appropriate balance might be and how you think the law can achieve that.

! Don't be tempted to...

- Simply go through all the provisions and explain what they are; you must comment on whether they help families achieve a balance.

- Assume that there is one appropriate balance for all and the law should set this down; acknowledge the importance of flexibility and choice.

- Ignore academic commentary. It is difficult in an exam to remember what academics have said but you cannot really answer this question fully without reference to the ongoing debates.

? Question 3

(a) Nikolina is a translator. Her employer requires that the personnel should be committed to professional development and attend regular training to make sure all language use remains accurate and current. The employer has various occupational schemes which reward experience. Nikolina is currently on maternity leave. She is worried about how this 'career break' will affect her rights at work. She also wants to know whether she can exercise her professional skills or work occasionally during maternity leave.

(b) Julian is a junior manager for the same employer. His sister recently fell off her horse and sustained injuries which mean she is now disabled and relies on the assistance of others. Julian would like to ask his employer for flexible working hours, but at a recent staff meeting the director expressed concern that the economic crisis will affect the business and he will therefore be counting on all staff to 'do their bit'.

Answer plan

→ Intro: outline that the question is about rights at work related to family friendly rights and caring responsibilities.

→ Nikolina: she is on maternity leave so presume she is aware of her rights there. The question requires consideration of:
  − right to return to work
  − (KIT) 'keeping in touch' days
  − general concerns about impact of career break on careers.

→ Julian: there are three separate issues:
  − flexible working − he can request it but there is no right to it
  − he can take time off in an emergency if his sister is dependent on him
  − potential for discrimination by association following the decision in *Coleman* (overlap with equality law here).

Diagram plan

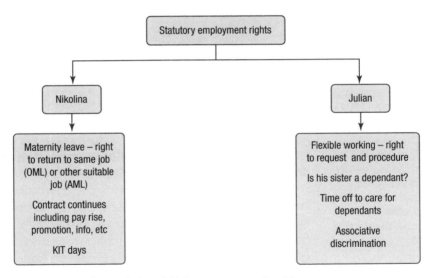

A printable version of this diagram plan is available from www.pearsoned.co.uk/lawexpressqa

Answer

Nikolina and Julian wish to know what their statutory rights are at work. As the issues raised are different for each, we will deal with them in turn.[1]

Nikolina

Nikolina is on maternity leave and is concerned about how this affects her rights at work.[2] Much research has shown that taking time out to raise a family can have a detrimental effect on career progression and the government has recognised that, too. As long ago as 1998, the White Paper *Fairness at Work*, stated: 'we need to achieve a society where to be a good parent is not in conflict with being a good employee'.[3]

A number of rights do help to achieve a balance, although how effective they really are is open to some debate. As Nikolina is currently on maternity leave, we shall presume that she is aware of her rights and entitlements in relation to taking leave and any pay she might get either under statutory provisions or her contract.[4] When she returns to work she has the right to return to her old job. There is no exception to this if she has taken only ordinary maternity leave of 26 weeks (Maternity and Parental Leave Regulations 1999, reg 18). If she has also taken additional maternity leave (a further 26 weeks), she is entitled to her old job back unless this is not reasonably practicable (see **Blundell v The Governing Body of St Andrew's Catholic Primary School** [2007] ICR 1451, EAT)). If this is the case she must be given an alternative position with terms no less favourable than her old position. Nikolina should therefore not worry about being demoted or receiving less favourable treatment on her return.[5] If she is not allowed to return to her job, this would count as an automatically unfair dismissal under the Employment Rights Act 1996 (ERA 1996).[6]

In addition, all contractual terms apart from those relating to pay continue while she is on maternity leave, so she should continue to benefit from things like gym membership, private health care or similar if she had such benefits before going on leave. Her holiday entitlement also continues to accrue, as does her continuity

---

[1] Give a very quick indication of the structure of your answer – you are showing that you recognise that the answer requires a consideration of statutory rights and that a number of issues will need addressing.

[2] Your whole answer should be written in the context of the question, so use the names used in the question and don't talk about rights etc in the abstract. Talk about Nikolina's rights.

[3] If you can remember a quote like this one, great, but even if you can't remember the exact wording you can still paraphrase.

[4] The question is not really asking about maternity leave and pay rights but more about what the consequences of making use of those rights might be, so don't waste time outlining maternity provisions.

[5] In a problem question like this you should always try to clarify exactly what the application of the law means for your 'client', so say that the law should protect Nikolina.

[6] In theory, therefore, her rights are protected and she should not be subject to any detriment but she will also want to know of any legal option if things do go wrong.

of service. She should also benefit from any automatic pay rises (coming into effect once she returns to work) and be made aware of any opportunities for promotion which might apply to her. For example, in **The National Union of Teachers v Ms L Watson** [2006] All ER (D) 84 (Aug), EAT, the claimant was on maternity leave when she learned about an opportunity for promotion. She applied but was not appointed; she argued this was due to her being on maternity leave and won her case.[7]

According to the scenario, Nikolina is keen to exercise her skills and work while on maternity leave.[8] Regulation 12A of the Maternity and Parental Leave Regulations 1999 gives her the right to ten 'keeping in touch' days or KIT days. These allow her to work for ten days during her maternity leave without ending that leave or her entitlement to maternity pay. These KIT days have been used to ensure women undergo a smoother transition back into the labour market, to reduce the isolation sometimes felt by new mothers and to allow them to keep their hand in. In Nikolina's case, KIT days could allow her to exercise her skills and keep her hand in.[9]

Nikolina can therefore draw on a number of legal rights to protect her position and make sure she is not disadvantaged by taking time off to start a family. However, in spite of these provisions the evidence still suggests that the labour market is not a level playing field for men and women and in particular for parents with child care responsibilities. Nikolina has to rely on her employer and her colleagues, as well as society more generally, to help her work out an appropriate balance between work life and home life.[10]

Julian

The Work and Families Act 2006 amended s 80F of ERA 1996 to extend the right to request flexible working to carers of adults. Section 80F provides statutory right to request a contract variation to make changes to working hours, working times, work places or other issues. One year's continuous employment is required to exercise this right (ERA 1996, s 108(1).[11]

Julian would therefore have to show that he has one year's service and that his sister is dependent on him as a carer. If so, he has the right to make a request for flexible working and a right to have that

[12]Here you apply the law to the scenario by saying what the legal provisions mean for Julian, showing that you understand how the law works.

[13]By stating the legal provision here you are indicating your knowledge of the law but can then go on to go through the procedure as it relates specifically to Julian.

[14]This is a little abstract because you have little information. You therefore have to write in quite a general way, which is OK but try to keep it as specific as possible.

[15]You need to clarify that Julian's sister falls within the definition to show your application of the law clearly.

[16]Julian would want to know if he is in any way protected if his employer does discriminate against him and, although you do not have time to deal with this in detail, you should still mention it.

[17]Conclude your advice for Julian by telling him specifically what you think he should do.

request considered by his employer. He does not, however, have a right to flexible working.[12]

The Flexible Working (Procedural Requirements) Regulations 2002 state the procedure to be followed for requests of this nature.[13] Julian's employer should arrange a meeting with Julian to discuss the request within 28 days of having received it. Within 14 days after the date of the meeting, the employer must write to Julian either to agree to a new work pattern and a start date; or to provide clear business grounds as to why the application cannot be accepted. The sort of reasons the employer could give might include additional costs or an effect on ability to meet consumer demand (see ERA 1996, s 80G).[14] However, if the employer agrees to a contract variation, it must provide a written note of the contract variation agreed to and the date on which it is due to take effect.

Under s 57A of ERA 1996, which relates to emergency time off to care for dependants, 'dependants' are defined as: the spouse or partner; child; parent; someone living with the employee as part of his/her family and others who reasonably rely on the employee for help in an emergency may also qualify. Under s 57A there is therefore little doubt that Julian could take time off to deal with an emergency relating to his sister. [15]

It is also important to note that if Julian is discriminated against at work because of his sister's disability, he is afforded some protection[16] following the case of **Coleman v Attridge Law** [2008] All ER (D) 245 (Jul), ECJ, which confirmed that discrimination by association is covered by disability discrimination legislation. Therefore, if flexible working requests are granted to others but not to Julian he may, depending on the circumstances, have a claim under the Equality Act 2010.

In conclusion, therefore, Julian has the right to request flexible working and the employer must seriously consider the request; and if there are economic or business related reasons as to why the employer considers the request to be problematic for the business, it can legitimately be refused. However, this should not stop Julian from making the request. If it is refused, Julian must wait 12 months before he can make such a request again.[17]

Make your answer stand out

■ You could expand your discussion on whether Julian's sister is a dependant or not and add more detail in relation to time off for emergencies.

■ You could draw on some of the academic debate around work–life balance for Nikolina and flexible working and caring for Julian. Check what you have covered in your lectures.

■ Useful arguments are put forward in J. Kodz *et al* (2002) *Work–Life Balance: Beyond Rhetoric* (Report 384, Brighton: Institute for Employment Studies) or S. Dex and F. Sheibl, 'Should We Have More Family Friendly Policies?' (1998) 16(5) European Management Journal 586.

! Don't be tempted to...

■ Just cite the legal provisions and then jump straight to a conclusion without discussing how the law applies to the facts.

■ Cite lots of cases; pick a few to illustrate your points.

■ Ignore time off to care for dependants or possible discrimination issues. While not central, they are important provisions.

Question 4

Does the law achieve a fair balance between the needs of employers for work and the needs of employees for time off?

Answer plan

→ Intro: outline that this question is often asked in the family context but actually applies to all workers.

→ What are the key time off rights at common law? – Health and safety/mutual trust.

→ Discuss statutory rights – working time and breaks, holiday, family and other rights.

→ Compare and contrast the formal position of a good package of rights with whether it works on the ground.

→ Conclusion – discuss the correct balance, which may depend on context and whether you are an employer or employee.

Diagram plan

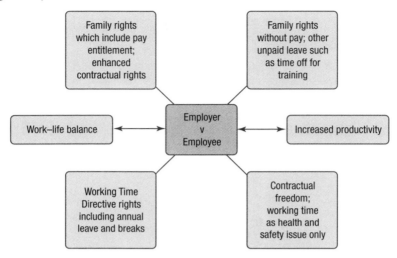

A printable version of this diagram plan is available from www.pearsoned.co.uk/lawexpressqa

Answer

[1]This introductory sentence acknowledges that you have fully understood the question and realise that it is about much more than family rights even though the issues raised are often discussed in a family context.

[2]You are putting your cards on the table straight away here by saying limits on working time and good work–life balance packages can be good for employees and employers. Be confident in your opinion!

[3]As there are common law and statutory provisions to consider, it makes sense to take them in turn, starting with the weakest protection first.

The question of balancing working time and time off has been discussed extensively in relation to family related rights but is of increasing importance to the workforce more generally.[1] At the basic level there must be some consideration of the employees' health and safety, with which excessive working hours without breaks and leave stand in conflict. In addition, however, regulation of working time, flexible working and annual holiday entitlements can serve to help employees balance their working life with other interests and commitments. While this is of obvious benefit to the employee, it may also benefit the employer by increasing productivity of employees while at work and by engendering a sense of loyalty in the workforce. Flexible and generous packages can create significant goodwill, which employers can then rely on where necessary. [2]

The common law now appears to recognise that the employment relationship is more than a simple wage/work bargain. The implied duty of mutual trust and confidence in particular suggests that both parties should behave in such a way as not to undermine that relationship.[3] A useful example of how this may impact on the area of the employment contract under discussion here is the case of **Johnstone v Bloomsbury Health Authority** [1992] QB 333, CA,[4] where an express contractual term which appeared to allow the employer to insist on excessive working hours for junior doctors was qualified by the duty of mutual trust and confidence so as to allow for long working hours but not hours so excessive that they would damage the employees' health. In addition, there is of course a duty of care owed by the employer to the employee; and where that duty is breached, an action in negligence may lie. Health and safety legislation as well as the common law duty to provide a safe system of work may also protect the employee from being required to work for such long periods that their health is at risk.

Historically, though, the employer and employee were free to contract as they saw fit, giving the employer significant power to impose contractual terms requiring long working hours with few breaks and little annual leave. As long as there was no harm to the employee and the complaint was merely not having any time outside work, little could be done.[5] However, as employment relationships and employment law developed, major statutory provisions were enacted to protect employees' rights. The Working Time Regulations 1998 which implement the Working Time Directive regulate the maximum hours that can be worked in a week, set rules for rest breaks and annual holidays and make special provisions for young workers. Workers are therefore now entitled to work no longer than 48 hours per week on average (reg 4.1); they are entitled to a full day off in every seven days (reg 11), should get a break of 11 hours in every 24 hours worked (reg 10) and are also entitled to a break of 20 minutes for every six hours worked (reg 12).[6] Working time during periods of work is therefore carefully regulated and the regulations aim to safeguard against excessive working.[7]

However, paradoxically, given that the Working Time Regulations are intended to be a health and safety measure, individuals can opt out of the 48-hour maximum working week (reg 5) and there are further exceptions for those whose working time is unmeasured and who determine their own working time. Research has shown that although working hours initially fell following the enactment of the Working Time Regulations, they are once again on the rise. Whether this is a genuine question of choice for those workers opting out or falling within the unmeasured working time exception is a matter of some debate.[8]

[4] If possible, try to use examples that relate as directly as possible to what you are discussing. There are many cases about mutual trust and confidence you could use here but the one chosen explicitly deals with the question of excessive working hours and is therefore particularly useful.

[5] You need to acknowledge the importance of contractual freedom. Common law still takes the view that employer and employee can contract as they wish, including terms about hours and time off. This is tempered only by mutual trust and confidence. Statute thus has to step in to regulate and this is your next point for discussion.

[6] You just need to summarise the main provisions – no need to set them out in detail or your essay will be too descriptive.

[7] A brief comment on the regulations before you move on to a little more analysis is useful to highlight what you think and guide the reader into the analysis.

[8] Here you are showing that there are problems with this legislation and if you have the time this section could be expanded a little.

[9]Do not presume that what the law says is what actually happens. Acknowledge that things may be different in practice and that this renders the law less helpful/useful than it might otherwise be. It shows you have thought about this.

The right to annual holidays has increased over the years and now stands at 28 days per year (regs 13–13A). This annual leave must be paid and, other than at the end of the employment relationship, the employer cannot pay the employee in lieu of the holiday. The annual leave entitlement allows employees to take time off throughout the year although employers may place restrictions on when leave can be taken and how much can be taken at any one time. In practice this may therefore restrict an employee's ability to take time off as he or she would like.[9]

[10]Here you are indicating that you have dealt with the rights you consider key but are acknowledging that there are others which are also important. This is not a question about family rights so there is no need to set them out in detail, although you could add a short explanation if you had the time.

There are additional rights to time off which can be important for individuals, such as the right to time off for union activities and public duties or for further training. These rights allow employees time off for activities which may be work related or help employees to further their career or support activities and causes important to them. In addition, a whole host of family rights helps parents to find and maintain a work–life balance which works for the family unit.[10]

[11]This is a key point and one often forgotten by students. Leave is only of limited use if it is unpaid, so you cannot ignore pay provisions in your assessment of leave provisions.

The effectiveness of leave provisions cannot usefully be assessed without also considering the pay provisions made for such leave.[11] Where leave is unpaid, such as in relation to the last portion of maternity leave or in relation to leave to care for dependants, as well as in relation to some union activities and for training, it is unrealistic to expect a large uptake of the leave right. Clearly the statutory framework provides significantly more opportunities for leave than was previously the case and also significantly more protection from suffering detriment where these rights are accessed but much of this access and protection is only formally available. When assessed on the ground, many leave rights do not come with linked right to pay during that leave, which renders them at best unattractive and at worst useless for employees.[12]

[12]A clear statement of what you think of the legal provisions and their implementation on the ground. Be bold, don't sit on the fence.

[13]You mentioned contractual freedom above as a potential negative; here you are bringing your argument full circle by looking at the positives.

However, it is worth returning to the importance of contractual provisions in employment law.[13] Employers are of course at liberty to offer more favourable contractual terms to their employees and this is often done in relation to maternity leave and pay, for example. Many employers, especially in larger organisations, have recognised the importance of attractive all-round packages to keep their employees happy, loyal and hard working.

The law has, through a statutory framework, signalled that it is important to recognise that employees are people with lives outside of work rather than simply human resources to be worked as much as possible. The law has balanced working time and time for private life to some extent and contractual provisions can push that balance further to the benefit of the employee, which in turn may also be for the benefit of the employer. However, where exactly the balance should be drawn may largely depend on whether you are an employee or an employer because some of the regulations may appear rather too employee focused for small businesses in particular.[14]

[14]Although you haven't made much of this throughout the answer, it is worth flagging up that how you feel about where the balance should be may depend on your current position or role as either employer or employee.

✓ Make your answer stand out

- You could add discussion of the debate in the UK about the Working Time Directive. See, for example, Fitzpatrick, *Straining the Definition of Health and Safety* (1997); TUC, *Slaying the Working Time Myths* (2009).
- You could make more of the distinction between regulating working time when actually at work in terms of breaks, etc, and taking actual time off.
- A few case examples would help to illustrate the points made. Consider *British Airways v Starmer* [2005] IRLR 862, EAT regarding flexible working and the extent to which it should be allowed.

! Don't be tempted to…

- Explain all working time and time off rights in detail. If you do this you will not have time for analysis.
- Concentrate just on family rights; although this question is often asked in that context, this particular one is much wider.
- Sit on the fence. Build up your own academic argument which draws on your knowledge of the law and wider debate and then set out to convince the reader.

? Question 5

Samantha and Joshua both work for Mr Snips hairdressers. Joshua has been working 55 hours a week for the last 15 weeks to try to build up a client base. He now wants to reduce his hours to a more sustainable 40 hours but has been told that if he does so he cannot take his annual leave because the work still needs to be done. Joshua has also been criticised for taking 20 minutes for his lunch. Mr Snips allows 15 minutes.

Samantha is told that, because of staff shortages, she must work seven-hour shifts with one 15-minute break for lunch for each of the next 10 days. When Samantha protests that two of those days were booked as annual leave, she is told that she is not entitled to any leave because she has not yet completed six months' service. Samantha is 17 years old. Advise Joshua and Samantha.

Answer plan

➡ Identify the area of law: the question relates to various aspects of working time.

➡ Joshua: 48-hour working week – consider if this has been exceeded and whether Joshua can insist on working fewer hours.

➡ Joshua: lunch break – consider his entitlement to rest breaks.

➡ Joshua: annual leave entitlement – can he take leave?

➡ Samantha: 40-hour maximum working week (young worker) – assess whether this is being exceeded.

➡ Samantha: rest break – what is she entitled to at the age of 17?

➡ Samantha: discuss her annual leave entitlement and whether it can be subject to a minimum service requirement.

Diagram plan

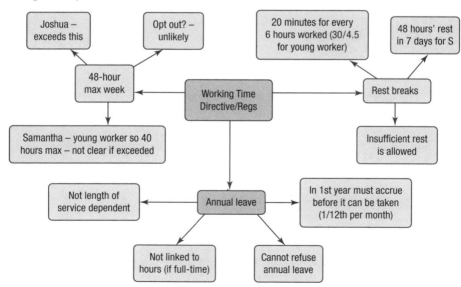

A printable version of this diagram plan is available from www.pearsoned.co.uk/lawexpressqa

Answer

This question requires an examination of the application of the Working Time Regulations 1998 (WTR) (which implement the Working Time Directive in the UK). In particular, the issues of annual leave, rest breaks and maximum working hours per week need to be considered.[1] The WTR apply to workers, which includes not only employees but also those carrying out work under a contract that obliges them to carry out the work personally for another party who is not a customer or client (**Redrow Homes (Yorkshire) Ltd v Wright, Roberts and Others** [2004] EWCA Civ 469, CA). While it is not entirely clear whether or not Joshua and Samantha are employees, the scenario suggests that they fall within the definition of 'worker' even if they do not meet the more stringent test of 'employee'. The WTR thus apply to them and they will be advised in turn.[2]

Joshua has been working 55 hours per week for 15 weeks. However, reg 4(1) of the WTR provides that a worker's working time should not exceed 48 hours (on average) for each seven days unless the worker has specifically agreed to opt out of the provision. To allow for some flexibility, the number of hours worked is averaged out over a reference period of 17 weeks (reg 4(3)). The scenario makes it clear that Joshua is working for 55 hours per week so we do not need to be concerned with the definition of working time in this case.[3] There is also no mention of Joshua having agreed an opt out and indeed his desire to reduce his hours would indicate that he does not wish to opt out of the 48-hour maximum working week.[4] The issue to be considered, therefore, is the reference period and whether or not the maximum hours have been exceeded.[5] We are not given information as to Joshua's working hours before the last 15 weeks but even if he did not work at all (without taking annual leave) his average working hours for the last 17 weeks would still be just above 48 hours. It is therefore clear that his rights under the WTR have been breached in relation to the maximum hours he can be asked to work.

His rights have further been breached in relation to the 15-minute lunch break allowed by Mr Snips. Regulation 12 stipulates that a worker who works more than six hours per day is entitled to a rest break of not less than 20 minutes. Joshua was therefore perfectly entitled to take 20 minutes for his lunch break.[6]

[1] Here you clearly identify the area of law to be dealt with.

[2] You need to establish that the legal provisions apply and although it is not entirely clear whether the clients are employees, you do not need to establish that for the regulations to apply, so just move on.

[3] You do not need to discuss what constitutes working time here because the scenario is quite clear on what is being worked by Joshua.

[4] Although you don't have concrete information on the opt out, consider the facts: someone who is actively seeking to reduce their hours is unlikely to opt out!

[5] This sentence is just a useful signpost as to the issue you need to deal with.

[6] Again, the law is stated in the context of the scenario, saving time and demonstrating a clear understanding of the provisions.

[7]This is an important point, often missed. Workers can still be required to work up to the maximum allowed; there is no automatic right to work 40 hours.

[8]You have to speculate a little here because you do not have enough information to give a definitive answer on how much leave he has accrued. That's fine but don't make up facts that are not given.

[9]By stating this, you set yourself up so you do not have to repeat those bits that are the same – you can simply refer back.

[10]Here you are saying why the provisions might be different.

[11]Again, you need to speculate a little here, which is fine just as long as the scenario could support everything you say.

[12]This is a further example of how you can state the law in the context of a scenario without separating out the application of the law from the explanation of it.

In relation to reducing his working hours to 40 per week, he does not have a right to do so under the WTR: the right extends only to not being forced to work more that the average weekly maximum.[7] So, while he can reduce his hours to fall below that limit, he cannot insist on working 40 hours per week and must negotiate this with Mr Snips. However, reducing his hours to fall below the maximum set by the WTR has no bearing on his annual leave entitlement. Workers are entitled to 28 days' paid annual leave per leave year (WTR, regs 13–13A). During a worker's first year of employment, a worker can only take leave once it has accrued in sufficient quantities (reg 15A). We are not told how long Joshua has been working for Mr Snips but the fact that he has been building a client base might indicate that he is a relatively new worker.[8] If that is the case, he would only be able to take the leave that has accrued, which would be 1/12th of the leave for every month worked. In other words, he could take 2.3 days off for every month worked.

The considerations relating to Samantha are similar to those examined above.[9] However, as Samantha is only aged 17, the provisions for young workers apply to her.[10] Regulation 5A thus stipulates that she is not to work for more than 40 hours per week on average. The average is calculated using the same reference period as for Joshua. We are not given sufficient information on whether the average will be exceeded over the reference period but if Samantha has been working close to the 40-hour limit it is quite likely that it will.[11] However, there are additional issues with her being asked to work for ten consecutive days. She is entitled to a break of 48 hours in a seven-day period unless technical or organisational reasons justify a lesser period of no less than 36 hours. It is possible that Mr Snips can justify the lesser period for such a reason but, even so, Samantha must be given 36 hours off. She is also entitled to a rest break of at least 30 minutes after having worked for 4.5 hours in any one day.[12] Mr Snips is therefore clearly breaching her rights relating to rest breaks and probably also the maximum average working week for young workers. In addition, Samantha is entitled to her annual leave regardless of her length of service. As with Joshua above, she will be entitled to 1/12th of her total entitlement for every month that she has worked. Provided she has worked for a month at least, she will be entitled to her two days off. She is entitled to these two days in addition to the 48 hours' rest she is entitled to, so even

[13]A useful summary of Samantha's rights, which then leads into a possible limitation or qualification of those rights.

if Mr Snips allows her to take her rest breaks, she can still insist on taking two days' holiday.[13] However, workers are not free to take their annual leave when they please without reference to the employer. Regulation 15 stipulates that the employer can require the worker to take all or part of his leave on particular days if notice at least twice as long as the number of days' leave to be taken is given. Likewise, a worker must give notice at least twice as long as the proposed leave. The employer may then give counter-notice, equivalent to the number of days' leave. It is therefore possible for Mr Snips to insist on Samantha taking her two days on certain days but he cannot stop her from taking the leave.

[14]As lawyers we have a tendency to think legal solutions are the best but remember that many issues can be resolved informally.

Both Joshua and Samantha should first try to talk to Mr Snips, point out their rights and try to resolve the issues that way.[14] However, once all workplace policies and procedures have been exhausted, and if Mr Snips still refuses to let them take their statutory leave and rest entitlements and makes them work longer than the WTR maximum allowed, they can bring a complaint to the employment tribunal (ET) within three months of the breach of their rights. ETs can award compensation that they consider just and equitable in the circumstances having regard to the employer's fault and any loss sustained by the worker (reg 30). If the complaint is one of a failure to grant annual leave, compensation is limited to the pay for this period.[15]

[15]The final paragraph contains the practical advice for the clients you are advising: what should they do next?

 Make your answer stand out

- You could add more explanation of rest break – i.e. a definite break not subject to employer's recall (*Gallagher* v *Alpha Catering Services* [2004] EAT).
- Clarify the position of annual leave in relation to the reference period for calculating average weekly hours (i.e. the reference period is extended).
- Include the calculation for average hours worked for Joshua.

> **!** **Don't be tempted to...**
>
> - Deal with the explanation of the law first and then the application to both clients second – you are likely to miss something or not make clear which bit applies to which client. The issues are different enough to warrant separate treatment.
> - Ignore the fact that Samantha is only 17. If you are told a client's age in a scenario, there is usually a reason for it!
> - Explain other regulations in the WTR which are not relevant here – we do not need to know everything you know about the regulations, just what is relevant here.

? Question 6

Pete and Sanjiv work for Ania in her small family business.

(a) Pete, who, because of family commitments, is no longer able to work Saturday mornings as he is required to do by his contract, is given six weeks' pay in lieu of notice. He is not given two weeks' holiday pay (which he claims is due) as Ania tells him she is deducting it for 'poor timekeeping'.

   NB you should ignore the issue of the dismissal itself, and concentrate only on the issues relating to the payment made to Pete.

(b) Sanjiv, who earns £250 gross for a five-day week, has £25 deducted from his wage packet. Ania tells him that this is because of two till shortages on consecutive days, for which Sanjiv must take responsibility.

Answer plan

→ Intro: outline that the question concerns an examination of the law relating to pay entitlement and deductions.

→ Pete: consider two issues:

→ Is Ania entitled to pay him in lieu of notice? Examine to what extent this depends on his contract and consider that even without a clause there is no loss, so claim is pointless.

→ Holiday pay: assess whether he is entitled by examining the relevant provisions. Consider if the deduction is lawful applying ERA, s 13.

→ Sanjiv: consider if the deduction is lawful – does it fall within ERA, s 13 and do ss 17–22 regarding retail workers apply? Examine whether Ania has fulfilled formalities and therefore whether the deductions are lawful.

Diagram plan

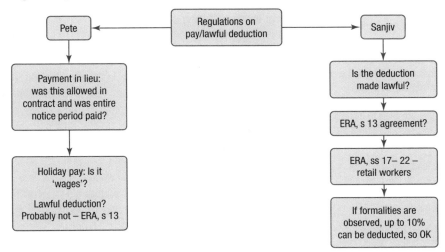

A printable version of this diagram plan is available from www.pearsoned.co.uk/lawexpressqa

[1]You have identified the area of law and set out the structure so straight away the marker knows you have understood the law and they know what to expect from your answer.

[2]This might be an obvious restatement of the question but it is worth showing the examiner that you have taken this on board. Many students miss this.

[3]Get the obvious and easy issues out of the way quickly and without detail so you can focus on those areas that are controversial.

[4]You don't really have a choice but to assume this, given the limited information in the scenario.

Answer

This question relates to employees' entitlement to pay and the lawfulness of deductions made from wages in certain circumstances. The issues arising for Pete and Sanjiv are slightly different and will therefore be dealt with in turn.[1]

Pete has been dismissed and been paid six weeks' pay in lieu of notice. For the purposes of this question we are asked to ignore the dismissal and focus merely on issues of pay.[2] We are not told how long Pete's contractual notice is or whether his contract contained a clause allowing payment in lieu of that notice. If such a term exists, payment in lieu of notice is lawful and, as long as Pete has been paid for his entire notice, he has no complaint regarding this issue.[3] However, if his contractual notice period is longer, he is entitled to be paid for the full notice period. If no contractual notice period has been set down, the statutory minimum period will apply and a tribunal can consider what is reasonable given the circumstances. We are not given sufficient information about Pete's position in the business to be able to work out whether or not six weeks would be reasonable. We will thus assume that six weeks is the notice he was entitled to.[4]

[5]It is important that you acknowledge both the technical breach of contract in this situation and the pointlessness of bringing a claim.

[6]Clear statement of the law, which is then quickly followed by its application to the scenario. If you tackle it this way you are likely to focus on the law that is important for the problem at hand.

[7]This leads into the main question on this point and it is useful to state exactly what the legal issue is.

[8]First issue to consider is whether holiday pay is covered by the relevant provisions. Start at the beginning and work logically through each issue. If holiday pay wasn't covered, you'd have to go no further, so this approach ensures you cover everything you need to but do not go off track.

[9]Again, logically deal with one section at a time.

[10]You don't have sufficient information to deal with this point, so it is fine to raise the point, say you need more information and then move on.

[11]You do not have to spend a long time on enforcement and remedies unless specifically asked but you should mention what the course of action would be.

[12]In other words, the law you have already set out in relation to Pete applies here too and there is no need to go over it again.

If Pete's contract does not contain a term which expressly allows for payment in lieu of notice, Ania is technically in breach of contract for paying him instead of letting him work out his notice. It is, however, not worth bringing a claim on that basis because Pete will not have suffered loss and no damages would be awarded.[5]

In relation to the holiday pay due, reg 14 of the Working Time Regulations 1998 (WTR 1998) stipulates that, if employment is terminated during a 'leave year', the employer must make good any annual leave still owed by a payment in lieu. Pete is therefore entitled to the two weeks' pay if we presume that he has an accurate record of his annual leave entitlement and what he has taken to date.[6] The question arising, therefore, is whether or not Ania can lawfully deduct the holiday pay for poor timekeeping.[7] Deductions from wages can be made only if they fall under specific rules in the Employment Rights Act 1996 (ERA). ERA, s 27 defines 'wages' as any sums payable to the worker in connection with his employment and clearly includes holiday pay. The holiday pay being withheld from Pete therefore comes under the relevant provisions.[8] The ERA stipulates (s 13) that deductions are lawful only where they are required by statute or where the employee has signed a written agreement to that effect. Clearly there is no statutory provision that applies here and we have no information regarding a written agreement authorising Ania to withhold payment of wages in the event of poor timekeeping.[9] It would be unusual for such an agreement to exist and we must thus assume that the deduction is unlawful. However, even if there was such an agreement, the case of **Fairfield Ltd v Skinner** [1992] ICR 836, EAT suggests that the ET can look at the circumstances surrounding the deduction to decide whether the amount of a particular deduction was justified. In this case we would need additional information on the extent of the poor timekeeping to be able to advise Pete further.[10] Assuming, however, that the deduction is unlawful Pete can bring a claim to an employment tribunal within three months to claim the missing pay.[11]

Sanjiv has had £25 deducted from his pay for till shortages. In this context, the same regulations apply to deductions from wages during employment as they do at the end of the employment.[12] Section 13 of ERA thus applies and the first question to consider is whether or not Sanjiv's contract contained a clause stating that deductions could be made for till shortages or whether there was a separate

[13]The scenario suggests this by referring to till shortages but it is not absolutely clear so you could also argue that the provisions for retail workers do not apply

written agreement to that effect. If not, the deduction will be unlawful and Sanjiv could ultimately bring a claim to the ET; although for £25 this hardly seems worth it. If a written agreement exists, Sanjiv's situation seems to fall within ERA, ss 17–22, which relate specifically to retail workers.[13] As well as requiring a contractual term under ERA, s 13, the maximum amount which can be withheld must not exceed one-tenth of the gross amount of wages payable on that pay day. In addition, Ania should inform Sanjiv in writing prior to deducting the amount and must provide him with a written demand for payment on the pay day. We do not know if Ania has complied with these formalities but if she has the deduction of £25 is lawful as it is no more than 10% of his weekly gross wage. If she has not, the deduction is not lawful and Sanjiv can challenge it.[14]

[14]You can't be more specific than that but you can give an 'either/or' sort of answer here as the point you are making is not complicated.

 Make your answer stand out

- Expand the discussion relating to whether or not a deduction might be justified following *Fairfield*. Consider the amount of time lost due to poor timekeeping and whether withholding two weeks' pay could be justified.
- Justify more clearly why Sanjiv might fall within the retail worker provisions – this is not made entirely clear in the scenario.
- Provide more detail on statutory notice periods and the courts' interpretation of reasonable notice periods.

! Don't be tempted to…

- Assume there is a contractual clause allowing payment in lieu – it might not matter in terms of outcome but it matters in law.
- Ignore Sanjiv's potential claim because it is for such a small amount; you must still apply the legal principles.
- Jump to conclusions which are not borne out by the facts; there is lots you don't know in this scenario, such as whether there are written agreements about deductions and whether a demand for payment has been issued – it is fine to say you need more information.

❓ Question 7

Examine the effectiveness of the protection afforded to whistleblowers under the Public Interest Disclosure Act 1998.

Answer plan

➔ Intro: outline the gap left by common law and introduce the PIDA.

➔ Explain what a protected disclosure is:
  – a qualifying disclosure which is made to specified persons.

➔ Comment on the scope of protection: it is quite narrow.

➔ Examine the requirement of 'good faith' in making a disclosure.

➔ Highlight the available remedies.

➔ Conclusion: the protection is quite limited because of the narrow list of persons that can be disclosed to and the good faith requirement.

Diagram plan

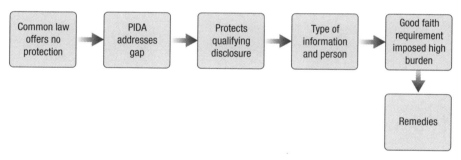

A printable version of this diagram plan is available from www.pearsoned.co.uk/lawexpressqa

[1] In an essay question which asks about the evaluation of a piece of legislation it can be really helpful to set out how the legislation addresses a gap in the common law. You show that you have a good understanding of the context of the provisions you are evaluating.

Answer

The common law provides little protection for those employees who disclose confidential information about their employers or employment.[1] According to **Camelot Group plc v Centaur Communications Ltd** [1998] CA even the option of leaking

²This sentence really sets out the problem the PIDA needed to address. It shows you have identified the relevant issues and have set the criterion for your assessment of the PIDA.

³Examiners are looking for accurate knowledge of the law and here you are highlighting that you know the law well because you know its original source and where the provisions can now be found.

⁴This is a useful indication of what you are moving onto next, which helps your structure flow.

⁵Bullet pointing like this is accepted by most examiners and it can save time in an exam.

⁶ Giving a couple of case examples here shows that you have a full understanding of the law rather than just the statute. It also begins to build your argument about the effectiveness of the provisions.

⁷Little comments such as this one show that you are analysing the law throughout and not just stating the provisions.

information secretly might not be enough to protect the employee, and discovery is likely to lead to dismissal.[2]

The Public Interest Disclosure Act 1998 (PIDA) seeks to draw a better balance between the interests of employers in having their confidences respected and the public interest in allowing employees to disclose certain types of information without fear of dismissal or detriment. The Act takes effect by inserting Part IVA into the Employment Rights Act 1996 (ERA).[3] These provisions identify which disclosures are to be protected and grants remedies to workers and employees who are subjected to dismissal or detriment for making such a disclosure. To fully assess the effectiveness of the provisions, we must first consider what disclosures are protected.[4]

Only a 'protected disclosure" is covered by the Act. A protected disclosure is a 'qualifying disclosure' which is made under the circumstances outlined in ERA, ss 43A–43L. A qualifying disclosure (s 43B) is one that in the reasonable belief of the worker tends to show that one of the following has occurred or is likely to occur:

- the commission of a criminal offence;
- the failure of a person to comply with a legal obligation;
- a miscarriage of justice;
- the endangering of a person's health and safety;
- damage to the environment; or
- the deliberate concealment of information concerning any of the above.[5]

Parkins v Sodhexo [2002] IRLR 109, EAT[6] decided that the disclosure of a simple breach of contract could form the basis of a qualifying disclosure as long as there was a reasonable belief that the breach had occurred or was likely to occur. This suggests quite wide-ranging protection.[7] In **Kraus v Penna** [2004] IRLR 260, EAT, the EAT decided that 'is likely to' required more than a possibility or a risk of the relevant occurrence. Rather the disclosure should show that the event was probable, or more probable than not. A disclosure that a proposed course of action 'could' breach a legal obligation did not satisfy this test. Here protection seems weak as there may be good reasons to disclose a possible breach in order to prevent it.

These qualifying disclosures are most likely to be protected if they are made to:

[8]You are bullet pointing again, which should be fine expecially because you are also listing your legal authority as you do so.

- the employer; or a person designated to receive them; or the person solely or mainly responsible for the failure in question s 43C;[8]
- a legal adviser (s 43D);
- a Minister of the Crown (s 43E);
- a prescribed person (s 43F).

It is possible for qualifying disclosures to be made to other persons but the circumstances where they may be protected are much more restricted. In such cases there are separate rules in s 43H for disclosures of an exceptionally serious nature and in s 43G for those that are not.

[9]It would be possible to explain what the courts think 'good faith' is in the abstract and then just cite the case as authority but setting it out like this makes it less abstract and reduces the chances of you getting confused while writing too.

All but one of these disclosures have a requirement of good faith. The only exception to this is a disclosure made to a legal adviser. In **Street v Derbyshire Unemployed Workers' Centre [2004]**[9] the Court of Appeal considered what was meant by 'good faith'. The tribunal felt that it must mean more than 'honest' due to the overlap with the requirement that the disclosure must in most cases also be based on a reasonable view that the information disclosed was substantially true. The tribunal should only find that a disclosure was not made in good faith when the predominant purpose of making it was some ulterior motive. A disclosure motivated by personal antagonism was allowed to stand as being not in good faith.

[10]A couple more case examples help illustrate the point you are making. All the time you are building your argument about the effectiveness by showing what is or is not protected.

In **Brown v Welsh Refugee Council** [2002] All ER (D) 21 (Jun), EAT[10] disclosure of suspected fraud by an employer to the organisation's management committee was a protected disclosure. In **Miklaszewicz v Stolt Offshore Ltd** [2002] the Court of Session upheld an EAT decision that, where the protected disclosure that led to dismissal was made before the Act came into force, this was covered by the Act. Mr Miklaszewicz had been employed by Stolt and came to work for them again when the company he worked for was taken over by them. The dismissal related to a disclosure made during the earlier employment. Here protection for the employee appears wide ranging.[11]

[11]Try to keep the analysis going throughout and then pull it all together in the conclusion.

Where conduct is of an *exceptionally serious* nature, a wider group of disclosures may be protected. However, in such cases the person making the disclosure must show a reasonable belief in the truth of the disclosure, that it was reasonable to make the disclosure in that way and that it was not made for personal gain. Disclosures to the media, for example, especially if made in return for money, are therefore rarely protected. If the conduct is not of an exceptionally serious nature it might still be that a disclosure to a person outside the list in ss 43A–43F *is* protected, but according to s 43G additional requirements apply and in particular the disclosure must be reasonable.

[12]To be effective there must be a remedy, so you need to mention what protection there actually is.

Dismissal following a protected disclosure is automatically unfair (s 103A). There is also protection against the worker suffering detriment or victimisation because of making a protected disclosure. This is set out in s 47B(1).[12]

[13]There has not been a huge amount of commentary throughout the essay, so you really need to make your points explicitly in the conclusion to highlight your analysis and critical thinking. Without this last paragraph examiners will probably conclude that you have not fully answered the question.

The law as set out above goes some way towards protecting whistleblowers [13] but that protection is limited. In particular it is restricted because of the limited range of people a disclosure can be made to and the requirement of good faith, which places a high burden on the whistleblower and focuses attention on the motives of the employee rather than the issue that the whistleblower is trying to raise. This does not encourage a culture of whistleblowing and is unlikely to lead to many reports of employer wrongdoing. Increasingly, though, the value of whistleblowing has been recognised and policies are now common. In addition, a re-think of this area of law to bring it in line with general anti-discrimination provisions might make it more effective longer term (see Lewis, 2001).

 Make your answer stand out

- Comment on the fact that workers as well as employees are protected from suffering detriment and the provisions include an extended definition of worker in s 43K.
- Consider remedies in further detail. For example, *Melia* v *Magna Kansaei* [2005] EWCA Civ 1547, CA which confirmed that damages can be awarded for injury to feeling for detriment suffered prior to dismissal.
- Explain that it is not possible to contract out of the provisions (see s 43J).
- Public Interest Disclosure (Prescribed Persons) (Amendment) Order 2003 (SI 2003/1993): you could give one or two examples of who disclosures can be made to.

! Don't be tempted to...

- Set out all the provisions relating to whistleblowers in detail – you will run out of time and your answer will be too descriptive.

- Sit on the fence; you need to decide if you think the protection is effective or not. If you don't, the examiners cannot award as many marks for your critical thinking and evaluating skills.

- Ignore remedies available – they are an important aspect of how effective the provisions are. Students often forget to mention remedies but doing so gets easy marks.

Equality law

How this topic may come up in exams

Discrimination law is a major area of any course on employment law. Given the differences in origin and extent of protection provided by the United Kingdom's discrimination law, assessment questions will often focus on the development of protection, proposals for reform and general application of the law to problem scenarios. In short, discrimination law, regardless of whether it relates to employment or housing, concerns itself with the differential treatment of individuals or groups of individuals on the basis of specified irrelevant considerations, i.e. sex, race, disability, sexual orientation, marital status, gender reassignment, religion or belief, age or disability.

Attack the question

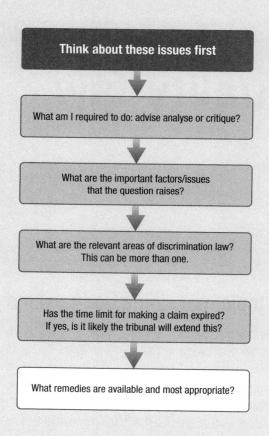

Think about these issues first

What am I required to do: advise analyse or critique?

What are the important factors/issues
that the question raises?

What are the relevant areas of discrimination law?
This can be more than one.

Has the time limit for making a claim expired?
If yes, is it likely the tribunal will extend this?

What remedies are available and most appropriate?

A printable version of this diagram plan is available from www.pearsoned.co.uk/lawexpressqa

Question 1

Discuss the extent to which the United Kingdom's accession to the European Union has impacted upon the law relating to sex and racial discrimination.

Answer plan

→ Intro: discuss the development of sex and race discrimination law in the UK, the influence of the United States of America (US) and European Union (EU) on the law.

→ Discuss the origins of the Sex Discrimination Act 1975 (SDA 1975) and Race Relations Act 1976 (RRA 1976).

→ Analyse the extent of the original protection (definition of sex and race) and its ever widening scope (transsexuals, transgendered, nationality).

→ Discuss contemporary changes in the law, i.e. the Equality Act 2010 (EA 2010).

Diagram plan

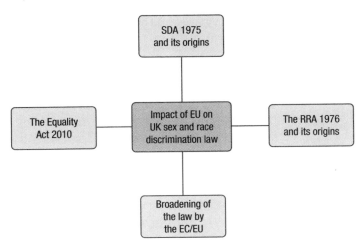

A printable version of this diagram plan is available from www.pearsoned.co.uk/lawexpressqa

[1]This is a short and clear introduction that identifies the fact that, in addition to the EC, the US has influenced UK discrimination law. It also sets the scene by outlining that the discussion centres on two major pieces of legislation and the extent of the protection provided.

[2]Importantly, you will need to outline the fact that this is a more widely available claim not delimited by prescribed statutory restrictions.

[3]Breaking up your answer by headings will help distinguish the arguments you make and provide a logical structure to your answer.

[4]This point will achieve more marks because it shows the ability to formulate a rational argument as to why the origin of the Act was perhaps misunderstood.

[5]Using abbreviations can save time in examinations because you avoid wasting time by writing out the name of the Act in full every time you refer to it. When using an abbreviation, make sure that the first mention of the Act is in full with the abbreviated version in brackets immediately after it – this tells the marker that from now on you will be referring to the same Act as an abbreviation.

[6]A case is added to strengthen the argument, showing that as well as directly legislating (by Regulations or Directives), the European Union affects domestic UK law indirectly through the jurisprudence of the European Court of Justice.

Answer

Discrimination law in the UK has its origins in a number of sources that range from the United States of America (USA) to the European Community (EC) or what is now known as the European Union (EU). In this answer I will discuss two important pieces of legislation: the Sex Discrimination Act 1975 (SDA 1975) and the Race Relations Act 1976 (RRA 1976).[1] It should be noted that, amongst others, both these statutes have now been repealed and replaced by the Equality Act 2010 (EA 2010). Both Acts were fundamental pieces of law that sought to protect individuals from discrimination in employment. Unlike other statutory protections – for example, most instances of unfair dismissal – protection from discrimination is afforded to workers regardless of length of service, thus it is operational at the following three stages: pre-employment (advertisements for jobs, interviews): during employment; and post-employment.[2] The impact of discrimination law on the employment relationship in the UK has been profound. However, the origins of some areas of discrimination law remain misunderstood or somewhat elusive.

Sex Discrimination Act 1975[3]

The SDA 1975, contrary to the belief of many, was not a piece of discrimination law that had its origins in the European Union or European Community (as it was previously known). The UK joined the EC in 1973, two years prior to the enactment of this Act, hence misunderstanding can be partially attributed to the coincidence of the date of accession of the UK to the EU and the date of the SDA's enactment.[4] In fact, the UK had been proactive in providing protection from some forms of discrimination much earlier than even the EC: the Equal Pay Act 1970 (EqPA 1970)[5] (now repealed by the EA 2010) was a good example of this – especially as the European Court of Justice (ECJ) extended this Act's version of indirect discrimination to EU law (see **Jenkins v Kingsgate (Clothing Productions) Ltd (Case 96/80)** [1981] ECR 911, ECJ.[6] The SDA 1975 has its origins in the USA and was intended to protect from both direct and indirect (or hidden) discrimination.

The SDA 1975 and the EqPA 1970 complemented each other with the former providing protection from discrimination in employment and the

[7]Here there are a number of important points, all attracting more marks. First, the argument draws comparisons between the SDA 1975 and the EqPA 1970 and shows how systems of law interact to inform each other, i.e. dualism (wider reading and understanding of transnational legal systems); and, second, how direct European Union legislation (Directives) initiate change in domestic UK law.

latter dealing with the actual terms of the employment contract. One distinct feature of the SDA 1975 was to set up the Equal Opportunities Commission (EOC) albeit the new Equality and Human Rights Commission (EHRC) was created to amalgamate this with the Commissions for Racial Equality, Disability Rights and Equal Opportunities. In 1986 another Sex Discrimination Act was passed to rectify the failure of the 1975 Act to meet the requirements of the European Equal Treatment Directive (76/207) (see **Commission of the European Communities v United Kingdom (Case 165/82)** [1984] 1 All ER 353, ECJ).[7]

One of the main problems with the original law stemmed from the restricted definition of 'sex' employed by the SDA 1975. As a result the Act applied only to individuals that were born male or female, i.e. the term was limited by biology (see **White v British Sugar Corporation** [1977] IRLR 121, Ind Trib) and thus did not protect, amongst others, transsexuals. In **P v S and Cornwall County Council** [1996] IRLR, 347, ECJ the court held the dismissal of a transsexual who was undergoing gender reassignment to be discriminatory. This decision was followed in **Chessington World of Adventures v Reed** [1997] IRLR 556, EAT. The effect of these decisions was to accord the SDA 1975 as being in compliance with Directive 76/207. However, this extension was limited and still did not go far enough to cover sexual preference (see **Grant v South West Trains** [1998] IRLR 206, ECJ).[8]

[8]This touches on the European doctrine of supremacy and demonstrates wider reading – it evidences how domestic law is required to be compliant with European law. More importantly, the argument shows the impact of European law on domestic UK employment law.

Race Relations Act 1976

[9]Here you will gain marks (a) for tracing the origin of the RRA back to the US CRA 1964 and (in the next paragraph) (b) by developing an argument relating to the extent of protection and its subsequent extension by EU law.

The origin of contemporary law relating to racial discrimination, prior to the EA 2010, was found in the Race Relations Act 1965. This was modelled on the American Civil Rights Act 1964 – to the current day it contains the definition of direct racial discrimination.[9] Growing unrest regarding the rights of ethnic minorities in the UK produced this Act to deal primarily with much civil unrest, racial hatred and incitement of the same. The Act was of little benefit in promoting racial equality, partly because its application was limited to those acts of discrimination that were committed in public spaces. This Act was subsequently amended by the Race Relations Act 1976 which allowed individuals with complaints recourse to employment tribunal proceedings and established a Commission for Racial Equality (CRE), as referred to above. The latter has been superseded by the new Equality and Human Rights Commission (EHRC).

Although the definition of discrimination on racial grounds in s 3(1) of the RRA 1976 included colour, race, nationality and ethnic or national origin, it did not cover religion. This situation was remedied by the Employment Equality (Religion or Belief) Regulations 2003 (SI 2003/1660), which were enacted to implement Council Directive 2000/78/EC; the regulations have now been revoked and replaced by s 10 of the EA 2010. Furthermore, racial discrimination on the grounds of nationality was introduced into the RRA 1976 by reason of the House of Lords' decision in **Ealing London Borough Council v Race Relations Board** (CRE) [1972] 1 All ER 105, HL where the council refused to put a Polish national onto their social housing register despite the fact that the European Community Treaty (the Treaty of Rome, now amended by the Treaty of Lisbon)[10] protected the right of European Member State nationals to move freely throughout the European Union.

[10]Show that you are up to date by highlighting the fact that the Treaty of Lisbon amended the Treaty of Rome – this will achieve more marks.

The Equality Act 2010

Both major pieces of legislation, and other similarly important anti-discrimination legislation, have been repealed and replaced or unified into a single Equality Act 2010. The Act is not a move away from protection afforded directly or indirectly by European law but a promotion of it: one of the effects of the change is now to make the European definition of indirect discrimination applicable to all characteristics protected from discrimination. In short, the law has been consolidated, the aim being to provide clear and consistent protection including protection from combined discrimination (previously referred to as 'dual characteristics') and to simplify the law for employees and employers to promote compliance.[11]

[11]You will gain extra marks for showing how the new EA 2010 is not a departure from the protections, both domestic and European, that have been developed over so many years. It may be useful to point out that the Equality Act 2010 also revokes the Sex Discrimination (Amendment of Legislation) Regulations 2008 (SI 2008/963).

Conclusion

In conclusion, the UK has pursued a number of measures designed to prevent discrimination, sometimes as a result of EU initiatives and sometimes of its own volition; the EqPA 1970, SDA 1975 and RRA 1976 were all good examples of this responsive and proactive approach. It is also evident that the UK's accession to the EU has had, amongst others, a basic twofold effect: first, to clarify and extend the application of discrimination law in areas in which

[12]This is a short and succinct conclusion – the extent of the impact that the UK's accession to the EU has had on the law is clearly stated without being limiting.

there existed ambiguity or no protection; and, secondly, to provide protection from further types of discrimination, i.e. sexual orientation and nationality.[12] What is clear is that UK and EU law do, to an extent, complement each other.

 Make your answer stand out

- Outline that the SDA 1975 and RRA 1976 provisions virtually mirrored one another, facilitating greater consistency in interpretation and court decisions.

- Discuss the fact that in the case of *Porcelli* v *Strathclyde RC* [1986] IRLR 134 SC it was held that the SDA 1975 covered sexual harassment as direct discrimination even though its provisions did not explicitly state that it did so – this shows how domestic UK courts respond to the requirements of EU law.

- Add that Directive 97/80 amended the definition of indirect sex discrimination, as an example of how EU law effects change to domestic UK law.

- Raise the fact that the law was deficient in relation to discrimination on the grounds of pregnancy; men could not become pregnant and thus a range of conflicting cases arose as to who the comparator would be – this issue was settled in *Webb* v *EMO Air Cargo (UK) Ltd* [1995] IRLR 645, HL.

- State that racial discrimination on the grounds of national origin was covered in the Race Relations Act 1968 prior to the House of Lords' decision in *Ealing London Borough Council* v *Race Relations Board (CRE)* [1972] which resulted in the prohibition of racial discrimination on the grounds of nationality. This shows how UK law changed without, to an extent, the direct intervention of EU law.

! Don't be tempted to...

- Go into too much detail regarding cases; it is the development of the law on sex and racial discrimination that is being discussed.

- Avoid discussing the consolidation of the law in the Equality Act 2010 – this is where the 'new' law with some changes lies, and therefore it is important that you understand the purpose and functioning of the Act.

- Discuss too many points – for example, the deficiencies in sex discrimination law; instead select a few points and discuss in relative depth.

? **Question 2**

Sabina is a Turkish woman employed by the Winchester Local Health Trust (WLHT). She has been living as a man for the last six months with a view to undergoing gender reassignment surgery next year. She now calls herself Ali. On the direction of WLHT, Stefan dismisses her on the basis that it would be impossible for WLHT to provide facilities for Sabina/Ali once she has had her gender reassignment surgery.

Mustafa is an orthodox Muslim male of Somalian origin. He is also employed by the WLHT. His supervisor, Stefan, has taken a dislike to him since he started and has called him, amongst other things, 'Paki' and 'Blackie', and has made derogatory references to Mustafa's smagh (headdress). He has frequently assigned Mustafa 'back office data entry' tasks so that he does not mix with other staff or service users.

Advise Sabina/Ali and Mustafa of their rights, if any, in discrimination law.

Answer plan

→ Sabina/Ali:
- analyse the facts as falling under ss 4 and 7 (protected characteristic, the definition of gender reassignment and clauses 62–63 of the explanatory notes) of the Equality Act 2010;
- briefly discuss the issue of the trust's vicarious liability for the acts of its employees; and
- outline the potential claims Sabina/Ali has, along with claim limitations, i.e. time within which a claim must be made, the possible remedies and their discretionary nature.

→ Mustafa:
- analyse the facts as falling under ss 4 and 9 (protected characteristic, the definition of race and clauses 68–69 of the explanatory notes) of the Equality Act 2010;
- briefly discuss vicarious liability under ss 109 and 110 of the Equality Act 2010; and
- summarise the possible claims Mustafa may have, their respective limitations (for example, any time limit), and the remedies available to him (discuss s 124 of the EA 2010, which specifies the remedies available).

→ Conclude with the advice (in summary) for both Sabina/Ali and Mustafa.

Diagram plan

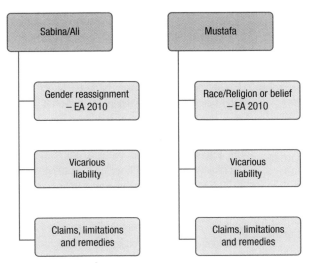

A printable version of this diagram plan is available from www.pearsoned.co.uk/lawexpressqa

Answer

[1]An introduction such as this can be difficult to construct, hence there is a brief summary of the provisions that will be discussed but little detail as to how. This is important, as the introduction must differ from the conclusion.

This question relates to the rights of Sabina/Ali and Mustafa under discrimination law. The advice for Sabina/Ali will be based upon a combination of protection provided by ss 4 and 7 of the Equality Act 2010, vicarious liability in the law of tort and her possible claim, any limitation on the same and the remedies available to her. The advice for Mustafa will be based upon, amongst other provisions, ss 4, 9 and 10 of the Equality Act 2010, once again vicarious liability in the law of tort, his possible claim and any limitation on the same and the remedies available to him.[1]

[2]Begin with advice to Ali/Sabina rather than Mustafa; she appears first in the question and her case involves less technical issues and case law.

Sabina/Ali[2]

Employees undergoing gender reassignment can pose much difficulty for employers where discrimination law is concerned. Here the law seeks to find a balance between preserving the rights of the individual, the employer and other employees. Section 4 of the Equality Act 2010 outlines those characteristics that are

[3]Often in examinations you will be allowed to take a statute book in with you. However, in instances in which you are not, the wording of the provisions is important. Where you cannot remember the exact wording, you should steer away from attempting to quote verbatim – paraphrasing a long provision to make it more digestible and direct to the point is more advisable.

[4]Showing how the law developed and referencing relevant case law will help you achieve more marks as this shows greater understanding of the rectification of the deficiencies in the law.

[5]Do not go into depth regarding the principles of vicarious liability but outline the trust's liability succinctly – this saves time in an exam.

[6]You should state explicitly that the claim for discrimination of this type is satisfied. It is important to include, in concluding your advice, what the time limitation for a claim such as this is and possible remedies Sabina/Ali is entitled to – outlining the type most likely to be awarded. You should choose your wording carefully; remember all remedies are at the discretion of the employment tribunal.

protected from direct and indirect discrimination, harassment and victimisation. Gender reassignment is one such characteristic: s 7 of the Equality Act 2010 (EA 2010) states that a 'person has [this] protected characteristic if [they are] proposing to undergo, is undergoing or has undergone a process (or part of a process) for the purpose of reassigning [their sex] by changing [the] physiological or other attributes of sex.[3] The Equality Act 2010 has removed the need for medical supervision. Sections 13 and 19 of the EA 2010, respectively, state that an employer may not directly or indirectly discriminate against a worker on the basis of gender reassignment. The Equality Act 2010 protects transsexuals from all forms of discrimination and is not, unlike the previous law (see **P v S** [1996] All ER (EC) 397, ECJ and the Equal Treatment Directive 76/207/EEC), deficient in this endeavour.[4]

Section 7 applies to an individual who is 'undergoing or has undergone part of a process' for reassignment of their gender: this clearly covers Sabina/Ali. This is a clear instance of direct discrimination and it must be proven that the WLHT has treated her less favourably because of her protected characteristic. In the scenario Stefan has dismissed Sabina/Ali on the direction of the WLHT, hence the trust is vicariously liable so long as Stefan was not acting outside the course of his employment – the standard principles of vicarious liability apply here[5] (see **Tower Boot Co Ltd v Jones** [1997] 2 All ER 406, CA and **Lister v Hesley Hall Ltd** [2001] UK HL 22, HL).

The advice to Sabina/Ali would be that a claim for discrimination on the grounds of gender reassignment is satisfied. She should apply to the employment tribunal within three months of the last discriminatory act; failing to do so will result in her claim being statute barred unless she can persuade the employment tribunal to exercise its discretion to extend this period because it is just and equitable to do so. The remedies available to Sabina/Ali, should her claim be successful, are a declaration, a recommendation (on the trust's future conduct) or compensation (s 124 of the EA 2010) – the latter of which is most likely and on which there is no maximum cap.[6]

Mustafa

Race discrimination under the EA 2010 (or racial discrimination as it was referred to under the Race Relations Act 1976 (RRA 1976)) involves a complex set of rules that include a range of different variables. This characteristic is also protected from direct and indirect discrimination, harassment and victimisation under s 4 of the Equality Act 2010. Section 9 of the Equality Act 2010 states that race includes 'colour, nationality and ethnic or national origins'. It also states that this reference to this particular protected characteristic includes a reference to a particular racial group that is defined by race in which the individual may fall. The issue relating to Mustafa does not concern religious discrimination and hence s 10 does not require consideration.[7] Sections 13 and 19 of the EA 2010 provide protection against direct or indirect discrimination against a worker on the basis of race (as defined: see clauses 68–69 of the Act's explanatory notes).

Here the issue is whether Mustafa is protected because he has been subjected to discrimination on the grounds of his 'ethnic origin'. Prior to the enactment of the EA 2010, Lord Fraser in **Mandla v Dowell Lee** [1983] 1 All ER 1062, HL outlined the conditions, amongst other considerations, that must be satisfied for the purposes of the RRA 1976 (now repealed) for a group to be eligible to refer to itself as a racial or 'ethnic group' in a broad cultural and historic sense. Although the RRA 1976 has been repealed, the reasoning will, in absence of evidence to the contrary, continue to be a useful reference: the conditions are '… a long, shared history, of which the group itself is conscious as distinguishing it from other groups, and the memory of which it kept alive and it must have a cultural tradition of its own, including family and social customs and manners, often but not necessarily associated with religious observance'.[8]

It seems that the alleged discrimination Mustafa has suffered relates to his race, nationality or national origin (Somalian), all of which are protected by ss 4, 9, 13 and 19 of the EA 2010. The EA 2010 prohibits both direct and indirect discrimination, the latter of which may be defended through justification (a proportionate means of achieving a legitimate aim). The facts suggest it is a case of direct discrimination, therefore the question is: would Mustafa have been treated differently but for his race? The facts seem to suggest this was the case, and segregating an individual from others is specifically prohibited by the Act (s 13). It seems that the WLHT has treated Mustafa less favourably than it would have treated someone that did not belong to his race. In addition, s 26 of the EA 2010 clearly

[7]Clarify that the applicable law is that relating to race discrimination and not religion or belief – in so doing you focus your argument and show wider reading, which will achieve more marks.

[8]A fuller quote, other than the one that is outlined above, would be difficult to remember.

[9]The brief mention that Stefan's conduct is likely to amount to harassment will gain you extra marks because you will have demonstrated consideration of a range of possible arguments.

prohibits the derogatory comments Stefan has made to Mustafa, with such racial insults being classed as harassment (and detrimental: see **De Souza v Automobile Associations** [1986] IRLR 103, CA).[9]

Furthermore, under s 109 of the EA 2010 (see also s 110) the WLHT will be vicariously liable for torts, but not criminal offences, committed by Stefan unless it can show that it 'took all reasonable steps to prevent [Stefan] from doing that thing or from doing anything of that description' (s 109 of the EA 2010); see also **Marks and Spencer plc v Martins** [1998] IRLR 326, CA and **Canniffe v East Riding of Yorkshire Council** [2000] IRLR 555, EAT. It should be noted that the vicarious liability of an employer under this new provision does not depend upon the employer's knowledge or approval.

If Mustafa is successful in his claim for race discrimination, then the employment tribunal is likely to make the following remedial awards: a recommendation or compensation (s 124 of the EA 2010) – the latter will normally include damages for injury to feelings, psychiatric harm and loss of earnings.

✓ Make your answer stand out

- Make reference to R. Wintermute, 'Recognising New Kinds of Direct Discrimination: Transsexualism, Sex Orientation and Dress code' (1997) 60 MLR 343, which discusses the growth of direct sex discrimination.

- Mention that s 136 of the EA 2010 changes the burden of proof requirements in claims of race discrimination.

- When discussing the dicta of Lord Fraser in *Mandla* v *Dowell Lee* [1983] 1 All ER 1062, HL, refer to the characteristics that he thought would also be relevant in determining 'ethnic group' for the purposes of the RRA 1976 and now the new Act, namely (a) either a common geographical origin or descent from a small number of common ancestors, (b) a common language, which did not necessarily have to be peculiar to the group, (c) a common literature peculiar to the group, (d) a common religion different from that of neighbouring groups or from the general community surrounding it, and (e) the characteristic of being a minority or being an oppressed or a dominant group within a larger community.

- Briefly outline the discretionary nature of the remedy of compensation, a breakdown of its various elements and the fact that it is the tortious measure of damages that are awarded.

Don't be tempted to...

- Go into too much detail regarding the facts of the scenario or the case law: for example, *Mandla* v *Dowell Lee* – give it context and apply the principle, for example 'in this case Lord Fraser outlined the considerations that'.
- Make too many references to legislation or quote too much dicta from cases – this may detract from the focus and weaken the answer.
- Discuss the development of the law too much as this will detract from the clarity of the answer and from your focus.

❓ Question 3

Frank is employed by Trampy Travels (a travel agency) as a travel sales adviser. As part of his job he is required to answer telephone enquiries and spend one afternoon of his five-day working week entering data relating to travel insurance sales. Frank has just been diagnosed as suffering from Myalgic encephalomyelitis (ME) also known as Chronic Fatigue Syndrome (CFS). Symptoms of this disorder include muscle and joint pain, cognitive difficulties, mental and physical exhaustion, digestive problems, and depression and muscle weakness. He has informed his employer in writing of his condition and they have refused to provide him with a modified telephone and headset. A few weeks later Trampy Travels dismisses Frank because it says that he now takes too many comfort breaks to visit the lavatory (at least one an hour), does not answer enough telephone enquiries and has greater difficulty in concentrating on data entry when processing travel insurance, for which they cannot provide support.

Advise Frank of his rights, if any, in discrimination law.

Diagram plan

A printable version of this diagram plan is available from www.pearsoned.co.uk/lawexpressqa

Answer plan

→ Outline that you will be discussing a potential claim under disability discrimination law.

→ Discuss the changes from the Disability Discrimination Act 1995 (DDA 1995) and its amendment by the European Union's Framework Directive on the Equal Treatment in Employment and Occupation Directive, and what additional protections are now afforded to the disabled as a result of the enactment of the Equality Act 2010 (EA 2010).

→ Outline the protection from disability discrimination under s 4 and its definition under s 6 of the EA 2010; analyse the elements (physical or mental impairment, substantial adverse effect, long-term adverse effect and the ability to carry out normal day-to-day activities) in relation to Frank.

→ Discuss whether Frank can claim direct or indirect discrimination (ss 13 and 19 of the EA 2010), discrimination arising from disability (s 15 of the EA 2010) or a breach of the duty to make reasonable adjustments (ss 20–22 of the EA 2010)

→ Outline which potential claims Frank may make, whether there are any limitations on these (i.e. time), and what remedies he can claim (mention s 124 of the EA 2010).

Answer

This question relates to the rights of Frank under discrimination law. The advice for Frank will be based upon a combination of protections provided by the Equality Act 2010 (EA 2010) including less favourable treatment, justification and reasonable adjustment; and, where a claim is established, advice will be given on any limitation periods for submitting a claim and the remedies available.

[1]Setting a context to begin with can be very helpful in focusing the question but also in putting in place a framework in which extra marks can be gained. Here the short discussion relates to the development of disability protection – this will relate directly to later discussion on the Equality Act 2010 and its consolidation of what was rather a piecemeal area of the law.

The Disability Discrimination Act 1995 (DDA 1995) (now repealed) was the United Kingdom's first statutory measure designed to prohibit discrimination against the disabled, giving rights in relation to (amongst other things) employment (see Part II of the Act). Although heavily amended, it was a proactive piece of legislation by a then Conservative government under the premiership of John Major. It preceded the European Framework Directive on the Equal Treatment in Employment and Occupation which, in addition to positive discrimination, required an employer to make 'reasonable accommodation' for the disabled. This meant that an employer was required to take steps (when necessary) to ensure that a disabled person had access, could partake, undergo and advance in training unless this would place a 'disproportionate burden' on it.[1] The extent

[2]Valuable extra marks can be earned by outlining the breadth of the protection provided by the current law.

of protection now ranges from direct and indirect discrimination, discrimination arising from disability and a duty to make 'reasonable adjustments'.[2]

In this scenario Frank has been diagnosed as suffering from ME/CFS. The issue here concerns the legitimacy of his dismissal: can Trampy Travels dismiss Frank on the basis of him now taking too many comfort breaks or of his lack of concentration, where the data entry part of his job is restricted to one afternoon a week? Without further information it is difficult to ascertain whether these factors are causally connected to Frank's disability; this could affect his potential claims.[3] Is Frank protected by the EA 2010? Section 4 of the Act outlines the characteristics that are protected from direct and indirect discrimination, harassment and victimisation. Disability is one such characteristic: s 6 of the EA 2010 states that a person has a disability if '[they have] a physical or mental impairment [which] has a substantial and long-term effect on [their] ability to carry out normal day-to-day activities'. This definition includes past and present disabilities. Frank must prove that (a) he has a physical or mental impairment, (b) which has a substantial adverse effect that is (c) a long-term adverse effect relating to (d) his ability to carry out normal day-to-day activities (see **Goodwin v The Patent Office** [1999] IRLR 4, EAT).

[3]The question requires you to make some factual assumptions: first, that there is an increase in the number of comfort breaks Frank takes since his diagnosis; and, secondly, that his disability has affected his concentration and performance. Hence, you can gain extra marks for outlining that there is a lack of information as to whether the factors for which Frank is being dismissed are actually caused by his disability and that this could impact on any claim(s) he may make.

It is for the employment tribunal, and not medical witnesses, to decide whether Frank is disabled for the purposes of the EA 2010 (see **Abadeh v British Telecommunications plc** [2000] All ER (D) 1456, EAT). Does Frank have a physical or mental impairment? The term 'impairment' is given its ordinary and natural meaning and may consist of an illness or be the result of it. Here, the answer is undoubtedly yes, Frank has an illness that amounts to both a long-term physical and mental impairment: see **Greenwood v British Airways plc** [1999] IRLR 600, and Sch 1 (Disability), para 1 to the 2010 Act.[4] Does this affect his ability to carry out normal day-to-day activities? Once again the answer is yes: from the activities that the DDA lists, Frank's disease affects, amongst other things, his continence and ability to concentrate. Does this have a substantial long-term adverse effect on his ability to carry out normal day-to-day activities?[5] The answer here is also yes: ME/CFS cannot be cured and hence will last for the rest of Frank's natural life (Sch 1 (Disability), para 2 to the EA 2010). The effect will be deemed as being a substantial long-term adverse effect

[4]Here you are showing your knowledge of the law and the fact that a list of eight factors no longer requires consideration as outlined in Sch 1 to the EA 2010.

[5] You will see that there are instances in which rhetorical questions appear. In an answer such as this they are difficult to avoid because they act as structuring mechanisms that relate to the style of writing in aiding the narrative flow, but avoid using them regularly as a rule.

even if its symptoms are being corrected by medical intervention (Sch 1 (Disability), para 6 to the EA 2010 and **Kapadia v London Borough of Lambeth** [2000] IRLR 14, EAT).

The EA 2010 prohibits employers from discriminating against the disabled by, amongst other things, dismissing an individual or subjecting them to a detriment: see **Kirker v British Sugar plc** [1998] IRLR 624, HL. Frank may make a number of potential arguments. The first is that he has been treated less favourably because of his protected characteristic (direct discrimination which cannot be justified) when compared to someone who does not have that particular disability and that the relevant circumstances of the comparator[6] are the same or not materially different from his own (s 23 of the EA 2010) – for example, the comparator would not have been treated less favourably for taking 'too many' comfort breaks or lack of concentration. The second is that he has been treated less favourably because of something that has arisen as a consequence of his disability; that he has, without justification, been treated less favourably when compared to someone to whom the reason does not or would not apply (s 15 of the EA 2010). Here, Frank's less favourable treatment is his dismissal – Trampy Travels cannot argue that they did not know or could not reasonably have known of his disability as he informed them in writing.

Finally, Trampy Travels will have discriminated against Frank if it has failed to comply with its duty to make reasonable adjustments (EA 2010, ss 20–21), as a result of which Frank has been substantially disadvantaged. Here, Trampy Travels has knowledge of Frank's disability and therefore should have taken reasonable steps to prevent this effect (EA 2010, s 20(5)); the sufficiency of the adjustments is a question of fact for the employment tribunal. In accordance with the statute, adjustments should have been made to the structure and organisation of Frank's job role as Trampy Travels could have allocated the data entry part of his employment to another employee (**Environment Agency v Rowan** [2008] IRLR 20, EAT and **Southampton City College v Randall** [2006] IRLR 18, EAT) and it should have provided him with the auxiliary aid (special telephone and headset) or at least given him the option to contribute towards its payment.[7]

The advice to Frank would be to claim for discrimination, within three months of his dismissal (EA 2010, s 123), on the basis

[6]This is a technical term and hence should be used to describe the person with whom the treatment of the disabled person is being compared.

[7]The main thrust of the argument is presented here: knowledge, reasonable adjustment and its sufficiency. Mentioning how the law deals with the issue of the cost burden shows a wholesome understanding of the issues that are often involved. Both these will help achieve better marks.

that he was dismissed as a consequence of his disability and that Trampy Travels had failed in its duty to make reasonable adjustments. The remedies available to Frank, should his claim be successful, are a declaration, a recommendation or compensation. In a claim such as this, compensation will also include an award for injury to feelings, financial loss and interest; it should be noted that, like other discrimination claims, there is no limit on the amount that can be awarded.

✓ Make your answer stand out

- Highligh the fact that certain types of condition, i.e. alcoholism and smoking, will not amount to impairment for the purposes of the EA 2010 unless they were originally the result of prescribed drugs or treatment.
- Mention that s 13 of the EA 2010 now provides that a non-disabled person cannot claim direct discrimination where a disabled person is treated more favourably, for example, through reasonable adjustments.
- Discuss the fact that the employer can ask Frank to contribute to the cost of adjustments: for example, to pay for the telephone or headset.
- Outline that the principles of vicarious liability apply to disability discrimination (EA 2010, s 109).
- Mention that compensation for injury to feelings varies and often includes aggravated damages to reflect the way in which the employer has behaved. In making an award the tribunal will take into account the age and vulnerability of the claimant and how severe the discrimination was.
- Refer to P. Thane (2010) *Unequal Britain: Equalities in Britain Since 1945* (London: Continuum International Publishing Group Ltd), to show you are up to date with reading in this area.

! Don't be tempted to…

- Go into too much detail on the statute or case law (at this stage the latter will only have started to appear in reports); simply state the relevant principles, for example 'the EA 2010 provides', and apply them to the scenario.
- Concentrate your discussion on one possible claim (direct discrimination) to the detriment of others (reasonable adjustment). Even where you know that the claim is a weak one, you should discuss and state that – remember when you do to try to keep the answer as succinct as possible.

? **Question 4**

Mobile Phones Inc has introduced a training scheme aimed at promoting equal representation of gay people at managerial level. Surinder, a deputy store manager, applies to partake in this opportunity. Since learning of Surinder's sexuality the store manager, Brian Norman-Pratt, has sent a memo to all members of staff (including Surinder) requiring them to send all gay customers to Surinder. He has also made a string of comments such as 'they support each other them gays' and 'I like you, you'll never go off on paternity leave as you will obviously never have children' – Surinder resigns as a result.

Fran, Surinder's friend, also works as a deputy manager for Mobile Phones Inc – Brian Norman-Pratt advises her that she should relinquish all ties with Surinder as this would hinder her progression in the company. Furthermore, he refuses her access to a management-training day. Fran is disgusted by Brian Norman-Pratt's suggestion; she does not resign but wishes to make a complaint.

Matilda is 25 years old; she applies for a job with Mobile Phones Inc as a sales adviser. She is sent a letter refusing her an interview on the basis that she is 'too young and inexperienced to undertake such a responsible role'.

Advise Surinder, Fran and Matilda of their rights, if any, in discrimination law.

Answer plan

→ Briefly outline the relevant provisions on sexual orientation discrimination and age discrimination.

→ Surinder:
  - mention the protection provided by ss 12–13, 19 and 26–27 of the Equality Act 2010;
  - discuss the protection from discrimination provided and whether harassment has also occurred;
  - advise of any potential claims, limitations on those claims and remedies available.

→ Fran:
  - assess whether Fran is a victim of associated discrimination;
  - discuss whether she has suffered harassment;
  - advise of any possible claims, the limitations that may exist on them and any remedies;

→ Matilda:
  - analyse whether Matilda has been the victim of age discrimination and whether her employer has any possible justifications;
  - discuss whether she has suffered indirect sex discrimination (EA 2010, ss 11 and 19);
  - advise of any likely claims, the limitations on them and the remedies available.

Diagram plan

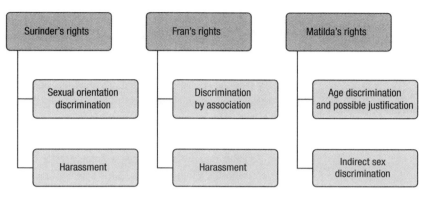

A printable version of this diagram plan is available from www.pearsoned.co.uk/lawexpressqa

Answer

[1]You can gain valuable marks by including a succinct introduction: this sets the scene for the discussion by outlining the elements that will be discussed in the answer without going into too much depth.

This question relates to the rights of Surinder, Fran and Matilda under discrimination law. The advice for Surinder will be based upon a combination of protections provided by the Equality Act 2010 (EA 2010) including harassment – concluding with any possible claims he may have, the limitations on them and the remedies available. The advice for Fran will be based on protection from associated discrimination under the EA 2010. Finally, the advice for Matilda will be based upon the EA 2010, her potential claim(s), any limitation on the same and the remedies available to her.[1]

Surinder[2]

[2]Dividing up the advice by headings will show an examiner the clarity in the structure that you have chosen to use; this will gain you marks for presentation of a chronological and clear argument.

Section 4 of the EA 2010 states those characteristics that are protected from direct and indirect discrimination, harassment and victimisation. Sexual orientation is one such characteristic: s 12 of the EA 2010 defines this as 'a person's orientation towards persons [of the same, opposite or either sex]'. The Act protects those with a sexual orientation towards the same or opposite sex or both sexes, thus covering gay men and women, heterosexual (**McClintock v Department of Constitutional Affairs** [2008] IRLR 29, EAT) and bisexual men and women; the provisions do not, however, cover

[3]Here you are showing knowledge of the fact that the regulations also cover those who are assumed to be of a particular sexual orientation: for example, a 'camp' male may be assumed to be a homosexual when in reality he may be a heterosexual. This will earn you extra marks.

[4]By recognising the limitations of the regulations you will gain extra marks; here the point relates to the failure of a claim where the connection between the act complained of and the sexual orientation of the complainant is difficult to prove.

[5]The situation with Fran is much clearer, therefore do not spend unnecessary time on this part of the question; keep your advice short enough whilst evidencing your understanding.

sexual practices or conduct. In short, Surinder must prove that on the grounds of his sexual orientation or perceived sexual orientation[3] he has been treated less favourably because of a protected characteristic (direct discrimination contrary to s 13 of the EA 2010). The condition here is that the relevant circumstances of the person chosen as the comparator need to be the same or at least not materially different as his own. In this instance the likely discrimination results from Brian Norman-Pratt's instruction to all members of staff requiring them to send all gay customers to Surinder and his making offensive generalisations.

Further, Surinder may wish to pursue a complaint for harassment on the grounds that Brian Norman-Pratt's conduct and comments had the effect of violating his dignity, creating a hostile, degrading, humiliating or offensive environment. He is likely to succeed in this latter claim so long as he can prove that, having regard to all the circumstances, including his perception, it would be reasonably considered as having the above effect. Harassment covers verbal, non-verbal, physical and non-physical conduct, hence comments such as 'you'll never go off on paternity leave as you'll obviously never have children' and 'they support each other them gays' is certain to amount to harassment. Prior to the enactment of the Equality Act 2010 there existed a technical flaw in the regulations under which the Equal Treatment Directive was implemented: where discriminatory acts rendered it impossible to link the conduct to the individual's sexual orientation, then the previous law did not cover the person.[4] Under the EA 2010 Surinder would be afforded protection. (See **English v Thomas Sanderson Blinds Ltd** [2008] EWCA Civ 1421, CA and, for discussion on harassment, see the Scottish Court of Session case **Porcelli v Strathclyde Regional Council** [1986] IRLR 134, Ct of Sess.)

Fran[5]

Secions 5 and 13 of the EA 2010 protect Fran from direct discrimination because she is associated with someone who has a protected characteristic, so this may be a claim she wishes to pursue. The concept of associated discrimination is fairly new. Recently, in **Coleman v Attridge Law and Another** (Case C–303/06) [2008] All ER (D) 245 (Jul), ECJ the European Court of Justice held that the

[6]This information gives some context to your answer and will help you achieve extra marks; it also shows that you are up to date with reading in this area.

[7]Clarifying that this was a disability discrimination case, yet it applies to other forms of discrimination, shows a deeper understanding of the area of law.

[8]This will gain extra marks; it also highlights that you understand that the decision was primarily aimed at that area of discrimination law but has far-reaching repercussions.

general framework for equal treatment created by the Equal Treatment Framework Directive 2000/78/EC also prohibits associated direct discrimination: for example, the mother of a gay male or carer of a disabled person.[6] (This was a disability discrimination[7] case, also reported as **Attridge Law (a Firm) v Coleman** [2007] *The Times*, 12 Jan; see also **Ghaidan v Godin-Mendoza** [2004] UK HL, 30, HL.) Although the above case relates to the Disability Discrimination Act 1995 (DDA 1995), the decision confirmed that the principle applied to areas of discrimination law where such protection is not provided such as sex and gender reassignment.[8] In addition, or in the alternative, Fran may wish to make a complaint of harassment as outlined above in relation to Surinder's potential claims; this is also likely to be successful.

Matilda

Here Matilda may have two possible claims: one for discrimination because of her age and the other for indirect sex discrimination. Section 4 of the EA 2010 provides that age is a protected charac-teristic; s 5 defines it as a person belonging to a particular age group whether of the same or a range of ages. Hence, the extent of coverage is akin to comparable areas of discrimination law, barring instances in which age discrimination is conditionally permissible (EA 2010, s 13). Employers can objectively justify differences in treatment on the basis that there is a genuine and determining occupational requirement that has a legitimate objective and is proportionate (EA 2010, Sch 9 (Work exceptions), Pt 1, para 1 and **Hampton v Lord Chancellor** [2008] IRLR 258, ET).

[9]The argument here is succinct and shows the breadth of the law because it covers the discriminator's perception without going into too much detail – this will achieve better marks.

Matilda must, however, prove that she was treated less favourably on the grounds of her age (or perceived age) and that the employer had no objective justification in so doing (EA 2010, ss 13 and 19). Mobile Phones Inc, without justification, has committed an act of age discrimination by making an assumption that links her experience and capability to her age (see **Wilkinson v Springwell Engineering Ltd** [2007] Unreported ET 2507420/07).[9]

Matilda's second potential claim is for indirect sex discrimination contrary to s 19 of the EA 2010; Mobile Phones Inc has applied an indirectly discriminatory provision, criterion or practice (PCP) to which fewer women than men can comply – for example, more women may lack experience or qualifications because they have taken a traditional role in family life. Mobile Phones Inc will have to prove that it has an objective justification (see **Weber von Hartz v Bilka-Kaufhaus** [1986] IRLR 317, ECJ) – it is unlikely that Mobile Phones Inc will be able to do this. The most appropriate remedy here is likely to be compensation – Matilda must claim within three months of the discrimination about which she has complained.

Conclusion

The advice to Surinder, Fran and Matilda would be that they all have potential claims that they can pursue under current discrimination law. The remedies available to them, should their claims be successful, are a declaration, a recommendation or compensation.

 Make your answer stand out

- Surinder:
    - by discussing the limitations of the now revoked Employment Equality (Sexual Orientation) Regulations 2003.
- Fran:
    - through exploring why the now revoked Employment Equality (Sexual Orientation) Regulations 2003 covered associated discrimination and the effect of the ECJ's decision in *Coleman* v *Attridge Law and Another (Case C–303/06)* on the current law.
- Matilda:
    - by further discussing the instances in which differential treatment may be justified on the basis of an objectively and reasonably justified legitimate aim;
    - through outlining the general exceptions set out in Sch 9, Pt 2 to the EA 2010.

! Don't be tempted to…

- Analyse Fran's claims in too much depth as the issue is simpler than those relating to Surinder and Matilda.
- Discuss the cases in depth or go through the legislation.
- Discuss or analyse the justifications in relation to Matilda's claims as this is not required; it is enough to state that none apply – this latter point shows that you know and have considered them.

📝 Question 5

Although ss 4–5, 13 and 19 of the Equality Act 2010 prohibit age discrimination, the Act provides a wide range of 'exceptions' under Sch 9 (Work exceptions), Pt 2 (paras 7–16) under which such discrimination may be lawful. Discuss, with reference to case law, at least one of those exceptions (whether past or present).

Answer plan

→ Brief overview of the law on age discrimination under the Equality Act 2010 (EA 2010):
  – age as a protected characteristic under ss 4–5, direct and indirect discrimination under ss 13 and 19, their purpose and effect.

→ Critically analyse at least one major exception:
  – retirement (Sch 9 (Work exceptions), Pt 2, paras 8–9) and positive action (ss 158–159).

→ Examine whether the protection provided is adequate and if the new law addresses some of the criticism levied on the Employment Equality (Age) Regulations 2006.

Diagram plan

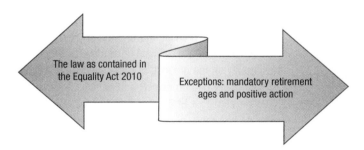

The law as contained in the Equality Act 2010

Exceptions: mandatory retirement ages and positive action

A printable version of this diagram plan is available from www.pearsoned.co.uk/lawexpressqa

Answer

This question relates to an employer's ability to justify discrimination by proving that an instance of age discrimination falls into one or more of the exceptions provided by Sch 9, Pt 2 of the Equality Act

2010 (EA 2010). Prior to the enactment of the EA 2010 this area of discrimination law was governed by the Employment Equality (Age) Regulations 2006 (SI 2006/2408). The regulations saw a number of amendments by, amongst others, the Employment Equality (Age) (Amendment No. 2) Regulations 2006 (SI 2006/2931) and the Employment Equality (Age) (Consequential Amendments) Regulations 2007 (SI 2007/825), both of which extended their application.

The Equal Treatment in Employment and Occupation Directive (Directive 2000/78 EC) laid down the framework for the prohibition of various forms of discrimination including age (Article 1), thus introducing the principle of equal treatment. Hence, the extent of protection from age discrimination was similar to comparable areas of discrimination law (Article 3: in particular, see Article 3(1)),[1] barring instances in which age discrimination was, and still is, conditionally permissible. Section 4 of the EA 2010 states that age is one of the characteristics that is protected from direct and indirect discrimination; however, unlike other forms of direct discrimination, direct age discrimination can be objectively justified under s 13(2) where the employer can show that the difference in treatment is based upon it trying to achieve a legitimate aim through a proportionate means (see **Hampton v Lord Chancellor** [2008] IRLR 258, ET). The extent of this protection is clear from the wording of ss 13 and 19 of the EA 2010 which prohibit age discrimination against both applicants and employees – the claimant must prove that they were treated less favourably on the grounds of their age (or perceived age)[2] and that the employer had no objective justification in so doing. Schedule 9 (Work exceptions), Pt 2, paras 7–16 and ss 158–159 of the EA 2010 provide a number of exceptions under which differential treatment because of age may be permissible. Some of these are: retirement, positive action, national minimum wage, child care, service length related benefits, enhanced redundancy and life assurance.[3] What follows is a discussion on two of the most controversial: retirement and positive action.

The most contentious of the general exceptions related to the retirement age. The Act permitted an employer to discriminate on the ground of age, for example, where an individual was either older than or within six months of the employer's normal (or statutory) retirement age: the employer could refuse to recruit

[1] This shows knowledge on the extent of protection envisaged and provided by this Directive, hence it will gain you extra marks.

[2] Extra marks will be gained for outlining that an employer cannot argue that the discrimination resulted from an incorrect perception on its part – for example, it thought a 30-year-old man was actually 60 – this shows depth of understanding.

[3] This list merely introduces the exceptions: it is not cumbersome and is effective because it is followed by a clear articulation of the exceptions chosen for discussion – this evidences knowledge and focuses the examiner on the main points of your argument.

that individual. Furthermore, an employer could dismiss an employee who had reached the statutory or employer's normal retirement age. It could not, however, retire individuals below either of those two ages; any retirement ages that were below the statutory retirement age (currently 65) were required to have been objectively justified. The government hoped that these regulations would allow both parties to plan their respective futures in advance; the Act required employers to give relevant employees notice of retirement at least six months in advance – a failure to do so would result in employer liability to pay the aggrieved employee compensation. Furthermore, an employer still has the right to terminate employment prior to its normal or statutory retirement age. However, this would still be subject to the normal rules on fair dismissals – hence an employer could not argue that the employee was being retired early without risking liability.[4]

Much of the case law surrounding this exception concerned mandatory retirement ages, and whether they were contrary to Directive 2000/78 and possibly its spirit.* In **Palacios de la Villa v Cortefiel Servicios SA** (Case C–411/05) [2007] ECR-I 8531, ECJ the European Court of Justice (ECJ) held that Spanish legislation which introduced compulsory retirement ages, whose intention was to promote a better distribution of work to all age groups, was justified and compliant with Directive 2000/78. A similar issue was raised by the Incorporated Trustees of the National Council on Ageing Heyday and Age Concern in the United Kingdom (also referred to as the **Heyday Challenge**). The issue centred on reg 36 of the Employment Equality (Age) Regulations 2006 (now revoked): Heyday argued that employers could compulsorily retire employees at the age of 65 so long as they followed a retirement process. On that basis, the United Kingdom had in effect introduced a mandatory retirement age and this meant that it had failed to correctly adopt Directive 2000/78. The ECJ held that the 2006 Regulations were compliant with the Directive and it was for the United Kingdom's courts to decide whether or not an employer's related provisions could be justified as achieving a legitimate aim.[5]

[4]This is a good point to make because it is one that strengthens your argument, it contextualises the extent to which protection is provided and shows how the government has attempted to balance the rights of employees with the commercial interests of the employer or commercial entity (to be more precise).

[5]These are two very important cases, the first of which provides some support for the challenge in the second; the discussion here is a valuable example of when more detailed case facts should be highlighted. By discussing these in a precise and succinct manner you can highlight contemporary issues surrounding lawful instances of age discrimination – this will gain you valuable marks.

*The Employment Equality Regulations 2011 (Repeat of retirement age provisions) now prohibits employers from issuing any new notifications of retirement using the default retirement age and it has abolished the statutory retirement procedure.

(See also **Hampton v Lord Chancellor and Another** [2008] IRLR 258, ET, **Johns v Solent SD Ltd** [2008] EWCA Civ 790, CA and **Bloxham v Freshfields Bruckhaus Deringer** [2006] EAT.) Prior to the enactment of the Employment Equality (Age) Regulations 2006 and now the EA 2010, ET 2205086/2006, individuals aged 65 or above were effectively debarred from claiming unfair dismissal and/or redundancy – this is now no longer the case in most instances. Employers wishing to prescribe a compulsory retirement age may do so only if it is a proportionate way of achieving a legitimate aim.

The term 'positive action' is widely defined. Essentially, positive action can be termed as a method designed to help eliminate or counteract the effects of past discrimination and stereotyping. The EA 2010 permits employers to discriminate on the grounds of age in providing opportunities in work or training to particular groups of individuals: for example, training offered to older members of staff in the use of information technology. The condition here is that the under-representation needs to have been identified the previous year. Positive action is not a new concept: both the Sex Discrimination Act 1975 (s 47) and the Race Relations Act 1976 (ss 37–38), both repealed and replaced by the EA 2010 (see ss 158–159), had included provision for this.[6]

[6]This sentence shows knowledge of how the law has consistently progressed and this will gain more marks.

One of the main problems with positive action relates to its public perception: it is often confused with positive discrimination. The latter is an equivalent of 'affirmative action' in the United States of America – it generally involves recruiting or providing opportunity to individuals of a particular group regardless of whether they have the requisite qualification or skills – whereas the former involves a process of 'encouraging' the same individuals but solely on a merit basis. Like positive discrimination or affirmative action, positive action is a controversial issue – paradoxically much of the argument concerns the potential to breed the very xenophobic or disharmonious attitudes that it seeks to eliminate.[7]

[7]This is an important but perhaps a rather contentious point to make; it will gain you extra marks for showing awareness of surrounding issues (wider reading) and the social impact of age discrimination law.

In conclusion, the exceptions provided under Sch 9 (Work exceptions), Pt 2 to the EA 2010, which operate to render certain instances of age discrimination lawful, are still subject to certain safeguards whether established in European law (retirement) or on the basis of good practice and merit (positive action). Safeguards, such as those mentioned above, are required to balance business and individual interests; their effectiveness is evidenced by their ability to change and develop with the changing nature of employment.

✓ Make your answer stand out

- Retirement:
  - by discussing non-consensual dismissals: for example, an employee's right under the new law to request continuation of work beyond retirement and the effect of a retirement related dismissal being rendered fair so long as it had occurred on the retirement date after the employer had followed the now abolished statutory retirement procedure.
- Positive action:
  - by discussing that the term is widely defined and thus can include the introduction of training, policies or procedures that are specifically aimed at preventing types of discrimination.
- By mentioning J. Sprack (2006), *Guide to the Age Discrimination Regulations* (West Sussex: Tottel Publishing) – this shows you are up to date on reading in this area of law.

! Don't be tempted to...

- Discuss too many or all the general exceptions – this will weaken your argument and you are likely to discuss too much in too little detail.
- Relay the facts of all the cases in detail; these should only be discussed where relevant to support a point in discussion.

Equal pay

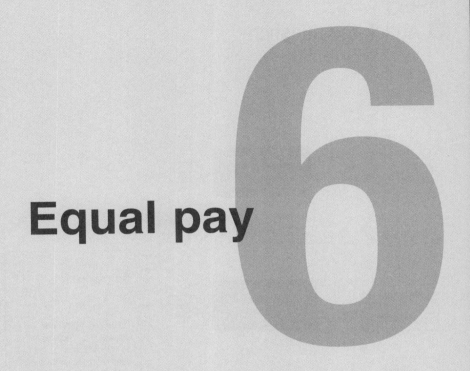

How this topic may come up in exams

Equal pay is a popular topic for examinations because it can test your understanding of complex legal provisions and case law as well as the influence of EU law on employment law in this jurisdiction. It is sometimes examined together with sex discrimination more generally. Problem questions are common and focus on working out whether a viable claim exists. Essay questions tend to focus on the EU influence in this area or on the effectiveness of equal pay provisions in actually achieving equal pay. Remember it is about equal pay between the sexes, not fair pay overall!

Attack the question

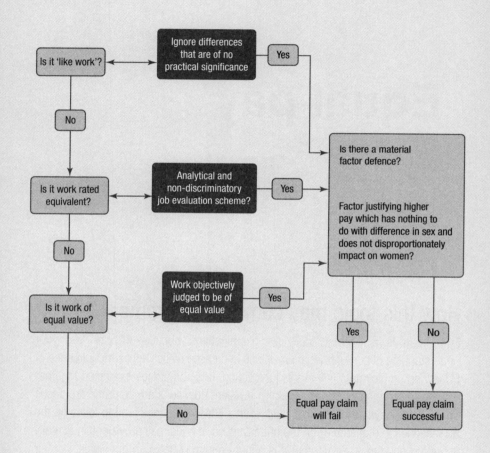

 Question 1

Assess the importance of European Union law in the development of equal pay law in the UK. Illustrate your answer with decided cases.

Answer plan

→ Discuss the importance of the Equal Pay Act 1970 (EqPA 1970) in providing a cultural shift and implementing EU law.

→ Set out the original provisions of EqPA 1970 re like work and work rated as equivalent.

→ Assess the impact of equal value work claims added as a result of ECJ decisions.

→ Consider the influence felt across a wide range of areas in relation to equal pay – use examples such as defining material factor and pay and single source.

→ Conclude by discussing how vital EU law is in shaping equal pay law.

Diagram plan

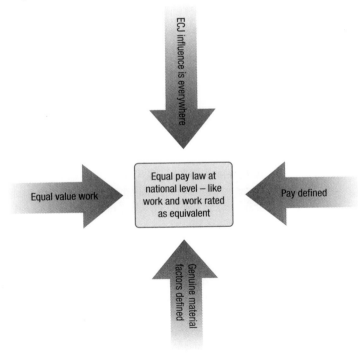

A printable version of this diagram plan is available from www.pearsoned.co.uk/lawexpressqa

Answer

The introduction of the Equal Pay Act 1970 (EqPA 1970) represented a huge cultural shift in the workplace and was the culmination of a long struggle to secure statutory recognition of the principle of equal pay.[1] EqPA 1970 is concerned with the establishment of equal terms and conditions of employment, as initially laid down in Art 141 EC[2] Treaty, which explicitly states that 'each Member State shall ensure that the principle of equal pay for male and female workers for equal work or work of equal value is applied'.[3]

The EqPA 1970 initially provided that a woman is entitled to equal treatment if she can establish one of the following:[4]

- she is doing like work with a man in the same employment (s 1(2)(a));

  or

- she is doing work rated as equivalent with that of a man following a job evaluation study (s 1(2)(b) and (5)).

The provisions are now contained in the Equality Act 2010 (EA 2010) in Chapter 3.

Section 65(2) of the EA 2010 provides that work is like work when it is of the same or broadly similar nature and any differences are not of practical importance (see also **Capper Pass v Lawton** [1976] IRLR 366, EAT). Additional responsibilities and duties can constitute a difference which justifies a difference in pay as seen in **Eaton v Nuttall Ltd** [1977] 3 All ER 1131, EAT but, as **Electrolux v Hutchinson** [1976] IRLR 410, EAT confirms, there must be evidence to support that different duties were actually performed. In addition, there must be an actual difference in the work, not merely the time when the work is carried out, as confirmed in **Dugdale v Kraft Foods** [1977] All ER 454, EAT.[5]

Section 65(4) of the EA 2010 provides further details in relation to work rated as equivalent and requires that a job evaluation scheme has been carried out. However, there is no provision to compel the employer to carry out such a scheme. So, where an employer was deliberately paying female dominated jobs less and male dominated jobs more even though the jobs may arguably have been of equal value, no claim could be brought. The work was not like work under s 65(2) of the EA

[1] Starting with a little bit of context can show that you understand the importance of the issue; don't get bogged down in this though – it must remain relevant to answering the question.

[2] It makes sense here to refer to old Treaty numbering because that was what applied then but do not worry if you have not learned this – you could also refer to Article 157 of the Treaty on the Functioning of the European Union (TFEU).

[3] Here you are highlighting the importance of EU law and signalling that you are focusing on the question and resisting the temptation to just outline the development of equal pay law.

[4] This section should set out the law as it was in the UK – that then allows you really to highlight the influence of EU law on the national provision and interpretation later on. The reference to the Equal Pay Act is accurate here because you are talking about the historical situation. However, the provisions are now contained in the Equality Act 2010.

[5] Your focus here is still the national law, so do not get drawn into the detail – you are only providing an outline.

2010 and the employer could simply refuse to carry out a job evaluation scheme and therefore block any potential claim. In addition, evaluation schemes would not necessarily result in objective classification of jobs and female dominated jobs may be systematically undervalued.

In **Bromley v Quick** [1988] EAT it was held that for such schemes to fall within s 65(4) of the EA 2010 they must be analytical – that is, they must analyse the jobs in terms of demands made under various headings – and in the **Danfoss Case** [1989] ECJ the ECJ confirmed that discriminatory schemes could themselves be challenged. These cases do not, however, solve the problems with evaluation schemes in relation to their questionable objectivity and the fact that they can quickly become outdated.[6]

[6]This paragraph really sets the scene and helps explain why national law was problematic, which then allows you to explain how EU law came to improve things.

In **Commission v United Kingdom** (Case 61/81) [1982] ECR 2601, ECJ it was held that British equal pay laws did not comply with the Equal Pay Directive, since it was only possible for a woman to claim equal pay for work of equal value if her employer had voluntarily agreed to a job evaluation scheme. Most employers did not undertake such schemes. To comply with this judgment, regulations were introduced in 1983 to amend the EqPA 1970.[7]

[7]Here's the major EU influence and it follows on logically from what came before; now you need to explain what the change actually was.

Section 65(6) of the EA 2010 now provides that where a woman is employed on work which is not like work or rated as equivalent under a job evaluation scheme, but which is, in terms of the demands made on her (for instance, under such headings as effort, skill and decision) of equal value to that of a man in the same employment, then she is entitled to have her contract modified so that the terms are not less favourable.

While the aim of the original section was laudable, it proved unpopular mainly because of the need for expert evidence to assess the value of the work. Tribunals can now decide cases without reference to experts and a questionnaire procedure has been introduced to help with matters but the need for a complex analysis remains.[8] **Pickstone v Freemans plc** [1988] 2 All ER 803, HL shows the importance of this section for potential equal pay claims. The employer argued that as there was a man doing the same work as Mrs Pickstone she could not bring an equal value claim comparing herself with another man. The House of Lords gave judgment for Mrs Pickstone, on the basis that a 'token man' defence would not be compatible with EU law and the Equal Pay Directive.[9]

[8]So the change was major but problems remain and you are showing you have a clear grasp of the issues here.

[9]The EU law has made a difference, though, despite the problems; and this example illustrates how.

[10]Here you are signposting the reader to your next big point – there are more EU influences than just the introduction of equal value work.

[11]And here are the illustrations to back up your statement, showing that you have learned the law and appreciate how it can play out in practice.

[12] A few more case examples, chosen because they are well known and important cases that made changes to how the law is interpreted nationally bring home the point that EU law is indeed everywhere in this field.

The influence of ECJ cases can be seen across all aspects of equal pay jurisprudence.[10] As well as being instrumental in bringing in the possibility of equal value claims, cases have also helped to clarify questions of genuine material factors that may act as a defence to an equal pay claim. In the Austrian case **Brunnhofer v Bank der Österreichischen Postsparkasse** (Case C–381/99) [2001] ECR I-4961, ECJ, the ECJ ruled that 'an employer may validly explain the difference in pay ... insofar as they constitute objectively justified reasons unrelated to any discrimination based on sex and in conformity with the principle of proportionality'. In **Grundy v British Airways plc** [2007] EWCA Civ 1020, CA the Court of Appeal held that there is no 'one size fits all' approach to assessing disparate impact and cases must be assessed on their facts.[11]

ECJ influence continues to be apparent.[12] The case of **Preston and Others v Wolverhampton Healthcare NHS Trust and Others (No. 2)** [2001] 3 All ER 947, HL was decided after a preliminary reference to the ECJ. The House of Lords ruled that part-time workers seeking admission to an occupational pension fund could include full- and part-time service with their employer from 8 April 1976. The ECJ decision in **Barber v Guardian Royal Exchange Assurance Group** (Case C–262/88) [1990] ICR 616, which decided that pension benefits are 'pay', opened the way for thousands of part-time workers to make retrospective claims for pension benefits. The case has potentially far-reaching and costly implications, because of backdating to 1976.The ECJ's ruling in **Levez v T H Jennings (Harlow Pools) Ltd (No. 2)** [2000] led to a change in the EqPA 1970, which previously limited back pay to two years. This was in breach of EU law as it was shorter than the limitation period for normal contractual claims. The effect of these decisions will to some extent be tempered by the six-month time limit to bring a claim, approved by the ECJ in **Preston**.

In **Lawrence and Others v Regent Office Care Ltd and Others** (Case C–320/00) [2002] All ER (D) 84 (Sep) the ECJ allowed for the possibility that the comparator could work for a different employer but the Court of Appeal required a 'single source' in **Robertson and Others v Department for Environment, Food and Rural Affairs** [2005] EWCA Civ 138, CA. The single source requirement was confirmed by the ECJ in **Allonby v Accrington and Rossendale College** [2004] ECR I-873, ECJ.

[13]The conclusion follows logically from the arguments made and illustrations given above and refers directly back to the question set so you can check for yourself that you have really answered it.

The influence of EU law and ECJ jurisprudence in particular on equal pay provisions in this jurisdiction cannot be underestimated. Not only has it made equal value claims possible, it has also played a significant part in defining important concepts such as pay and genuine material factors.[13] No doubt national tribunals will continue to rely on the ECJ for interpretative guidance.

✓ **Make your answer stand out**

- Discuss the importance of the *Barber* case in defining pay in more detail.
- Consider some academic commentary such as E. Szyszczak, 'Pay Inequalities and Equal Value Claims' (1985) 48 MLR 139.
- You could consider the importance of the EU principle of direct effect in providing a remedy for individuals who need to rely on the EU law directly.

! **Don't be tempted to...**

- List only the relevant ECJ cases; you need to set them in the national context.
- Explain the facts of the cases you are considering in detail; the principles are what is important here.
- Get drawn into an assessment of the effectiveness of equal pay law; that's not what the question is about.

Question 2

To what extent are the provisions in the Equal Pay Act 1970 (now contained in the Equity Act 2010) effective in ensuring that there is no sex discrimination in relation to pay?

Answer plan

→ Set out the main aims of EqPA 1970 and Equality Act 2010.

→ Explain like work, work rated as equivalent and equal value work provisions.

→ Consider the material factor defence.

→ Outline additional problems such as a lack of transparency or discriminatory evaluation schemes.

→ Conclude by assessing the differences between formal equality and what happens on the ground.

Diagram plan

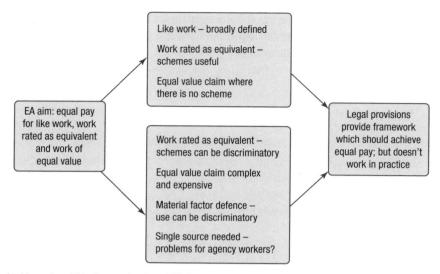

EA aim: equal pay for like work, work rated as equivalent and work of equal value

Like work – broadly defined

Work rated as equivalent – schemes useful

Equal value claim where there is no scheme

Work rated as equivalent – schemes can be discriminatory

Equal value claim complex and expensive

Material factor defence – use can be discriminatory

Single source needed – problems for agency workers?

Legal provisions provide framework which should achieve equal pay; but doesn't work in practice

A printable version of this diagram plan is available from www.pearsoned.co.uk/lawexpressqa

Answer

[1]A useful introduction which shows that you know what the EqPA 1970 is all about and is trying to achieve. It also acknowledges where the legal provisions can now be found.

The provisions of the Equal Pay Act 1970 (EqPA 1970) set out to ensure that men and women receive the same contractual pay and other benefits as a person of the opposite gender working in the same employment in relation to like work, work rated as equivalent and work of equal value. The provisions are now set out in Chapter 3 of the Equality Act 2010.[1]

A woman claimant must compare herself with a man, who must be under the employ of her employer or what is referred to as 'an associated employer'. The relevant comparison must normally be made with a man employed at the same establishment as the claimant woman. That said, a comparison may be made with a man at another establishment if both places are owned by the same employer (or an associated employer) and common terms and conditions of employment are applicable between the two establishments. The important issue here is that there must be a single source responsible for setting the pay and terms and conditions.

See **Lawrence and Others v Regent Office Care Ltd and Others** (Case C–320/00) [2002] All ER (D) 84 (Sep) ECJ, **Allonby v Accrington and Rossendale College** [2004] ECR I-873, ECJ and **Robertson and Others v Department for Environment, Food and Rural Affairs** [2005] EWCA Civ 138, CA.²

Section 65(2) of the EA 2010 provides that a woman will be considered to be employed on like work to that of a man if she is performing the same work as he is, or work of a broadly similar nature. In deciding whether a woman is employed on like work or not, consideration must therefore be lent to the nature of any differences between her work and the work of a man, how significant those differences are and how often they occur in practice (EA 2010, s 65(3) and **Capper Pass v Lawton** [1976] IRLR 366, EAT). Where a woman wishes to claim equal pay on the grounds that such a job evaluation study rated her job as equivalent to that of a man, the legislation requires, by s 65(4), that the study should have been undertaken to evaluate the demands made on a worker under various headings (e.g. skill, effort, decision making), the jobs to be done by all or any of the employees in a company or group of companies. Generally speaking, if a job evaluation study indicates that a woman's job is not the equivalent of a comparator man's job she will be unable to found her claim upon it.

European Union law additionally conferred equal pay rights where members of the opposite sex carry out work to which an equal value is attributed. It is judged that this represented a significant advance for the interests of women in the workplace, given that along with the possibility of making an equal pay claim based on 'like work' or 'work rated as equivalent' it thereafter became possible to found a claim based on 'work of equal value' even where no evaluation scheme was in place (EA 2010, s 65(6)).³

However, employers can defend equal pay actions on the basis that there is a genuine material factor which explains the difference in pay and that that factor has nothing to do with the sex of the employees (EA 2010, s 69). It should, however, be noted that even if an employer can demonstrate that a difference in terms of employment between a woman and a man is caused by a material factor other than the difference of gender, this will fail to create a defence if it concerns the application of a criterion which a significantly lower

[4]You are still setting out the law but are beginning to deal with issues which might hinder achieving actual pay parity; this then leads into your commentary. You do not need to separate the analysis from the description – in fact, integrating it is often better.

[5]State your view clearly and then go on to explain and justify it; this is much more convincing than listing a few criticisms but leaving the reader in the dark as to what you think.

[6]The previous paragraph deals with criticisms that are theoretical considerations about processes, procedures and implementation. This sentence and the next are probably your punch line – equal pay law has not really reduced the gender pay gap so it doesn't work!

[7]You have stated the evidence: now try to offer an explanation for the gender pay gap persisting.

proportion of women than men can satisfy. See **Brunnhofer v Bank der Österreichischen Postsparkasse** [2001] ECJ, **Barton v Investec Henderson Crossthwaite Securities Ltd** [2003] ICR 1205, EAT and **Grundy v British Airways plc** [2007] EWCA Civ 1020, CA, which confirm there is no 'one size fits all' approach to resolving this question and each case must be assessed according to the specific facts and context.[4]

The EA 2010 goes some way towards bringing about equality in law in relation to pay and pay related terms and conditions.[5] It is clearly unlawful to pay women less than men for like work and for work rated as equivalent. However, job evaluation schemes are not straightforward and may be inherently biased. While such schemes can be challenged, as in the **Danfoss Case** [1989] ECJ, many employees would not know the details of a job evaluation scheme and may not be in a position to question its legitimacy. Even where they are, they may not be able to afford lengthy and costly legal proceedings, which may be necessary to prove that a scheme is discriminatory. On the flip side, there is also no way of compelling an employer to carry out a scheme and there are still many examples of female-dominated jobs being systematically undervalued when compared with male-dominated roles. The introduction of the equal value provisions into the EA 2010 has gone some way to redress this but the need for experts in most cases makes this course of action unpopular and, again, often lengthy and costly.

Research evidence further confirms that the gender pay gap remains and has only marginally decreased in the last ten years or so.[6] Official figures show that in 2008 full-time female workers earned 17.1% less than their male counterparts and there are some sectors where this may be far worse. The gender pay gap is less likely to be reduced as long as there is secrecy about pay related terms and conditions in the workplace.[7] Transparent pay scales and bonus schemes as well as other benefits schemes go some way towards highlighting where equal pay issues may arise. This is for two reasons: first, employees are more likely to be able to compare their pay to that of their colleagues; and, secondly, employers are likely to be more conscious of where problems may arise and will therefore be in a better position to eliminate unconscious biases in their pay and reward structures.

In conclusion, it can be argued that, formally, equality seems to have been achieved but that the application of the provisions and principles on the ground is much more complex than a simple concept of equal pay for equal work might suggest. There is considerable way to go to eliminate sex discrimination in relation to pay but much of this work is best done through awareness raising and changing social attitudes rather than through the introduction of more complex legislative provisions.[8]

[8]Draw out your themes in the conclusion and briefly summarise your point.

✓ Make your answer stand out

- Add commentary: for example, J. Morrell *et al* (2001) *Gender Equality in Pay Practices* (EOC 1).
- Consider the news coverage in relation to equal pay such as 'Gender pay gap still as high as 50%, UK survey says', *Guardian*, 30 October 2009.
- You could strengthen your argument by restructuring the essay and starting with the issue of the continuing pay gap and then posing the question as to why it is continuing.

! Don't be tempted to...

- Assume that because the law covers most aspects of equal pay it will also work in practice; in this area of law in particular that is clearly not the case.
- Explain the cases in detail – you just need to show that you are aware of the key cases and how they apply.
- Just explain what the law is and then say 'therefore it is/isn't effective'; you need to explain why you think that.

❓ Question 3

Jayne works as a receptionist in a large hotel. She works part-time and usually works from 8 am to 1 pm. She has just found out that Pete, who works full-time on reception, receives £2 per hour more than she does. He works mainly nights from midnight to 8 am. Steve also works on reception: he has a certificate in customer service management and a degree in hotel management. He is being paid the same as Pete. Ania, who often works with Jayne but also sometimes works nights, has told Jayne that she gets an additional £1 per hour for night work.

Lydia works in the marketing department and earns £31,000 per year. Abhijit works in accounts and he has just received a pay rise which takes his pay to £45,000. Lydia complains because a job evaluation scheme rated hers and Abhijit's job as not similar on the basis that accountancy qualifications at degree level were harder to achieve than qualifications in marketing at the same level.

Advise Jayne and Lydia.

Answer plan

→ Outline the law relating to equal pay.

→ Jayne: Apply the like work provisions – are the differences between the work important enough to make it not like work? Focus on night work.

→ Jayne: Examine whether the material factor defence applies because of Pete's qualifications?

→ Advise Jayne.

→ Lydia: Assess whether the scheme is discriminatory on the basis that it makes a value judgement on the qualifications?

→ Lydia: Explain how a possible equal value claim would work.

→ Advise Lydia.

Diagram plan

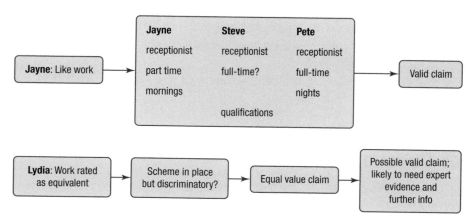

A printable version of this diagram plan is available from www.pearsoned.co.uk/lawexpressqa

Answer

¹You've identified what area
of law is relevant and then the
next sentence is even more
specific to the question. This
is really useful because it
avoids an answer which is too
general.

The problem question requires the application of the provision of the Equality Act 2010 (EA 2010), and in particular the Equal Pay provisions contained in Chapter 3, to Jayne and Lydia's situation.¹ In Jayne's case we need to consider the provisions relating to like work as Jayne appears to be doing the same or broadly similar job as Steve and Pete. According to s 65(3) of the EA 2010 and the case of **Capper Pass v Lawton** [1976] IRLR 366, EAT, any differences between the work Jayne does and the work Pete and Steve do are only to be considered where they are of practical significance, which should be reflected in the terms and conditions of service. Different responsibilities and different duties can be taken into consideration as in **Eaton v Nuttall Ltd** [1977] 3 All ER 1131, EAT, where additional responsibility could be said to be a difference justifying higher pay. However, as confirmed in **Electrolux v Hutchinson** [1976] IRLR 410, EAT, there must be concrete evidence of additional duties and responsibilities. There does not appear to be any such difference in the work carried out here.²

²This part sets out what
the legal issues in relation
to like work might be but,
as the scenario is not too
controversial on this point,
you do not need to spend too
much time on this.

Pete works nights, which may be considered a difference in the work done. However, cases such as **Dugdale v Kraft Foods** [1977] 1 All ER 454, EAT and **National Coal Board v Sherwin** [1978] IRLR 122, EAT confirm that when the work is carried out is irrelevant and basic pay should be the same. It seems, therefore, that Jayne is doing like work and should therefore be paid the same.³ However, employers can resist an equal pay claim if they can show that the difference in pay is due to a genuine material factor rather than the difference in sex. In **Strathclyde Regional Council v Wallace and Others** [1998] 1 All ER 394, HL the House of Lords, applying a strict interpretation of the statutory wording, decided that 'there is a valid defence under [what is now s 69 EA 2010] if a difference in pay is explained by genuine factors not tainted by sex discrimination'.⁴ It would therefore be legitimate to pay an additional premium for the night shift as is suggested by Ania. However, the scenario suggests that this premium for unsociable hours accounts for only £1 per hour additional pay and also that the pay provisions are not very transparent in this case.⁵ Where such premium is paid, it should be made clear that it is in fact a premium. It is also not clear whether Pete only works nights and, if not, what his pay is when he works a day shift.

³Apply the law to the specific
scenario – make your thought
process explicit.

⁴You have established that
there is a potential like work
claim – now consider the
possibility of a defence by
stating the relevant law in the
context of this scenario …

⁵ … and then apply it to the
facts given.

[6]Here you are moving on to the next possible material factor defence – again, state the law and then apply it. This shows off both your legal knowledge and your ability to apply that knowledge to a scenario.

Steve's additional qualifications, which appear relevant, may explain his higher wages.[6] In **Brunnhofer *v* Bank der Österreichischen Postsparkasse** (Case C–381/99) [2001] ECR I-4961, ECJ the ECJ ruled that 'an employer may validly explain the difference in pay … insofar as they constitute objectively justified reasons unrelated to any discrimination based on sex and in conformity with the principle of proportionality'. Additional qualifications seem an objectively justified reason to increase pay but, in order to satisfy the proportionality test, the qualifications would have to be relevant to the duties carried out. That test seems to be satisfied by Steve.

[7]Don't forget to conclude with your specific advice for the person you are asked to advise!

In conclusion, Jayne should challenge her pay, initially with the employer informally or through a grievance procedure and if she is unsuccessful then by bringing a tribunal claim.[7]

[8]A succinct summary of the complex legal issue facing Lydia shows you understand the issues. Don't overcomplicate matters – be as simple as you can when restating the problem you are dealing with.

Lydia's situation is potentially complex. Her claim seems to relate to a 'work rated as equivalent' claim under s 65(4) of the EA 2010. However, where a job evaluation scheme has been carried out under s 65(4) and jobs have been rated as not similar, a claim cannot succeed under this heading.[8] Lydia would have to challenge the validity of the evaluation scheme, which could prove a lengthy and costly way forward because of the expert input required to do so. There is some suggestion that her challenge might be successful as in **Bromley *v* Quick** [1988] 1 CR 47, CA it was held that job evaluation schemes must be analytical to fall within s 1(5). The **Danfoss Case** [1989] ECJ confirms that even unconsciously biased schemes can be deemed discriminatory. It may be that the greater weight placed on accountancy qualification compared to marketing qualification is evidence of such a bias in this case.[9]

[9]You do not have a lot of information in the scenario – do not be tempted to make it up but base your answer on what is available and if you cannot say much then leave it at that.

[10]You are offering a possible solution: now explain how it would work. Doing it this way round makes sure you keep focused on the question and do not get drawn into a general discussion.

If Lydia can show that the scheme is discriminatory, she can bring an equal value claim under s 65(6) of the EA 2010 even though a job evaluation scheme already exists.[10] Under this heading she is entitled to have her job evaluated in relation to the comparator's job under certain headings such as skills level, responsibility, efforts and decision making. The assessment would usually be made by an expert although tribunals have had the power to make a decision without reference to an expert since 1996. The expert who is appointed by ACAS would prepare a report for the tribunal. Parties would be allowed to make representations to the tribunal relating to the report and the tribunal would then make its decision as to

[11]You do not need to go over an explanation of material factors again. You have already explained them and given examples above and there are no additional possibilities suggested in the scenario.

[12]Conclude with your advice, which can include practical advice as well as guidance on the exact legal provisions if you think this is appropriate.

whether or not the work is of equal value. Lydia's employers would still be able to rely on a material factor defence if they can show that the difference in pay between her and Abhijit has nothing to do with sex.[11] We do not know from the scenario whether such a factor might exist or not and thus cannot speculate further.

Lydia should be advised to question the validity of the job evaluation scheme and ask her employers to reconsider. If she is not successful she can bring a claim based on the provisions for work of equal value but she would first have to show that the job evaluation scheme was in itself discriminatory. She must also be aware of the possibility of a material factor defence and the possibility of a rather lengthy and potentially costly legal battle.[12]

✓ Make your answer stand out

- Analyse the differences between Jayne's job and the others in a little more detail and comment more on the fact that Jayne works part-time. Consider *Bilka-Kaufhaus GmbH v Karin Weber von Hartz* [1986] ECJ, for example.
- Consider the basis on which Lydia's job could be compared to Abhijit's in order to assess an equal value claim.
- Comment on s 65(5) of the EA 2010 regarding biased evaluation schemes.

! Don't be tempted to...

- Set out all the equal pay law first before advising – you only have to deal with the specific areas relevant to the scenario.
- Speculate in relation to the material factor defence in relation to Lydia; you don't have any relevant information.
- Ignore the practicalities of equal play claims – the problem is often the implementation, not the legal provisions themselves.

❓ Question 4

Katherine works for the EnviroCo as a technical specialist. She has a temporary contract through an employment agency. The agency is her employer. She is paid the same basic pay as other technical specialists, who are mainly male, but does not have access to any of the bonus payments or the generous pension provisions offered by the EnviroCo.

Timothy works in the IT department of EnviroCo and is paid £22,000 per year. Justyna works in Human Resources for the same company and is paid £28,000 per year. Timothy argues that he should be paid the same as Justyna because their work is of equal value. The company does not agree, arguing that the qualifications and skills required are completely different and, in any event, although the IT department is staffed mainly by men and HR is female dominated, this is not exclusively so, which means the difference in pay is clearly not based on sex.

Advise Katherine and Timothy.

Answer plan

→ State that the problem concerns the application of equal pay law.

→ Katherine: Discuss the need for there to be one employer and the single source issue. Can she claim?

→ Timothy: Assess if there is a scheme and whether he can claim based on that.

→ Timothy: Explain that if there is no scheme it would be an equal value claim.

→ Timothy: Consider that there is no token man (in this case woman) defence possible.

Diagram plan

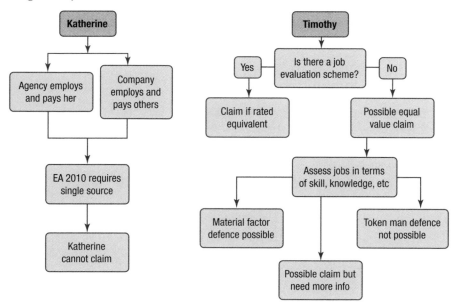

A printable version of this diagram plan is available from www.pearsoned.co.uk/lawexpressqa

Answer

The problem question requires the application of the equal pay provisions to Katherine and Timothy's situation. The Equality Act 2010 (EA 2010) sets out to ensure equal pay for like work, work rated as equivalent and work of equal value (EA 2010, s 65).[1] Equal pay can be claimed with employees of the opposite sex employed by the same employer. While that provision initially seems uncontroversial, it has raised a number of questions.[2] In **Lawrence and Others v Regent Office Care Ltd and Others** (Case C–320/00) [2002] All ER (D) 84 (Sep) ECJ the question of whether a comparator could be taken from someone working in the same organisation but employed by different employers was answered in the negative. **Allonby v Accrington and Rossendale College** [2004] ECR I-873, ECJ confirmed this and Mrs Allonby, whose contract with the College had been terminated and who had been re-engaged through an employment agency, could not claim equal pay with male colleagues still employed by the college. In order for the equal pay provisions to apply, there has to be a single source responsible for the pay. However, it was also held that the provision denying access to the statutory superannuation scheme, which was also at issue in **Allonby**, was in breach of equal pay provisions because this was not reliant upon the claimant working for the same employer as the comparator.[3]

Applying this to Katherine's situation, it seems clear that she cannot claim equal pay with her male colleagues[4] as she is employed by an employment agency and there is no single source responsible for her pay. Furthermore, the pension scheme appears to be a company scheme rather than a statutory one and therefore does not fall within the scope of the **Allonby** decision. In other words, the pension scheme is reliant on the claimant working for the same employer as the comparator, which is not the case for Katherine. Her claim will therefore fail.[5]

Timothy's claim relates to work of equal value. The first point to note is that most claims for equal pay are brought by women but that does not mean that men cannot claim where an appropriate situation arises. The aim of the EA 2010 is to achieve equal pay between the sexes, not merely to achieve equal pay for women.[6]

[1] Introduction which sets out the basic provisions of the EA 2010 leads you nicely into the specifics of this question.

[2] It seems an obvious point but it actually isn't uncontroversial and it is worth pointing this out because that is what makes it legally interesting.

[3] This paragraph gives a useful overview of the law relating to the single source using cases to build the argument. Now you need to apply that law.

[4] Many students would simply say this but you need to justify how you come to that conclusion more clearly. It's all about making your thought process explicit.

[5] Now you have given your explanation, so you can confidently state your conclusion.

[6] Perhaps an obvious point but many a student has taken the wording of the EqPA 1970 a little too literally and excluded Timothy from being able to claim!

Timothy is thus not excluded from bringing a claim because he is a man. Secondly, there does not seem to be a job evaluation scheme in place. The scenario gives no information in relation to this and we must therefore presume no such evaluation has taken place. The provisions of the EA 2010 do not compel employers to carry out such evaluations and Timothy cannot insist on such a scheme being put in place. However, if an analytical evaluation has been carried out and has been carried out correctly without being in itself discriminatory, Timothy's claim would fail unless his job and Justyna's had been rated equivalent.[7]

[7]This is a background point to your main legal argument but one that does need dealing with. Wherever possible, try to explain the law in the specific context of the question as shown here – it saves time.

In the absence of a scheme, Timothy must rely on the provisions relating to work of equal value. Section 65(6) of the EA 2010 states that where work is the same in terms of the demands made under such headings as effort, skill and decision making, for example, that work is of equal value. Although written from a woman's point of view in the original Equal Pay Act 1970, the EA 2010 has recast the provision in gender neutral language, clarifying that the provision applies equally the other way round. Timothy is thus entitled to have his and Justyna's job compared under a number of headings in order to determine whether or not the jobs are of equal value.[8] This exercise will usually be carried out by an expert appointed by ACAS, who will report to the tribunal.

[8]So here is the solution to Timothy's problem, which is stated clearly. To advise fully, you should now explain a little how it works.

Timothy must be aware that the employers could defend an equal pay claim, even where the jobs are held to be of equal value, if there is a genuine material factor that can explain the difference in pay and has nothing to do with sex discrimination.[9] The scenario does not give any information in relation to such a factor. However, employers have on occasion pointed to the fact that a member of the opposite sex is appointed on the same pay as the claimant and concluded that therefore the difference in pay cannot be related to sex discrimination.[10] This 'token man defence' (or, in Timothy's case, token woman defence) was held to be unlawful in **Pickstone v Freemans plc** [1988] 2 All ER 803, HL, where the employer argued that, as there was a man doing the same work as Mrs Pickstone, she could not bring an equal value claim comparing herself with another man. The House of Lords disagreed and gave judgment for Mrs Pickstone.

[9]Once you have dealt with Timothy's rights, consider any possible defence he should be aware of.

[10]Which is the argument Timothy's employers seem to have made, so you need to engage with it directly.

Timothy should thus seek further advice on the demands of his and Justyna's jobs before deciding on whether an equal pay claim may

[11]Finish with your specific advice, which shows you have fully answered the question you were set.

be appropriate. If he does decide to go ahead, he needs to bring a claim to the employment tribunal.[11]

 Make your answer stand out

- Explain the 'token man defence' in more detail and include a discussion as to why the courts will not allow it (it would allow an easy way for employers to avoid equal pay legislation).
- Consider the similarities and differences that might exist between the IT and marketing department and which might form the basis of an equal value claim and base this discussion in the context of s 65(6) of the EA 2010.

! Don't be tempted to...

- Spend a lot of time discussing Katherine's position in relation to like work. This part is straightforward – there is no single source, so no claim can be brought.
- Ignore the possibility of a job evaluation scheme completely – there is no indication that one is in place but you should acknowledge the possibility.

Wrongful dismissal

7

How this topic may come up in exams

Wrongful dismissal is quite a popular topic for examiners and it lends itself well to problem questions. As scenarios are usually relatively straightforward, questions usually also require some consideration of remedies and the sort of damages claimants might be entitled to. Essay questions are also possible and are usually phrased around the role of wrongful dismissal as an avenue for a claim given the statutory unfair dismissal jurisdiction. In fact there is often overlap between wrongful and unfair dismissal questions so it might be useful to consider the questions in this chapter in conjunction with the chapter on unfair dismissal.

Attack the question

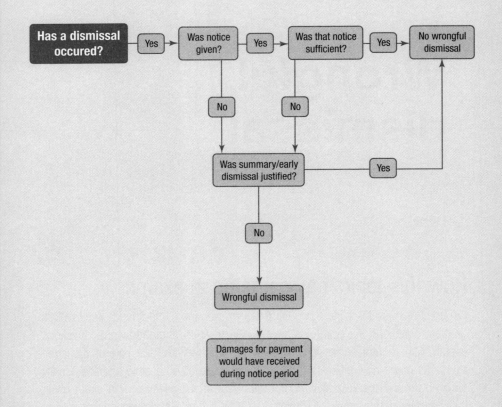

❓ Question 1

Sickeze is a pharmaceutical research and development company. Ric is a graduate scientist working in one of the plant's 'clean' areas where some of the most important research is undertaken. Ric learns that his wife has been having a relationship with his close colleague, Steve. He confronts Steve the next day at work and they argue. Steve complains about Ric's aggressive behaviour. The research and development manager dismisses Ric on grounds of gross misconduct. Written into the company handbook is that fighting is a dismissable offence. The handbook also states that, in the case of graduate employees, dismissals may take place only with the approval of the director of research, which did not happen in this case. Ric has a six-months' notice entitlement in his employment contract and he is dismissed summarily without a payment in lieu of notice.

Advise Ric as to the possibility of claiming for wrongful dismissal.

Answer plan

→ Explain wrongful dismissal is a common law concept.

→ Set out the elements necessary to claim: dismissal which is in breach of contract and not justified.

→ Consider whether or not the dismissal in this case is justified.
  - does the argument amount to fighting and therefore gross misconduct?
  - consider whether the dismissal should have been carried out by the director of research.

→ Conclude whether the dismissal was wrongful or not and, if appropriate, consider damages.

Diagram plan

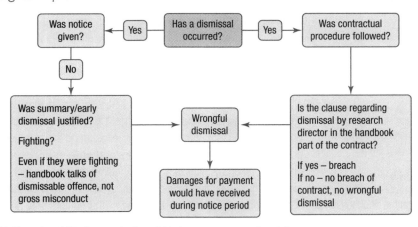

A printable version of this diagram plan is available from www.pearsoned.co.uk/lawexpressqa

Answer

Wrongful dismissal is a common law action which is based on a dismissal that occurs in breach of contract. The most common reason for dismissals being in breach of contract is lack of notice or sufficient notice given to the employee. In order to successfully bring a claim for wrongful dismissal, an employee must show that they were dismissed, that the dismissal was in breach of contract and that this breach was not justified.[1]

[1] A succinct explanation of wrongful dismissal.

In Ric's case, it is clear that he has been dismissed and also that he has been dismissed without the notice that he is contractually entitled to.[2] He should have received six months' notice but instead was summarily dismissed for gross misconduct. The only question requiring further examination is therefore whether or not the summary dismissal was justified.[3]

[2] Deal with issues which are answered for you quickly. Do not spend time considering whether a dismissal has occurred if you are told it has.

[3] Identify the issue that does need discussion.

Immediate dismissal can be justified by the employer in certain circumstances. Gross misconduct is misconduct that is so serious that it will justify summary dismissal. What amounts to gross misconduct will vary depending on the nature of the employer's business. ACAS recommends giving examples of acts which the employer would consider amount to gross misconduct. This will illustrate clearly to the employee what conduct will not be tolerated. It will also assist the employer, as the employment tribunal will be more likely to consider that a dismissal for these offences is justifiable.[4] In this case the employer seems to have done so by including some guidance in their handbook. The handbook suggests that fighting is a dismissable offence. However, it is not clear whether Ric and Steve were actually fighting. The scenario suggests that an argument ensued and Steve complained about aggressive behaviour but there is no evidence in the scenario that points to physical violence or anything more than a heated argument. However, even if it was shown that Ric was fighting, the handbook states only that it is a dismissable offence, not that fighting amounts to gross misconduct and therefore justifies a summary dismissal.[5] Arguably, therefore, while dismissal may be an option taken by Sickeze, summary dismissal is not automatically justified. It seems questionable whether or not gross misconduct has really been made out in this case.[6] Other factors may be taken into consideration when assessing whether or not the behaviour

[4] A clear explanation of gross misconduct and you are also highlighting your awareness of policy and good practice before then applying that to the scenario.

[5] You need carefully to apply the law and good practice to the scenario given.

[6] Consider your conclusion on this point and then justify it – try not to sit on the fence but, on balance, make up your mind.

was serious enough to warrant immediate dismissal. It would be prudent to consider where the argument took place, whether it was witnessed by colleagues or customers, whether the behaviour put any of the research or equipment at risk and also whether there had been previous issues relating to Ric's behaviour. However, overall, on the evidence given, it seems that a summary dismissal in these circumstances is too harsh a sanction and a warning may have been more appropriate.

[7]So here we have a possible w------ful dismissal not b [...]

The second issue arising in relation to the dismissal is the fact that Ric was dismissed by the research manager rather than the research [...] The handbook clearly states that the director must approve [...] e employee. In this case we are told that [...] nay be a breach of Ric's contract in itself.[7] [...] e handbook or even the entire handbook [...] ontract of employment and therefore forms [...] etween Ric and Sickeze, then the correct [...] dismissal has not been followed in Ric's case. [...] at the entire handbook will have contractual [...] ate v ASLEF (No. 2) [1972] CA; Dryden v [...] th Board [1992] IRLR 469, EAT) but individual [...] andbook may be held to be contractual. If the [...] elf or Ric's section 1 statement refer to any of [...] the handbook, they are likely to be construed [...] er, even in the absence of such a reference, a [...] fic and relates to an important aspect of the [...] ip is also likely to form part of the contract. [...] International Ltd [2006] All ER (D) 65 (Oct) [...] e Court of Appeal concluded that where a staff [...] handbook [...] details of enhanced redundancy pay there was a presumption of contractual status. Similarly, one might argue here that where the handbook refers to a specific dismissal procedure, this is specific and important enough to be of contractual status. On that basis, being dismissed by the research manager rather than the research director was in breach of Ric's contract.[8]

[8]You need to establish that the handbook or at least the relevant terms are in fact contractual; once you have done that, the breach is clear.

[9]You then need to state what all that means for the client, what they should do about it and what remedies they might expect.

Ric should therefore be advised that it is unlikely that his behaviour amounted to gross misconduct and that therefore a summary dismissal was not justified; and, in addition, that the dismissal by the manager was in breach of contract as well. A wrongful dismissal claim is thus likely to succeed.[9] If that is the case, the remedy available to Ric is the usual contractual remedy of damages. He would be entitled to the pay he would have received during his notice period and he is under an obligation to mitigate his loss. Earnings from any new job would thus be taken into consideration when calculating his damages and if he had made no effort to secure employment or refused employment when offered to him, this could be taken into account and his damages could be reduced.

✓ Make your answer stand out

- Add more case law examples, highlighting the issues raised and backing up your points; focus on recent cases and those discussed in your lectures.
- Expand your discussion on what sort of conduct might be gross misconduct in the case and whether or not summary dismissal was justified. Consider, for example, the importance of the location of the fight: was it in front of clients or in an area where things might get broken?
- You could expand the explanation of remedies and how to get them by including a discussion of tribunal and court jurisdiction.

! Don't be tempted to…

- Slip into a consideration of unfair dismissal; just answer the question set.
- Focus purely on the lack of notice and thus conclude that the dismissal was wrongful.
- Ignore the breach of procedure; you must consider if this is a breach of contract.

❓ Question 2

Happy Print is a newly established design and print company. Shona works in the web design team. Following an argument with the design manager one Tuesday afternoon, she is dismissed with immediate effect, told to pack her things and informed that she will be paid up until the end of that week. Shona has a six-months' notice entitlement in her employment contract. Eight months after the dismissal, shares in Happy Print are floated and employees are entitled to large gains provided that they are employees at the time of the flotation. Furthermore, bonuses were also paid the month after Shona left. The company handbook says that all bonuses are paid at the discretion of the company and depend on current employment with the company.

Advise Shona as to the possibility of claiming for wrongful dismissal and the remedies available to her.

Answer plan

→ Explain that wrongful dismissal is a common law concept.

→ Set out the elements necessary to claim: dismissal which is in breach of contract and not justified.

→ Consider whether or not the dismissal in this case is justified.

→ Conclude whether the dismissal was wrongful.

→ Consider damages:
  – pay
  – bonuses
  – payout from flotation
  – duty to mitigate loss.

Diagram plan

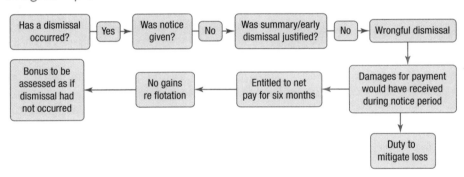

A printable version of this diagram plan is available from www.pearsoned.co.uk/lawexpressqa

[1]Keep the introduction as specific to the problem question as possible. So, what do you have to prove or discuss to answer the question Shona requires an answer to?

[2]If the scenario is straightforward (such as this one), say so. The question is clear on this issue because it wants you to focus on the remedies issue. You still have to justify your answer, though, and this comes next.

Answer

This scenario requires an examination of the law relating to wrongful dismissal. This common law action relates to a dismissal which is carried out in breach of the employment contract. We must therefore establish whether or not Shona has been dismissed in breach of her contract and, if so, what remedies are available to her.[1]

In this scenario it appears fairly clear that Shona has been wrongfully dismissed.[2] She has been dismissed with immediate effect and will be paid only until the end of the week. Even if this is considered payment in lieu of notice, it is nowhere near sufficient to meet her six months' notice requirement. We are given no information relating to exactly why Shona was dismissed. We are told she argued with her manager. Without any further information we cannot be certain but it does not seem like her dismissal is justified. However, if Shona did behave in a way that amounted to gross misconduct, it is possible that summary dismissal was justified. In the absence of additional information we must presume that this is not the case. Shona should therefore be advised to bring a claim for wrongful dismissal.[3]

Damages in wrongful dismissal claims are calculated in the same way as for breach of any other contract. The basic rule is that the employee must be placed in the same position as if the contract had been performed.[4] The employee will therefore be entitled to their full net salary for the contractual notice period, and to be reimbursed for the loss of other benefits for the notice period including, for example, employer's pension contributions, loss of use of a company car, private health insurance, contractual bonuses, commissions, etc. Damages for wrongful dismissal will be assessed by reference to loss suffered during the period of notice which the employer should have given.[5] In Shona's case this period is six months and we are not told of any other benefits besides the bonus and payment following flotation. We must thus presume she is not entitled to any further payment in relation to other benefits, although this should be confirmed with her.[6] There is no doubt that Shona would first of all be entitled to six months' pay (less the pay she received for the Wednesday – Friday following her dismissal on the Tuesday).

However, Shona was dismissed without any proper disciplinary process and **Edwards v Chesterfield Royal Hospital NHS Foundation Trust** [2009] EWHC 2011 (QB), HC suggests that in appropriate cases, where the employee has been dismissed without proper notice and without the benefit of a proper disciplinary process, the damages may include the income which would have been earned during the time the disciplinary process would have taken place as well as during the contractual notice period.[7]

The benefits following flotation can be dealt with quickly. As those benefits arose after the end of Shona's notice period, she will not be entitled to any payment resulting from the flotation.[8]

The bonus payments are thus the only issue requiring further consideration. The basic principle is that loss of contractual bonus falling

[3] Some speculation is inevitable when you are given so little information – just go with what you have and do not try to second guess the question.

[4] Set out the basic purpose of damages in wrongful dismissal.

[5] This section has set out basic principles; now you must apply them to the facts given.

[6] It is safe to presume that if the question wanted you to deal with specific benefits it would have mentioned them but in 'real life' you would, of course, check.

[7] This is worth stating as it would increase Shona's entitlement by a little while, although how long is difficult to assess.

[8] You need to mention it but as this is clear-cut, don't waste time on it.

due in the notice period will be payable. The handbook in Shona's case states that bonuses are paid at the discretion of the company. In **Clark v BET plc** [1997] IRLR 348, HC, BET argued that Mr Clark would have received no bonus at all or a bonus of only 6% on the basis that they were entitled to perform the contract in a manner most favourable to them. However, the judge held that the court should assess, without unrealistic assumptions, what position the employee would have been in had the employer performed its obligation. Looking at past bonus awards and predicted future profitability of the company, the judge held that Mr Clark would have continued to achieve significant bonuses. Similar reasoning was applied in **Clark v Nomura International plc** [2000] IRLR 766, CA: a city employee recovered £1.35m damages for loss of bonus. In **Horkulak v Cantor Fitzgerald International** [2004] EWCA Civ 1287, CA the Court of Appeal considered a term in the employee's contract stipulating that the employer 'may in its discretion pay you an annual discretionary bonus'. The Court of Appeal held that this was subject to an implied term that the discretion would be exercised genuinely and rationally.

[9]Consider what the case law says regarding bonuses but then make sure you apply that to the scenario – this comes next.

Moreover, it was not correct to assess damages on the basis of the minimum amount that might be awarded genuinely and rationally but rather the amount that the employee would probably have received had he remained in employment.[9] Applying the principles from the cases to Shona's position would suggest that she is entitled to the bonus payment she would have received had she still been in employment and that discretion in calculating that bonus pay must be exercised genuinely and rationally without taking into account the fact that Shona has been dismissed.

[10]Summarise where you have got to before moving on to the next issue. It helps the reader follow your thought process.

In summary then, Shona would be entitled to six months' notice pay and her bonus. However, she does have a duty to mitigate her losses.[10] In practice this means that she must try to find another reasonable job at the same or similar level of remuneration. If she does not apply for another job, she fails to mitigate her loss and any award made can be reduced. If there has been failure to mitigate, a reduction to compensation must be assessed by looking at what Shona should have done to get another job to mitigate her loss, and when she would have achieved an alternative income. A tribunal would then reduce the compensation by the amount of income which would have been earned. There is, of course, some guess work involved here but the case of **Roofdec Ltd v O'Keefe** [2008]

All ER (D) 195 (Dec), CA confirms that an arbitrary percentage reduction is not an appropriate way of assessing mitigation. The only circumstance where Shona would recover full wrongful dismissal compensation is if she genuinely tries to find alternative employment and fails. Damages may also be more substantial if, through no fault of her own, Shona does obtain other work but at a much lower level of pay.

✓ Make your answer stand out

- Expand your application of the case law relating to bonuses and consider how bonuses might be calculated in Shona's case.
- Consider the possibility of awarding additional damages for breach of procedure in more depth. What sort of procedure should have been carried out?
- Briefly consider what sort of conduct might have led to a justifiable dismissal and illustrate this with case law but note the first bullet point below.

! Don't be tempted to...

- Spend a lot of time on establishing wrongful dismissal – focus on remedies, that is really what the question is asking.
- Consider the flotation in detail; it falls outside the notice period.
- Slip into a discussion of unfair dismissal. The question clearly asks only about wrongful dismissal.

Unfair dismissal

How this topic may come up in exams

This chapter deals with the law relating to the statutory remedy of unfair dismissal; in short, the instances in which dismissals may be deemed as being fair (within the law) or unfair (contrary to the law). Unfair dismissal is a major topic and is likely to appear as a problem rather than an essay question. A good knowledge of the origin and sources of the law will aid your understanding of the subtle nuances that exist – this also helps to flesh out answers evidencing further reading. Unfair dismissals occur as the result of an employer's breach of statute rather than contract (wrongful dismissal). Employers can still fall foul of the law even if they have a potentially fair reason for dismissal. Depending on relevancy, your answer should also include a discussion on the remedies of reinstatement, re-engagement and compensation.

■ Attack the question

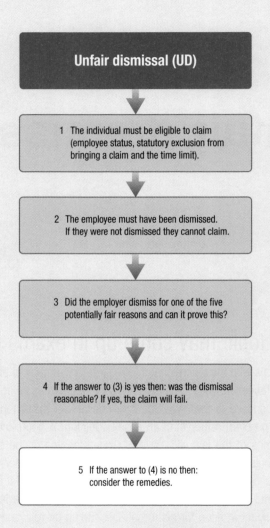

🖎 Question 1

The United Kingdom's law on unfair dismissal often favours the employer over the employee. Discuss.

Answer plan

→ Introduce unfair dismissal and its aims and purpose, the requirements (for example, the test for fairness and response), and remedies.

→ Discuss the arguments that support employee protection: for example, constructive dismissal and the decision in *Western Excavating (ECC) Ltd* v *Sharp* [1978] 1 All ER 713, CA.

→ Analyse the arguments that support protection of the employee by contrasting them with those that support the employer, for instance:
  - procedural fairness and the decision in *Polkey* v *AE Dayton Services Ltd* [1988] AC 344, HL; and
  - the range of reasonable responses test with a discussion of the decision in *Iceland Frozen Foods Ltd* v *Jones* [1982] IRLR 439, EAT.

→ Summarise the arguments and conclude whether or not the law on unfair dismissal does favour the employer over the employee.

Diagram plan

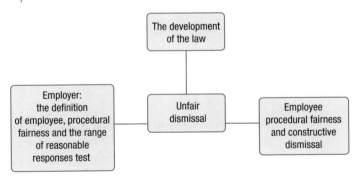

A printable version of this diagram plan is available from www.pearsoned.co.uk/lawexpressqa

Answer

Unfair dismissal was first introduced by the Industrial Relations Act 1971 as a direct result of recommendations by the International Labour Organization. The consolidation and development of the law in this area of employment can be traced by reference to the Contracts of Employment Act 1963, the Redundancy Payments Act 1965, the Trade Union and Labour Relations Act 1971, the Employment Protection (Consolidation) Act of 1978 (repealed), the Consolidation Acts of 1996 and now the relevant statutory provisions in which the current law is contained, namely Part X of the Employment Rights Act 1996 (ERA 1996)[1].

Although every employee in the United Kingdom (UK) has the right not to be unfairly dismissed, this is subject to a number of exceptions and exclusions that are often argued to favour either the employer or employee (for example, the requirement for one year's worth of continuous employment). It is these factors that this essay will discuss.[2]

Much of the time the law was construed in favour of employees; however, there are many instances in which the judicial interpretation of the law has favoured the employer. It is often argued that the range of reasonable responses test founded in **Iceland Frozen Foods Ltd v Jones** [1982] IRLR 439, EAT allows an employer too wide a discretion to dismiss an employee so long as its decision is akin to that of a reasonable employer: for example, a reasonable employer would have decided to dismiss had it been confronted with the same facts. The result renders the opinion of the employment tribunal (ET) irrelevant. The criticism lies in the fact that this test, which is not explicitly mentioned in s 98(4) of the ERA 1996, favours the employer.[3] This is so even though Lord Denning followed the statutory wording of the provision when interpreting it.

The decision in **Western Excavating (ECC) Ltd v Sharp** [1978] 1 All ER 713, CA is further evidence of judicial interpretation of the law in favour of employers. Here Lord Denning, following statutory terminology, decided that constructive dismissal was in fact a breach of a fundamental term in the employment contract that evidenced the desire no longer to be bound by it. The decision overruled previous authorities that simply required proof that the employer had acted unreasonably – something that was far easier to prove. The result of this was to make it more difficult for employees to prove that they had been constructively dismissed and thus limiting the number of cases that would eventually succeed.[4]

[1] Reference to the International Labour Organization and the fact that the 1978 Act was repealed and replaced by the Employment Rights Act 1996 shows knowledge on the development of the law and wider reading.

[2] This paragraph provides context to the proceeding discussion; it acts to structure the answer.

[3] This discussion shows (a) understanding of the test, (b) that judicial interpretation of the law resulted in delimitation of the law in favour of the employer and (c) that perhaps it was not envisaged in this form by the statute. Reference to the fact that Lord Denning followed the statutory wording, which could detract from the strength of this argument, will gain extra marks.

[4] The decision from this case clearly favours the employer but the policy consideration is also implicit within it – this will gain extra marks.

In contrast, the law on procedural fairness has favoured the employee. In **Polkey v AE Dayton Services Ltd** [1988] AC 344, HL the court decided a dismissal where a fair procedure (or process) had not been followed would be unfair even though the employer could show that its decision fell within the range of reasonable responses. The narrow exception to this was where the employer could prove that it would have been futile to follow a fair procedure because it would have made no difference. The result of this decision was in favour of the employee since it raised the bar in relation to an employer's conduct in instances of dismissal because of the greater likelihood of some procedural unfairness existing. See also **Duffy v Yeomans and Partners** [1995] ICR 1, CA where it was decided that there would be no procedural unfairness where the employer could show that a reasonable employer would have done the same, and **British Labour Pump Ltd v Byrne** [1979] IRLR 94, EAT.

The Employment Act 2002 (EA 2002) partially reversed the decision in **Polkey**, which meant that a dismissal would no longer be regarded as being procedurally unfair where the employer (a) followed the minimum statutory dismissal and disciplinary procedures as contained in Chapters 1 and 2 of Part 1 of Schedule 2 to the EA 2002, (b) its decision fell within the range of reasonable responses and (c) it could show that following a fair procedure would have made no difference to its decision to dismiss (contrast this with the decision in **Mason v Ward End Primary School Governing Body** [2006] IRLR 432, EAT). Section 98A(1) of the EA 2002 was repealed by the Employment Act 2008, returning the law on procedural fairness to its prior position. Procedural unfairness will now normally render a dismissal unfair, but compensation can be reduced to reflect the likelihood of the dismissal having occurred had a fair procedure been followed (the **Polkey** reduction).[5] Hence, the bar has been reduced in favour of the employee once again.

[5]Outlining the change in the law shows an understanding of how the law has developed and how it tries to balance the right of the employee to be protected with the right of the employer's commercial interests – this will gain extra marks.

Lastly, it is often argued that litigation is unequal because of the unequal access to resources: i.e. employers will normally have insurance and thus can afford to litigate, whereas employees without such funds are more likely to rely on pro-bono support. Furthermore, remedies on a successful claim of unfair dismissal often favour the employer: for example, reinstatement is rarely awarded and hence

[6]You will achieve more marks if you present two possible opposing arguments as this shows a greater understanding of the issues tribunals must contend with.

employers wishing to remove an employee from a particular post succeed in their endeavour. The contrasting argument suggests that this is often because the relationship has broken down to the extent that it is irreparable.[6] Finally, compensation where awarded is subject to a statutory cap (maximum).

[7]Here mention is given to the fact that the UK has a common law system where judicial interpretation of the law can have such an effect – this will gain extra marks because it shows an understanding of the dynamics in which UK employment law exists.

In conclusion, UK employment law aims to regulate the relationship between employer and employee. Often judicial interpretation of the law leads to greater protection of one party over the other – such is the fallibility of a common law system.[7] Like any system of law, UK employment law continues to develop over time and thus the nature and extent of protection will continue to change: the decisions in **Polkey v AE Dayton Services Ltd** and **Western Excavating (ECC) Ltd v Sharp** are good examples of this. What is clear is that UK law seeks to balance the rights and interests of both parties to the relationship.

✓ Make your answer stand out

- Outline that the decision in *Duffy* v *Yeomans and Partners* [1995] ICR 1 CA was a return to the 'no difference rule' from *British Labour Pump Ltd* v *Byrne* [1979] IRLR 94, EAT.

- Discuss the elements of procedural fairness such as delay, investigation and consistency, the ACAS Code on Discipline and Grievance and state that natural justice forms part of it.

- Discuss conflicting authorities such as *Alexander* v *Bridgen Enterprises Ltd* [2006] ICR 1277, EAT or *Mason* v *Ward End Primary School Governing Body* [2006] IRLR 432, EAT where HHJ McMullen QC had decided that an employer could only rely on s 98A(1) of the Employment Act 2002 where the procedure breached was in written form or implied through custom and practice.

- Discuss 'some other substantial reason' in which an employer may dismiss an employee for refusing to accept contractual changes, with reference to case law, i.e. *Anglian Homes Ltd* v *Kelly* [2004] EWCA Civ 901.

- State that it is mooted that judicial discretion and precedent making in the United Kingdom has been eroded by Parliament because of the impact it has on the 'meaning' of the law and its purpose, and that future decisions are less likely to affect the law to the extent they have done in the past.

! Don't be tempted to...

- Discuss the historical background to unfair dismissal in too much depth – although it is relevant it should be given due context in relation to what the question is asking you to do.
- Cover too many issues in a descriptive and summary form; select a few, for which you should provide a more detailed answer (for example, fairness).
- Spend too much time relaying the facts of the authorities; it is the principle that they set that is most important and the relative impact in terms of whether it lends support to the employer or employee.

? Question 2

Terry has worked for Foods Asia Ltd as a supervisor for seven years on a permanent contract of personal service. Recently Terry suffered the loss of his partner, Philip, who died in a car accident a year ago, leaving him solely responsible for looking after their two daughters, Fran and Velda. His manager, Chanelle, has noticed a change in Terry's working behaviour: he turns up late, he is less productive and he often seems to be lost in a daydream. After having warned Terry on a number of occasions, she dismisses him when he does not process a large order, losing the firm hundreds of pounds of profit. Advise Terry on any potential claim that he may have for an unfair dismissal.

Answer plan

→ Discuss the basic requirements for a claim.

→ Briefly discuss eligibility to claim, discussing s 94 of the Employment Rights Act 1996, employee status and continuity of employment.

→ Discuss and analyse the type of dismissal: for example, express or implied or constructive dismissal by reason of a fundamental breach of contract.

→ Analyse the reason for dismissal and whether it falls into one of the potentially fair reasons to dismiss (s 98 of the Employment Rights Act 1996), procedural fairness under *Polkey* v *AE Dayton Services Ltd* [1988] AC 344, HL and the range of reasonable responses test in *Iceland Frozen Foods Ltd* v *Jones* [1983] IRLR 439, EAT.

→ Conclude with a summary of the advice and any remedies that Terry may claim on success: for example, reinstatement or re-engagement and compensation.

Diagram Plan

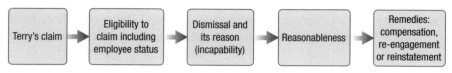

A printable version of this diagram plan is available from www.pearsoned.co.uk/lawexpressqa

Answer

[1]This typical answer format ensures that the main elements to a claim for unfair dismissal are covered and that valuable marks are not lost. These elements are: eligibility to claim, i.e. employee and continuity of service; dismissal and a reason for it; reasonableness; and remedies.

This question relates to the rights of Terry not to be unfairly dismissed and the protection provided by the law to that effect. The advice to Terry will be based upon protection provided by the Employment Rights Act 1996 (ERA 1996) that includes ss 94–95, 98 and 92.

Eligibility to claim [1]

Employees have the right not to be unfairly dismissed: protection against such dismissals is provided by s 94 of the Employment Rights Act 1996 under which all employees are entitled to a remedy. First, Terry must be able to prove that he is eligible to make this claim because it is limited to those individuals that are classed as employees who have been continuously employed for at least one year (qualifying period of employment). The only exception to the requirement for one year's continuous employment are dismissals that are considered to be automatically unfair.[2] It is clear that (a) Terry is an employee, and (b) he has been employed for the qualifying period with Foods Asia Ltd – the terms 'seven years … [and] … permanent contract of personal service' are evidence in support of this assumption.[3] In addition, it is clear that Terry does not fall into any category of employee that is statutorily excluded from making this claim (e.g. a Crown employee), and that he is bringing the claim within the prescribed three-month time limit.

[2]Stating the instance in which the eligibility criteria are waived will achieve extra marks – this shows a fuller understanding of how the law operates.

[3]By stating the evidence in support of the assumption you are making in favour of Terry's status as an employee, you will get valuable marks.

Dismissal and its reason

Terry must prove that he has been dismissed: from the facts above it can be ascertained that he has been expressly dismissed (also referred to as a direct or an actual dismissal) by his manager Chanelle; such dismissals fall under s 95(1)(a) of the ERA 1996.

[4]Outlining that there are five potentially fair reasons to dismiss an employee so long as the dismissal was carried out in a fair manner shows a good understanding of the law because it highlights (a) that the reasons are only potentially fair and (b) the extent of procedural fairness.

Employers who can prove that they have one of the five potentially fair reasons to dismiss and have dismissed in a fair manner (unless futile to do so – see **Polkey v AE Dayton Services Ltd** [1988] AC 344, HL) will have a defence to a claim.[4] In this instance the facts suggest that Foods Asia Ltd could argue that it had grounds upon which to dismiss Terry: here it would be incapability of performing his job functions to a reasonable standard, which encompasses skill, aptitude, health or any other physical or mental quality under s 98(2)(a) of the ERA 1996. The reason would be the facts known to or belief held by Foods Asia Ltd that cause it to dismiss Terry (see **Abernethy v Mott, Hay & Anderson** [1974] ICR 323, CA). His alleged carelessness would also be included within this. If an employer puts forward a sham reason then the employment tribunal (ET) will simply look behind it.

Reasonableness

[5]You will gain marks by discussing the issues and considerations for the employment tribunal once the fair reason has been established. Often students will stop short of this and lose valuable marks.

If Foods Asia Ltd can establish incapability (or any other of the five potentially fair reasons) as the reason for dismissing Terry then the ET will consider whether or not it did so in a manner that was fair and reasonable taking into account the size of the employer, the resources available to it and equity/merits of the case. In **Iceland Frozen Foods Ltd v Jones** [1983] IRLR 439, EAT it was decided that the ET should direct itself using the terms in s 98(4) of the ERA 1996, only consider the reasonableness of the employer's conduct and not fairness to the employee, it should not substitute its decision as to the right course of action over the one the employer actually took, and the majority of the time it should apply the range of reasonable responses test (see **Foley v Post Office** [2000] All ER (D) 1137, CA).[5]

[6]Discussing the test and its narrow exception shows that you have understood the law – this will gain extra marks.

The ET will consider whether Foods Asia Ltd believed the reason it has given and whether it had reasonable grounds upon which to formulate that belief (see **British Home Stores Ltd v Burchell** [1980] ICR 303, EAT), i.e. did Foods Asia Ltd act in a manner that was procedurally fair unless it was futile and useless to do so (see **Polkey v AE Dayton Services Ltd**)?[6] From the facts above, it is not apparent whether Foods Asia Ltd carried out any investigation into the order Terry did not place or how it dealt with his reduced productivity or the nature and extent of the warnings given to him, and more importantly whether it knew of the death of his partner, Philip. It would certainly be reasonable to expect Foods Asia Ltd to have conducted an investigation: this would almost certainly reveal the reason behind Terry's conduct, perhaps leading to a different course of action. Hence, in absence of such an investigation it is likely that Terry can establish a prima facie case for an unfair dismissal.

Remedy

In a successful claim of UD, the ET will consider the most appropriate remedy at its discretion. Often reinstatement is unlikely and re-engagement not possible due to organisational constraints, thus compensation is considered most suitable. On the facts, it may be possible for Terry to be reinstated so long as the job vacancy is still available. Where the ET awards compensation, then the award will consist of two elements: a basic and a compensatory award. The basic award is calculated using the same formula as that used for calculating a redundancy payment (using the claimant's age, wage and service). The compensatory award includes much more: for example, loss of past and future earnings, pension rights, benefits, etc (see **Norton Tool Co Ltd v Tewson** [1973] 1 All ER 183, NIRC).[7]

[7]A short analysis of the remedies available and the likelihood of their being awarded, including a short discussion on what compensation includes, will gain more marks because it shows a deeper understanding of factors that affect the award of a remedy.

Conclusion

In conclusion, it seems that Terry may be able to establish a prima facie case for an unfair dismissal. However, the success of this depends upon the manner in which Foods Asia Ltd dismissed him, i.e. did it conduct an investigation, what were the nature and extent of the warnings given, etc? On success, the most likely remedy to be awarded to him would be compensation.

✓ Make your answer stand out

- Outline that the time limit for bringing the claim may be extended if it was not reasonably practicable for him to bring the claim within the three-month limit prescribed.
- Discuss the fact that the giving of unjustified warnings can in itself amount to a constructive dismissal, stating the following authority: *Walker* v *Josiah Wedgwood & Sons Ltd* [1978] IRLR 105, EAT.
- Discuss that, where two or more grounds are put forward, the principal or motivating cause for the dismissal must be identified; refer to the authority of *Carlin* v *St Cuthbert's Co-operative Association Ltd* [1974] IRLR 188, NIRC.
- State that reasons for dismissal cannot be changed; the purpose of this is to give the employee enough time (a) to know the reason for dismissal and (b) to prepare a defence to it.
- State that in the United Kingdom the level of judicial discretion and precedent making has been reduced by Parliament, debates surrounding this issue suggest that the main reason for this is the impact they have on the law in terms of purpose, clarity and consistency.

! Don't be tempted to...

- Discuss any claims he may have in discrimination law as the question specifically refers to unfair dismissal.
- List and discuss all the potentially fair reasons for dismissal and their relative law.
- Question the principles set by the case law because this question requires you to apply them to the facts rather than assess them in essay style.

❓ Question 3

Jennifer has worked for Snuggles Ltd (a small family firm) for several years; she checks in stock delivered to the branch from Geneva, where it is manufactured. One day her line manager John Boyle sees Jennifer loading some snuggles into the back of her car. On being questioned on what she was doing with the stock Jennifer says, 'It's none of your business'. In fact, unbeknown to Snuggles Ltd, Jennifer works for a charity that distributes blankets to the poor during the winter. John Boyle dismisses her on the spot, saying, 'You're fired'. Advise Jennifer whether she can claim unfair dismissal.

Answer plan

→ Outline your intended discussion and include mention of the eligibility to make the claim, the reason for the dismissal and its reasonableness, and remedies.

→ Briefly discuss eligibility to claim discussing s 94 of the Employment Rights Act 1996, employee status and continuity of employment.

→ Discuss and analyse the type of dismissal such as express, implied or constructive (i.e. a fundamental breach of contract).

→ Analyse the reason for dismissal (theft) and whether it falls into one of the potentially fair reasons to dismiss (s 98 of the Employment Rights Act 1996).

→ Discuss procedural fairness under *Polkey* v *AE Dayton Services Ltd* [1988] HL and the range of reasonable responses test *Iceland Frozen Foods Ltd v Jones* [1983] IRLR 439, EAT.

→ Outline in the conculsion a summary of your advice and any remedies (compensation, re-engagement or reinstatement) that she may claim on success.

Diagram plan

A printable version of this diagram plan is available from www.pearsoned.co.uk/lawexpressqa

Answer

This question relates to the rights of Jennifer not to be unfairly dismissed and the protection provided by the law to that effect. The advice to her will be based upon protection provided by the Employment Rights Act 1996 (ERA 1996) that includes ss 94, 95 and 98.

Eligibility to claim

Employees have the right not to be unfairly dismissed: protection against such dismissals is provided by s 94 of the Employment Rights Act 1996 under which all employees are entitled to a remedy. First, Jennifer must be able to prove that she is eligible to make this claim because it is limited to those individuals that are classed as employees who have been continuously employed for at least one year (qualifying period of employment). The only exception to the requirement for one year's continuous employment are dismissals that are considered to be automatically unfair. It is clear that Jennifer both (a) is an employee and (b) has been employed for the qualifying period with Snuggles Ltd – the term 'several years' is evidence in support of this assumption. In addition, it is clear that Jennifer does not fall into any category of employee that is statutorily excluded from making this claim (e.g. an offshore fisherwoman), and that she is bringing the claim within the prescribed three-month time limit.[1]

[1]In addition to the standard eligibility to claim criteria (employment status as an employee and one year's continuity of employment), stating that certain categories of employee are prohibited from making this claim will achieve more marks.

Dismissal and its reason

Jennifer must prove that she has been dismissed: from the facts above it can be ascertained that she has been expressly dismissed (also referred to as a direct or an actual dismissal) by her line manager John Boyle; such dismissals fall under s 95(1)(a) of the ERA 1996.

[2]Stating that as standard most employee handbooks and contracts of employment will cover issues of gross misconduct – this will gain extra marks because (a) it seeks information to strengthen the argument and (b) it shows appreciation of the standard form of most documents of this sort.

The reason for the dismissal in this instance seems to be theft of stock. It is clear, according to the authority of **Sinclair v Neighbour** [1967] 2 QB 279, CA that theft from the employer will constitute gross misconduct. Often an employee's employment contract or their handbook will list the conduct that amounts to gross misconduct for the purposes of dismissal and discipline. In addition, although the facts above do not explicitly state this, her employment contract is more than likely to contain a term that refers to dismissal on the grounds of gross misconduct.[2]

Reasonableness

[3]Outlining that the employment tribunal will consider fairness and the terms by which it does so will achieve more marks because it shows a good understanding of the law.

At this stage the employment tribunal (ET) will consider the reasonableness of the dismissal. Fairness is a matter of fact and not law, and it is the responsibility of the ET to decide whether the dismissal was fair. In doing so, the ET will consider taking into account the size of the employer, the resources available to it and equity/merits of the case (see s 98(4) of the ERA 1996) and it should direct itself using the terms in s 98(4) of the ERA 1996 (**Iceland Frozen Foods Ltd v Jones** [1983] IRLR 439, EAT).[3]

Jennifer has been caught in the act and thus the need for investigation does not arise. However, Jennifer could argue that she has not been given the right to respond to the allegations nor appeal the decision to dismiss her. It is clear from the facts that Snuggles Ltd is a 'small family firm' and therefore is unlikely to have a detailed procedure in place; this does not affect the dismissal as such because s 98(4) allows the size and resource of the employer to be taken into account when the ET is assessing the reasonableness of the decision to dismiss.

In **British Home Stores Ltd v Burchell** [1980] ICR 303n, the EAT (as confirmed by the Court of Appeal) laid down a three-stage test in such cases. The questions the ET would pose are as follows: Did Snuggles Ltd believe that it was dismissing Jennifer for theft? Did it have reasonable grounds upon which to base that belief? The answer must be yes as Jennifer was caught loading stock into her car boot. Finally, did Snuggles Ltd act in a manner that was procedurally fair, unless it was futile and useless to do so (see **Polkey v AE Dayton Services Ltd** [1988] AC 344, HL)? In answer to this latter question, Snuggles Ltd could have conducted an investigation. The lack of such investigation is not necessarily fatal to Snuggles Ltd defending the claim; had it conducted the investigation, the true facts may have come to light.

[4] This brief discussion of the decision in *Polkey* and the narrow exception in which an employer may defend itself from a dismissal that would otherwise be considered procedurally unfair will get more marks because it shows a deeper understanding of the law.

In **Polkey v AE Dayton Services Ltd** the court decided that a dismissal where a fair procedure (or process) had not been followed was unfair even though the employer could show that its decision fell within the range of reasonable responses, with the narrow exception where the employer could prove that it would have been futile to follow a fair procedure because it would have made no difference.[4] It may be that Snuggles Ltd could argue that this case falls within that narrow exception.

Finally, in **Iceland Frozen Foods Ltd v Jones** it was decided that the ET should consider only the reasonableness of the employer's conduct and not fairness to the employee, it should not substitute its decision as to the right course of action over the one the employer actually took, and the majority of the time it should apply the range of reasonable responses test (see **Foley v Post Office** [2000] All ER (D) 1137, CA).

Remedy

In a successful claim of unfair dismissal, the ET will consider the most appropriate remedy at its discretion. Often reinstatement is unlikely and re-engagement not possible due to organisational constraints, thus compensation is considered most suitable. Where the ET awards compensation, then the award will consist of two elements: a basic and a compensatory award. The basic award is calculated using the same formula as that used for calculating a redundancy payment (using the claimant's age, wage and service). The compensatory award includes much more: for example, loss of past and future earnings, pension rights, benefits, etc (see **Norton Tool Co Ltd v Tewson** [1973] 1 All ER 183, NIRC).

[5]A short conclusion outlining the main crux of the argument (a summary of the advice and the basis on which you are giving it). This is a good way to conclude, although it could be amalgamated with the remedies paragraph.

Conclusion

In conclusion, it seems that Jennifer's claim rests on procedural fairness, i.e. the lack of investigation, failure to give her the right to respond or appeal; and the defence of Snuggles Ltd rests on it being able to prove that to follow such a procedure would have been useless or futile.[5]

 Make your answer stand out

- Discuss that the time limit for bringing the claim may be extended if it was not reasonably practicable for her to bring the claim within the three-month limit prescribed.
- Outline that the ACAS Handbook of Discipline at Work states that dismissals without notice for gross misconduct are valid.

! **Don't be tempted to…**

- Go into too much detail regarding the categories of employee that are excluded from claiming unfair dismissal.
- Discuss the facts of the cases *(Polkey* and *Iceland Frozen Foods)* in too much depth; simply state the principle that the case sets and its application.
- Simply repeat verbatim the entire advice (as set out in your answer) in the conclusion as this is simply duplication.

📝 Question 4

Examine the differences between unfair dismissal and wrongful dismissal.

Answer plan

→ Discuss wrongful dismissal as a claim for breach of contract (common law) and unfair dismissal as a statutory remedy with common law origins.

→ Examine jurisdictional differences with regard to the venue in which the claims can be heard (employment tribunal and/or ordinary courts and refer to the Employment Tribunals Extension of Jurisdiction (England and Wales) Order 1994).

→ Outline the time limit differences between the two claims.

→ Discuss the fact that procedural fairness is in issue only in unfair dismissal claims.

→ Analyse the differences in the remedies.

→ Critically examine why a fair reason that is discovered after an unfair dismissal has taken place cannot act retrospectively to make the dismissal fair; contrast with wrongful dismissal.

Diagram plan

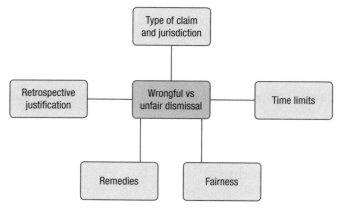

A printable version of this diagram plan is available from www.pearsoned.co.uk/lawexpressqa

Answer

[1]This is a short and clear
introduction that identifies
the nature and focus of
the discussion, namely the
difference between the two
claims. Although the question
asks you to examine the
difference between the claims,
if you add critical evaluation
to your answer then you will
gain more marks: for example,
discussing the reason for
retrospective justification in
wrongful dismissal claims.

[2]Dividing the answer up with
headings makes it easier
for the reader to follow the
argument because indirectly
this gives coherency and a
logical flow. It also acts to
remind you whether or not you
have covered all the points in
the most effective manner, i.e.
some topics may be related
and thus can be amalgamated.

[3]This additional comment
shows wider reading
and therefore a broader
understanding.

[4]These sentences are well
constructed because they
concisely cover the basic
limitation of the claims. This
will gain you extra marks.

The law relating to wrongful dismissal (WD) and unfair dismissal (UD) is not fully settled; the jurisprudence of the English courts has lent some clarity to it. In this answer I will discuss and examine the differences between two remedies relating to the dismissal of an individual from employment.[1] Often one set of facts will give rise to a variety of legal issues. Two examples of this are: employees dismissed for committing theft from work will be collaterally liable in criminal law; and an employee's resignation by reason of harassment may raise additional employer liability in the law of tort. The same is true for these two remedies that complement each other: they cover quite distinct categories of individuals (something discussed later in this answer).

Category of claim and jurisdiction[2]

The basic difference between these claims lies in the category of claim. A claim for WD is in short a claim for a breach of contract, in contrast to which a claim for an unfair dismissal is a claim for a breach of statute. It should be noted, however, that prior to being placed on a statutory footing UD was a concept created and developed by the common law.[3] An UD can only be claimed by employees who have at least one year's continuity of employment, unless the dismissal falls into one of the categories considered automatically unfair dismissals, where there is no requirement for any length of continuous employment. In contrast, wrongful dismissal can be claimed by anyone where there is a breach of contract and there is no minimum stipulated period for which a contract should have run.[4] A related issue concerns the venue in which the claims can be heard: although the ordinary courts and the ET have joint jurisdiction to adjudicate on employment related claims (see the Employment Tribunals Extension of Jurisdiction (England and Wales) Order 1994), a WD claim should be made in the ordinary courts and a claim for an UD in the ET. Often individuals may choose to pursue a particular claim because of the limit in remedy available: for example, in UD claims compensation is capped. Hence, an individual earning over the cap may wish to pursue a claim for a WD in the ordinary courts because the loss

[5]This shows depth of knowledge and a clear understanding of the considerations in relation to each claim when advice is required; this will gain extra marks not only for depth of understanding but also for wider reading.

[6]Here you can make the argument that those individuals whose claim is outside the limitation period may choose to pursue the WD claim. What is beginning to form is a critical analysis of the two remedies on the basis of the general factors bearing on why, where and when a claim is made – this will gain you better marks.

that they have sustained is greater than the compensation they would recover in an UD claim. In respect of this, it should be noted that the ordinary courts still retain the discretion to adjudicate on the matter; in reality they may choose to redirect the claim to the ET instead.[5]

Time limits

Another very important difference between the two claims concerns the time limit or limitation period in which the law permits a claim to be made. All UD claims must be made within a period of three months from the effective date of termination. The ET does have the discretion to increase this by a further three months where it believes there are just and equitable reasons for it to do so, or where certain impracticalities rendered it difficult for the claimant to issue the claim on time. Even though the discretion is retained, it is rarely exercised. In contrast, WD claims are subject to the normal limitation period for all general contractual disputes, namely within six years of the breach of contract; inevitably, this may be another reason for an individual choosing to make this claim instead.[6]

Procedural fairness

Interestingly, unlike claims for an UD, the issue of procedural fairness does not arise in claims for a WD. This can be partly attributed to the fact that one of the reasons for creating the remedy of UD was to rectify the failure of the law relating to WD to cover dismissals where the employer acted in a manner that was procedurally unfair. The law on this issue has seen much change: in **Polkey v AE Dayton Services Ltd** [1988] AC 344, HL the court decided that a dismissal where a fair procedure (or process) had not been followed was unfair even though the employer could show that its decision fell within the range of reasonable responses. The narrow exception to this was where the employer could prove that it would have been futile to follow a fair procedure because it would have made no difference. The Employment Act 2002 (EA 2002) partially reversed the decision in **Polkey**. The reversal was short-lived and the law on procedural fairness was reverted back to its previous position but with a reduction in compensation to reflect the likelihood of the dismissal

[7]This paragraph summarises the change in the law without too much detail. Stating the principle like this focuses the answer because the change is actually irrelevant to the present discussion.

[8]Mention here the stark contrast in remedies available for both WD and UD. Extra marks will be gained here for identifying the extent of the remedy of compensation (cap) on a successful claim of an UD.

having occurred had a fair procedure been followed (the **Polkey** reduction).[7]

Remedies

Finally, evidence of the distinction between WD and UD is further provided by the remedies available on a successful claim for each. The former, being a claim for a breach of contract, is remedied by compensation that seeks to put the employee in the position they would have been in had the contract been successfully performed, i.e. to compensate the loss incurred. In contrast, the remedies available on a successful claim for an UD are re-engagement, reinstatement and/or compensation. Often it is the latter that is awarded which, unlike in some claims for a WD, has a statutory cap (maximum).[8]

Conclusion

In conclusion, although the common law claims origin to both these claims, there are many differences between them. In short, UD was created to remedy the instances where WD provided no protection. What is clear is that both WD and UD have their own limitations: for example, compensation in UD claims is capped and the award of certain remedies increasingly unlikely.

 Make your answer stand out

- Mention that s 98A(1) of the EA 2002, which reversed *Polkey*, was repealed by the Employment Act 2008.
- Refer to surrounding debates, e.g. the Equality Act 2006 removed the upper age limit for claiming UD and thus claims are now not restricted to those under the age of 65.
- Discuss the point that, unlike in claims for a WD, in claims for an UD an employer cannot retrospectively justify a dismissal by putting forward a fair reason to dismiss an employee which it discovered after it had already dismissed them: refer to the authority of *W. Devis & Sons Ltd* v *Atkins* [1977] UK HL, 6.

> **!** **Don't be tempted to…**
>
> ■ Go into too much detail regarding cases; it is the differences between unfair dismissal and wrongful dismissal that are being discussed;
>
> ■ Discuss too many differences – this could have the effect of making your argument weaker. Pick the important points: for example, venue, time limit and fairness issues and discuss in relative depth.
>
> ■ Be too descriptive; remember to articulate the argument: for example, the ET has the discretion to extend the time limit but rarely does so.

? Question 5

Sharon has worked for Greene Antiquarian Books Ltd (GAB) as a buyer for one-and-a-half years. Tracy has worked for the company as a cleaner for the last 11 months on a fixed-term contract, and Garth has worked for it as a security guard for the last eight years. On Monday it came to the attention of the owner, Dorien Greene, that, instead of buying rare books for her, Sharon has been forwarding the details of such buys to GAB Ltd's main competitor Chris-Tees, and that Tracy has joined the Antiquarian Bookshop Employees' Union (ABEU,) something Dorien is not happy about. GAB Ltd has formally warned Garth for failing to properly vet those that enter the store. On Wednesday, Dorien discovers from the CCTV footage that on the previous day a customer set off the alarm as he entered the store but Garth failed to do anything about it. When questioned about this, Garth replies, 'I liked the old alarm-less system'. On the same Wednesday, Dorien dismisses both Sharon and Garth, and advises Tracy that her contract will not be renewed when it lapses on Thursday. Advise Sharon, Tracy and Garth whether they can claim unfair dismissal.

> ## Answer plan
>
> → Outline eligibility to make the claim, reason for dismissal and its reasonableness, and remedies.
>
> → Briefly discuss eligibility to claim, discussing s 94 of the Employment Rights Act 1996, employee status and continuity of employment.
>
> → Discuss and analyse the type of dismissal, i.e. express, implied or constructive (i.e. a fundamental breach of contract).
>
> → Analyse the reason – infidelity, trade union membership and capability – for dismissals and whether they fall into one of the potentially fair reasons to dismiss (s 98 of the Employment Rights Act 1996).
>
> → Discuss procedural fairness under *Polkey* v *AE Dayton Services Ltd* [1988] HL and the range of reasonable responses test from *Iceland Frozen Foods Ltd* v *Jones* [1983] IRLR 439, EAT.
>
> → Summarise your advice and any remedies that they may claim on success.

Diagram plan

Sharon	Tracy	Garth
• Eligibility to claim • Dismissal and its reason (fidelity) • Reasonableness including the lack of investigation and remedies	• Eligibility to claim including a lack of continuous service • Dismissal and its reason (trade union membership) • Reasonableness and automatic unfair dismissal and remedies	• Eligibility to claim • Dismissal and its reason (capability) • Reasonableness in view of the investigation • Remedies

A printable version of this diagram plan is available from www.pearsoned.co.uk/lawexpressqa

Answer

This question relates to the rights of Sharon, Tracy and Garth not to be unfairly dismissed and the protection provided by the law to that effect. The advice to the three of them will be based upon protection provided by the Employment Rights Act 1996 (ERA 1996) that includes ss 94, 95 and 98.

Eligibility to claim[1]

[1]This question is complicated by three possible claims. Better answers will deal with commonly satisfied elements together with discussion on the areas of difference. The style in which the answer is presented here aids the flow of the discussion and this will inevitably gain extra marks.

Employees have the right not to be unfairly dismissed: protection against such dismissals is provided by s 94 of the Employment Rights Act 1996 under which all employees are entitled to a remedy. First, Sharon, Tracy and Garth must be able to prove that they are eligible to make this claim because it is limited to those individuals that are classed as employees who have satisfied the requirement for one year's qualifying continuous period of employment. The exception to this requirement are dismissals that are considered to be automatically unfair.

It is clear that Sharon and Garth both (a) are employees and (b) have been employed for the qualifying period with GAB Ltd – the terms 'one-and-a-half years' and 'eight years' are evidence in support of this assumption. Although Tracy satisfies requirement (a), she does not have the requisite one year's continuity of employment; however,

[2]This sentence effectively summarises that Tracy's claim is for an automatically unfair dismissal; the analysis will gain marks for application of the difference in requirement between this and the ordinary unfair dismissal.

this does not necessarily mean that her claim fails. If Tracy argues that she has been dismissed by reason of her membership of the trade union, then she will satisfy one of the categories of reason that amounts to an automatically unfair dismissal and hence no minimum period of continuous employment is required.[2] In addition, Sharon, Tracy and Garth do not fall into any category of employee that is statutorily excluded from making this claim (e.g. if they were all offshore fisherpersons). The final element that must be satisfied is to ensure that their claims are issued within the prescribed three-month time limit.

Dismissals and their reasons

Sharon, Tracy and Garth must prove that they have been dismissed: from the facts above it can be ascertained that Sharon and Garth have been expressly dismissed (also referred to as a direct or an actual dismissal); such dismissals fall under s 95(1)(a) of the ERA 1996. For Tracy's purposes, she has been dismissed by virtue of s 95(1)(c) of the ERA 1996, which applies to contracts that come to a natural end, i.e. they lapse without being renewed.

The reason for each of the dismissals varies. In relation to Sharon, GAB Ltd will argue that the potentially fair reason it had for dismissing her was her conduct that resulted in a fundamental breach of the implied duty of fidelity or faithful service (ERA 1996, s 98). Section 86(6) of the ERA 1996 provides that in such instances employers may dismiss her without notice. Often an employee's employment contract or their handbook will list the conduct that amounts to gross misconduct for the purposes of dismissal and discipline. In addition, although the facts above do not explicitly state this, her employment contract is more than likely to contain a term that refers to dismissal on the grounds of gross misconduct. The potentially fair reason for Garth's dismissal seems to be capability (see s 98(3) of the ERA 1996): this includes the skill and aptitude by which the employee performs his job function and their inflexibility (see **Abernethy v Mott, Hay and Anderson** [1974] ICR 323, CA). Finally, in absence of evidence to the contrary it seems that the reason for Tracy's dismissal is her membership of the ABEU.[3]

[3]Identification and discussion of the likely 'potentially fair reasons', the requirements and evidence will gain marks – this shows a good appreciation of the law.

Reasonableness

At this stage the employment tribunal (ET) will consider the reasonableness of the dismissal. Fairness is a matter of fact and not law, and it is the responsibility of the ET to decide whether the dismissal was fair. In doing so, the ET will consider taking into account the size of the employer, the resources available to it and equity/merits of the case (see s 98(4) of the ERA 1996) and it should direct itself using the terms in s 98(4) of the ERA 1996 (**Iceland Frozen Foods Ltd v Jones** [1983] IRLR 439, EAT).

In relation to Sharon's dismissal, there is no evidence to suggest that an investigation has been carried out; neither has she been given the right to respond to the allegations nor appeal the decision to dismiss her. From the facts it seems that GAB Ltd is a small antiquarian bookshop and therefore is unlikely to have a detailed procedure in place; this does not affect the dismissal as such because s 98(4) allows the size and resource of the employer to be taken into account when the ET is assessing the reasonableness of the decision to dismiss. In contrast, Garth's dismissal seems to have occurred after investigation that includes a number of previous warnings and video evidence. However, once again it does not seem that he has been given a right to respond to the allegations nor to appeal against the decision to dismiss him. Tracy's dismissal is an automatic unfair dismissal for an inadmissible reason and it is for GAB Ltd to prove the contrary.

In **British Home Stores Ltd v Burchell [1980]** the EAT (as confirmed by the Court of Appeal) laid down a three-stage test in such cases. The questions the ET would pose are as follows: Did GAB Ltd believe that it was dismissing Sharon for conduct and Garth for capability reasons? Did it have reasonable grounds upon which to base that belief? In **Iceland Frozen Foods Ltd v Jones** it was decided that the ET should consider only the reasonableness of the employer's conduct and not fairness to the employee, and it should not substitute its decision as to the right course of action over the one the employer actually took. The answer in relation to Sharon is unclear as the facts do not state how Dorien discovered Sharon's infidelity. In contrast, the answer must be yes in relation to Garth as there seems to be a set of recorded warnings/video evidence against him. Finally, did GAB Ltd act in a manner that was procedurally fair, unless it was futile and useless to do so (see **Polkey v AE Dayton**

Services Ltd [1988] AC 344, HL)? There is no evidence to suggest that GAB Ltd conducted an investigation in relation to Sharon's conduct; had it conducted the investigation, alternative facts may have come to light. The lack of such investigation is not necessarily fatal to GAB Ltd defending the claim.

Remedy and conclusion

The facts provided suggest that Sharon and Garth may have a claim for an UD based upon procedural unfairness, i.e. the lack of investigation, failure to give the right to respond or appeal; and the defence of GAB Ltd rests on it proving the futility in following such a procedure. Tracy may have a claim for an automatically unfair dismissal unless GAB Ltd can prove that her dismissal did not relate to her membership of ABEU. If the claim is successful, the ET will consider the most appropriate remedy at its discretion: often reinstatement is unlikely and re-engagement not possible due to organisational constraints, thus compensation is considered most suitable.[4]

[4]Here the remedies and conclusion have been amalgamated: this results in a short concise advice – this will gain marks.

✓ **Make your answer stand out**

- Outline that the ACAS Handbook of Discipline at Work states that summary dismissals (without notice) for gross misconduct are valid.

- Discuss the fact that the non-renewal of a fixed-term contract is not in itself sufficient for the purposes of a wrongful dismissal claim.

- State that where a claim for UD fails, then a failure to give requisite notice to Sharon may be justified where the employer has proof that she has done the same in the past: refer to *Boston Deep Sea Fishing Ice Co* v *Ansell* [1888] 39 ChD 339, CA.

- Discuss the decision in *Polkey* v *AE Dayton Services Ltd* in terms of procedural unfairness and the narrow 'no difference' exception, which GAB Ltd could argue it falls within.

- When discussing the decision in *Iceland Frozen Foods Ltd* v *Jones*, mention that in the majority of cases the ET should apply the range of reasonable responses test (see *Foley* v *Post Office* [2000] All ER (D) 1137, CA).

- State that awards of compensation consist of a basic and a compensatory element. The basic award is calculated using the same formula as is used for calculating a redundancy payment (using the claimant's age, wage and service). The compensatory award includes much more: for example, loss of past and future earnings, pension rights, benefits, etc (see *Norton Tool Co Ltd* v *Tewson* [1973] 1 All ER 183, NIRC).

! Don't be tempted to...

- Advise on the claims of Sharon and Tracy but not Garth.
- Discuss the categories of employee that are excluded from making this claim in too much depth.
- Be too descriptive when discussing the cases (for example, the facts of *Polkey*). Remember to apply the principle and articulate the argument: for example, GAB Ltd may be able to argue that it falls within the 'no difference' defence.

Redundancy

How this topic may come up in exams

Not all employment law courses include redundancy and where it is included it is often taught together with the provisions relating to transfers of undertakings (see Chapter 10). Before you start, therefore, make sure that you know exactly what is on your syllabus. Although the questions provided here relate specifically to redundancy, you will often see problem questions overlap with unfair dismissal questions and we have flagged this up where appropriate. Essay questions tend to focus on explaining and evaluating redundancy procedures, whereas problem questions usually focus on the entitlement to redundancy pay.

Attack the question

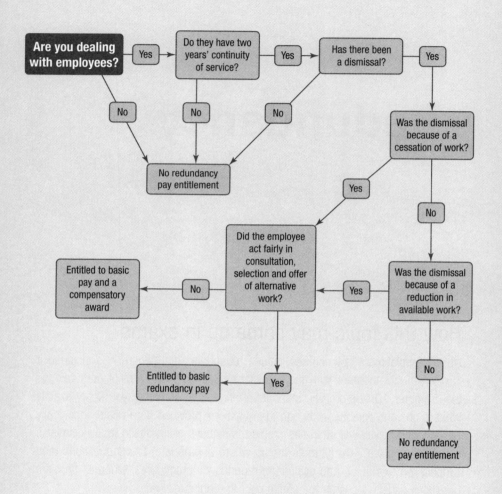

📷 Question 1

Outline the legal obligations employers are under when facing a redundancy situation and comment on the effectiveness of these obligations.

Answer plan

→ Define redundancy.

→ Assess each of the obligations in turn:
  - selection procedure, which must be fair
  - consideration of alternative employment
  - collective consultation
  - notification requirements.

Diagram plan

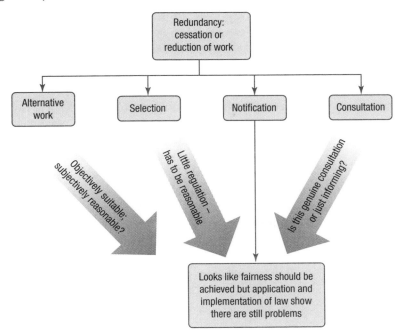

A printable version of this diagram plan is available from www.pearsoned.co.uk/lawexpressqa

Answer

[1]Your first sentence should always give a clear indication of what the essay is dealing with; this one does that.

This essay considers the legal framework governing employers' conduct in relation to redundancies and critically assesses the effectiveness of that framework.[1] The Employment Rights Act 1996 (ERA 1996) defines a redundancy as occurring if the dismissal of an employee is wholly or mainly attributable to:

(a)　the fact that his employer has ceased or intends to cease –

　　(i)　to carry on the business for the purposes of which the employee was employed by him, or

　　(ii)　to carry on that business in the place where the employee was so employed, or

[2]Setting out the definition of redundancy in law is useful. Do not try to memorise this word for word if you find that difficult. You can summarise the provision rather than reproduce it.

(b)　the fact that the requirements of that business –

　　(i)　for employees to carry out work of a particular kind, or

　　(ii)　for employees to carry out work of a particular kind in the place where the employee was employed by the employer, have ceased or diminished or are expected to cease or diminish. (ERA 1996, s 139(1))[2]

[3]You have set the context and now begin to explore which obligations apply.

Where a redundancy situation exists, employers must follow a procedure to ensure the fairness of redundancy selection.[3] Clearly, a selection procedure is not required where the entire workforce is to be made redundant because there is a complete cessation of business activities. In all other cases a selection procedure should be followed. There is no statutory selection procedure and employers are allowed some flexibility here. The focus is on the fairness and transparency of the procedure so that an employee can see how and why the decision has been made (**Cox v Wildt Mellor Bromley Ltd** [1978] IRLR 157, EAT) and the need not to discriminate directly or indirectly against certain groups of employees such as part-time workers or those on fixed-term contracts (**Whiffen v Milham Ford Girls' School** [2001] All ER (D) 256 (Mar), CA).[4] A once popular method for selection is the 'last in, first out' procedure, which protects those with longer service. This system has been increasingly questioned, though, and may fall foul of age discrimination legislation in some cases. Some kind of appraisal system or score card is now often used to select employees where compulsory redundancies are necessary.

[4]Your first example here is selection procedures and the law is set out first showing clear understanding of the provisions.

However, length of service should not be ignored. In **Thomas and Betts Manufacturing Co v Harding** [1980] IRLR 255, CA it was held that if the unit of selection is wider than a department, then an employee in one department may 'bump' a less senior employee in another department. **Lionel Leventhal Ltd v North** [2005] All ER (D) 82 (Jan), EAT confirms the need to consider bumping redundancies in appropriate cases.⁵

⁵The law you just set out is then illustrated with some examples, which show some of the considerations required and highlight that you also appreciate how the law plays out in practice.

If there is no procedure, then the overall reasonableness of the selection will be considered (ERA 1996, s 98(4)). Length of service is only one factor to be taken into account when assessing reasonableness. A useful illustration of this is **Hobson v Park Brothers** [1973] (Unreported), where a younger manager was kept on rather than a more senior manager because the younger one was thought to be more appropriate for the future task ahead.

Employers must also consider whether there is alternative employment that can be offered to the employee. Where the employer offers a re-engagement on the same terms, the employee will lose their right to redundancy pay if they unreasonably refuse such an offer. Where alternative employment is offered, the position must be objectively suitable and the employee will only lose his rights if he subjectively unreasonably refuses the employer's offer. In **Fisher v Hoopoe Finance Ltd** [2005] All ER (D) 51 (Jun), EAT it was held that an employer should provide potentially redundant employees with information about the financial prospects of any vacant alternative positions and, in addition, an employer must allow a trial period of at least four weeks if alternative employment has been offered.

Employers must consult collectively with recognised trade unions or, where there are no recognised unions, with employee representatives. According to the Trade Union and Labour Relations (Consolidation) Act 1992 (TULR(C)A 1992) if 20–99 employees are to be made redundant within 90 days of each other, consultation must occur at least 30 days before a decision is made and at least 90 days if there are over 100 redundancies anticipated. In **Hardy v Tourism South East** [2005] IRLR 242, EAT the company failed to consult and was found to be in breach of the consultation requirements even though it was planning on re-engaging some staff and redeploying others.⁶ Although there is no minimum statutory consultation period if there are fewer than 20 employees, each employee has a right to be

⁶This paragraph sets out and illustrates the next obligation and starts with a case example, which is a really useful way of highlighting a particular legal issue or problem.

9 REDUNDANCY

consulted. The timing of the consultation has been at issue in two cases that give inconsistent results: in **Middlesbrough Council v TGWU** [2002] IRLR 332 the Employment Appeals Tribunal (EAT) held that the requirement to consult when the employer is proposing to dismiss employees means that consultation must take place before a final decision has been made; in **MSF v Refuge Assurance plc and Another** [2002] IRLR 324, EAT the EAT held that the TULR(C)A 1992, s 188 requirement to consult occurs later in the process than is required by the relevant EU Directive, which requires consultation when the employer is contemplating redundancies. Good practice suggests that consultation should take place as early as possible.[7]

An employer must also notify the Department for Work and Pensions of impending redundancies at least 90 days before the first dismissal, where at least 100 employees are to be dismissed over a 90-day period; or at least 30 days before, where at least 20 are to be dismissed over a 30-day period. There is no duty where fewer than 20 are involved (TULR(C)A 1992, s 193).

Employers face a number of obligations in redundancy situations and the aim appears to be to help avoid redundancies wherever possible.[8] Many employers have procedures in place which will actually deal with potential redundancy situations much earlier by implementing early retirement or voluntary redundancy schemes and avoiding compulsory redundancies altogether.[9] Once a genuine redundancy situation has been reached, the obligations apply to ensure fairness. While this seems to have been achieved formally, selection procedures may still produce unfair or even discriminatory results and the consultation requirements do little to stop that, especially as it is not clear from the case law when consultation should begin. Consultation when decisions have already been made suggests that the provisions are not effective, whereas earlier consultation may result in fewer redundancies having to be made.[10]

[7] If time allows, this point could be expanded – what does in good time mean?

[8] To be able to assess the effectiveness you need to know what the aim is, so set that out clearly.

[9] Information like this shows your general awareness of context and industrial relations and lends some credibility to your argument.

[10] Make sure that your conclusion follows logically from what you said before. There is no point in arguing above that a selection matrix ensures fairness and concluding here that selection is problematic.

Make your answer stand out

- Set out more clearly at the beginning what you think the objectives of the obligations actually are – this will strengthen the analysis.
- Discuss the impact of statutory consultation procedure. See, for example, M. Hall and P. Edwards, 'Reforming the Statutory Redundancy Procedure' (1999) 28 ILJ 299.
- Add a comment in relation to the notification requirements. What do you think about the effectiveness of the requirement?

! **Don't be tempted to…**

- Simply list the requirements; you need to comment on them as you go through and then pull the analysis together at the end.
- Focus on one obligation such as consultation to the exclusion of others; you need to deal with all of them.

? Question 2

Stones Double Glazing Co has branches throughout England. The company has recently run into financial difficulties. All employees have been warned that the company may have to make some staff redundant and that it would be prudent to look for alternative employment. Advise the following staff of their entitlement, if any, to redundancy payments.

(a) Ramon has worked for Stones for six years; he has recently started living with his girlfriend and their baby, and has a large mortgage. He obtains a job with a local builder and hands in his notice.

(b) Gillian, a senior accounts clerk who joined Stones in 1984, is told that she is being made redundant because Mr Stone has learned to word-process his own letters, so his secretary, who began work for the company in 1999, will be taking over Gillian's payroll and invoicing duties.

(c) Dave, who is aged 58 and has worked as a fitter for Stones for 32 years, is given six weeks' notice of redundancy. He is told that he has failed to keep up to date with modern techniques, and such an old-fashioned approach cannot be tolerated.

(d) Carlos has been an Area Sales Manager in Bedford for ten years. He is told that fewer sales staff are needed in Bedford, so his job will cease to exist, but he's offered a post as a Senior Sales Executive in Northumberland, retaining his present salary. He refuses the offer as he would have to move house and change to a smaller company car.

Answer plan

→ Define redundancy.

→ Ramon: Explain that there has to be a dismissal, so no redundancy pay entitlement.

→ Gillian: Consider the key issue of reduction of work and the fact that it does not have to be a reduction in her area of work, therefore bumping redundancies are OK, so she is redundant.

→ Gillian: Does she have a possible challenge relating to fairness of procedure?

→ Dave: Address the issue of no reduction in work.

→ Carlos: Consider if the two jobs are broadly equivalent and, if they are, whether his refusal was subjectively reasonable.

→ Explain how pay would be calculated.

Diagram plan

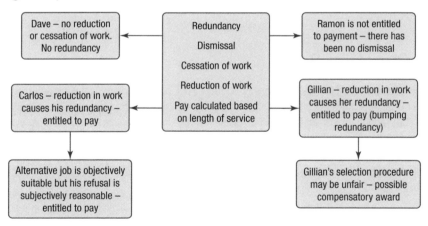

A printable version of this diagram plan is available from www.pearsoned.co.uk/lawexpressqa

Answer

¹True, and the next section sets it out. This sets the scene and allows you to refer back to the definition as you go through answering the question.

In order to advise each of the members of staff it is vital to understand the definition of redundancy.¹ The relevant provision can be found in s 139(1) of the Employment Rights Act 1996 (ERA 1996), which provides as follows: a dismissal is a dismissal by reason of

2It is unlikely that you would be required to memorise the whole section, so setting it out in your own words is fine.

3Here you are showing that you are aware of the criteria of eligibility but also that you have read the scenario. If information is clearly stated, you do not need to spend time setting out the legal provisions in detail – the question wants you to focus on other elements.

4This paragraph is a good example of explaining the law in the context of the question and sticking to the question without general discussion. This is what you are aiming for.

5A clear statement of exactly what the legal issue is can focus the mind and keep your answer relevant and also shows you really understand the problem.

6Make your points avoiding jumps in logic. You clarify that it's not that simple in the next sentence.

7Clear statement of the legal position on bumping redundancies, which shows you have recognised the issue you are required to address.

8Clear application of that legal position to the scenario shows you are engaging with the question and can apply the law rather than just having learned it.

redundancy if the dismissal is because of the cessation of business or a reduction in the need for work of a particular kind.[2]

If the employees can satisfy the definition given, they will be entitled to redundancy payments as the scenario confirms they are all employees (see ERA 1996, s 135(1)) with sufficient continuity of service (ERA 1996, s 155) to satisfy other eligibility criteria.[3] The position of each individual will therefore be considered in more detail next.

Ramon's personal (financial) circumstances are irrelevant when considering entitlement to redundancy pay and only the statutory criteria must be applied. Ramon has handed in his notice and therefore no dismissal has taken place. In order to qualify for redundancy payment, there must be a dismissal. **Morton Sundour Fabrics Ltd v Shaw** [1966] 2 ITR 84, CA confirms that no redundancy payment is payable to a worker who resigns under threat of redundancy. Ramon is therefore not entitled to any payment.[4]

In Gillian's case, her entitlement turns on whether there has been a cessation or diminution in the requirements of the business for employees to carry out work of a particular kind, either generally or at the employee's place of work.[5] However, it seems that there is no decrease in the need for accounts work so on the face of it Gillian is not redundant.[6] However, in **Murray and Another v Foyle Meats Ltd** [1999] 3 All ER 769, HL the House of Lords made it clear that, provided there is a causal link between diminution and dismissal, the dismissal is due to redundancy.[7] Applying this to Gillian, it can be argued that there is a direct causal link between a decrease in work and her losing her job. The reduction in typing work allows the secretary to take on extra duties, resulting in Gillian being redundant.[8] However, the fairness of the selection procedure that was used to select Gillian for redundancy can be questioned. The scenario seems to suggest that a 'last in, first out' approach was not used as the secretary has not been working for the company as long as Gillian but it is not clear what selection procedure was used. As there is very little legal definition of the selection procedure, employment tribunals (ETs) have a great deal of scope in deciding whether a selection procedure has been properly carried out. It does have to be fair and reasonable though. Fairness requires, according to **Cox v Wildt Mellor Bromley Ltd** [1978] IRLR 157, EAT, openness about how the selection criteria were chosen and applied in practice. In **Thomas and Betts Manufacturing Co v Harding** [1980] IRLR 255, CA it was unfair to dismiss a longer serving employee without explanation – this is a departure from 'last in, first out' which must be justified. There is no clear justification in the scenario given, so it is likely that Gillian will get the basic redundancy award and a compensatory award for unfair selection.

The question to consider in relation to Dave is whether there has been a reduction or diminution in the kind of work Dave is employed to do. In **North Riding Garages v Butterwick** [1967] 2 QB 56, CA the claimant's inability to adapt did not amount to redundancy, so Dave is not redundant and therefore not entitled to redundancy pay.[9]

[9]If you can deal with something quickly like here, do. The position is straightforward, so don't waste time on it.

Carlos's post is being axed due to a s 139(1)(b) reason: diminution in requirements at the place where the employee was employed by the employer. Therefore, there is a prima facie redundancy.[10] But Carlos has been offered, and has refused, alternative employment. His entitlement to redundancy payment depends upon the reasonableness of his refusal.[11] It must therefore be decided whether the alternative post offered was suitable. Following **Taylor v Kent County Council** [1969] 2 All ER 1080, QBD, the question to ask is whether the new post is substantially equivalent? Although the title has changed slightly, the scenario confirms that the salary will not change. However, Carlos would have to accept a smaller company car. No further information is provided regarding the equivalence of the positions but on the information given it can be argued that the two posts are substantially equivalent.[12]

[10]This statement directly applies the law to the question and thus keeps your answer focused and succinct.

[11]A clear statement of the legal issue but in the context of the question.

[12]Note that you are given some information which allows you to speculate but say the information you have is not conclusive.

The second question to ask is therefore whether Carlos was reasonable in refusing the offer. **Paton Calvert & Co v Westerside** [1979] IRLR 109, EAT confirms that this is a subjective test and the question should thus be considered from Carlos's point of view.[13] The new post is a very long way away and would not be accessible without moving house. Carlos can therefore reasonably refuse the job and is indeed redundant and entitled to redundancy pay.

[13]Again, a clear statement of the law in the context of the question, which leads directly to the application of the principle.

Those employees entitled to redundancy pay can calculate their entitlement as follows:[14] for each year of service up to a maximum of 20, where the claimant is aged between 21 and 40 the employees are entitled to one week's pay up to a maximum of £350; where the claimant is aged between 18 and 21, half a week's pay is taken into

[14]You should at least mention the calculation: you don't have the information necessary to do the actual calculations but clients would want to know how to work out what they are entitled to receive.

account; where the claimant is over 41, one-and-a-half weeks are used in the calculation. In addition, where there have been irregularities in the selection procedure, as is suggested in Gillian's case, the claimant may be entitled to an additional compensatory award.

 Make your answer stand out

- Spend a little more time considering the fairness of the selection procedure in Gillian's case. What factors might be deemed fair or unfair and how does that play out for Gillian?
- Consider the reasonableness of Carlos's refusal of the job in more detail.
- Provide advice on the calculation to be made for each person individually, as far as you can based on the information you have.

! Don't be tempted to…

- Repeat the explanation of redundancy for each scenario – if you set it out at the beginning, you can just refer back to it.
- Spend much time on areas which are straightforward, such as in the case of Ramon where there is no dismissal.
- Jump to the conclusion that because another job has been offered to Carlos there is no genuine redundancy. You need to consider the reasonableness of his refusal before you can decide this.

? Question 3

You are the Human Resources Manager in an advertising agency employing 150 people in the UK: 120 in a London office and 30 in a Manchester office. Max, the Chief Executive, has decided that it is necessary to reorganise the company in an effort to make cost savings. He has identified a reduced need for creative staff. He would like to reduce the creative team in the London office from 30 to 15 employees and the creative team in the Manchester office from 10 to 4 employees.

In addition, Max is proposing to reorganise the creative team in London. At present, the London creative team is split into three groups – media, telecoms and sport. Each group has ten members of staff – a creative director, two creative managers, five creative assistants and two researchers. Max is proposing to merge the three groups. He would like to retain one overall creative director, three creative managers (one for each of media, telecoms and sport), nine 'generalist' creative assistants who will work across media, telecoms and sport, and two generalist researchers. He would be happy for those employees currently employed as creative directors to be considered for the creative manager roles and, likewise, the creative managers may apply for one of the nine new generalist creative assistant roles. However, he does not feel that the researchers would have enough experience or skills to carry out the creative assistant roles, so he is not proposing to offer them the opportunity to apply for the creative assistant roles.

Max has chosen the following criteria, which he is proposing to apply to the various pools, in order to select the employees to be made redundant: (a) attendance; (b) commitment; (c) creativity; (d) experience in the media/telecoms/sport field (as applicable); (e) computer skills/experience.

Discuss.

Answer plan

→ Outline that the question is about managing redundancy situations.

→ Consider obligations:
 – Consultation: collective consultation is required if there are more than 20 employees affected. Are the two offices one establishment?
 – Selection: fair procedure –
  • consider how the staff will be pooled
  • discuss the selection criteria.

→ Summarise your advice to Max.

Diagram plan

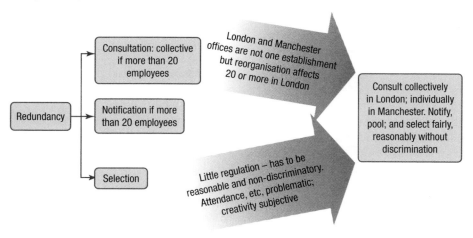

A printable version of this diagram plan is available from www.pearsoned.co.uk/lawexpressqa

Answer

This case requires us to consider what obligations Max is under in managing the redundancy situation in his business. One of the first questions to consider is the extent to which collective consultation is required in this case.[1] Sections 188–194 of the Trade Union and Labour Relations (Consolidation) Act 1992 (TULR(C)A 1992) (as amended) requires the employer to consult the authorised representatives of recognised independent trade unions (TUs) or other elected representatives about dismissal for redundancy and also to notify the Secretary of State where more than 20 employees are to be made redundant.

We must first determine whether or not the London and Manchester offices should be treated as one 'establishment' and therefore the redundancies across the two offices be added together. Collective consultation is required, beginning at least 30 days before the redundancies, where more than 20 staff are going to be affected by the redundancies; so where the offices are considered part of the same establishment, collective consultation will be required within this time frame. Where there are fewer than 20 employees facing redundancy, no time limit is specified and no collective consultation is required, although individuals are still entitled to be consulted.[2]

Provided that the two offices are distinct entities, each with a certain degree of permanence and stability, each assigned to perform distinct tasks and each of which has a workforce, technical means and a certain organisational structure allowing for the accomplishment of those tasks, then they will be separate establishments. If there is joint operational management at each site, it is likely that they form a single establishment. However, shared support functions – for example HR/payroll or finance – will not point towards a single establishment. Where the same or similar activity is carried out at each site for shared (internal or external) customers and/or where there is evidence of employees working across sites or being relocated on a temporary or permanent basis from one site to another, then the two sites are likely to be treated as one establishment.[3] There is not a huge amount of detail provided in the scenario but, given that one office is in London and one in Manchester and we are not told of any staff moving between offices,

[1] It doesn't really matter what issue you start with but this makes logical chronological sense because the process Max would go through is likely to start with consultation where it is required and the time limits are an important consideration.

[2] This sets out the law and the issue it raises in relation to the scenario. Keep the focus on the scenario – you are not talking about more than 100 employees being affected, so there is no need to discuss those provisions.

[3] Set out the issues that would help you apply the law in this scenario even if you do not have sufficient detail actually to do this exercise conclusively; you still need to show that you understand how this would work.

⁴Then apply the law by commenting on those aspects you do know something about. It is fine to say that you would need further information but state your conclusion based on the information you do have.

⁵Then back up your argument with legal authority such as the case given here. It shows a comprehensive understanding of the situation.

⁶Sentences such as this one are really useful signposts for the marker. They indicate that you have finished with one issue and are now moving on to the next. They lend structure and coherence to your answer and make it easy to read.

⁷Again, note how the law is set out in the context of the question rather than more generally. Clients want to know about their situation, not the law generally, so stick to what is strictly relevant.

it is likely that the offices can be treated as separate establishments.⁴ This reasoning can be supported by cases such as **Bass Leisure Ltd v Thomas** [1994] IRLR 104, EAT where the EAT held that the fact that an employment contract contains a mobility clause is not an argument for stating that an employee is not entitled to a redundancy payment because the place where she normally works is closing. The EAT held that the place where an employee normally works is a question of fact in each case.⁵ However, this will need checking and justifying carefully.

In addition, given the reorganisation Max has in mind, employees will be changing terms and conditions of employment as well as facing redundancies, therefore it is likely that more than 20 staff will be affected by the redundancies in the London office. Consultation must therefore take place at least 30 days before the first dismissal in relation to this office in any event.

Consultation must be carried out 'with a view to reaching agreement' with the representatives as to: ways of avoiding dismissals; ways of reducing numbers to be dismissed; ways of mitigating the consequences of any dismissals. Guidance was given by the High Court in **British Coal Corporation v Secretary of State for Trade and Industry, ex parte Price and Others** [1994] IRLR 72, DC, in which it was said that the person being consulted must have a reasonable opportunity to understand fully the subject-matter of the consultation and express his views, which must be genuinely considered by the other party. Agreement does not have to be reached but both parties, it seems, must try.

The next issue to consider is how to select for redundancies.⁶ **Cox v Wildt Mellor Bromley Ltd** [1978] IRLR 157, EAT highlights the need for a fair and transparent selection procedure and the first question to resolve is how the employees should be pooled. The fact that the company is proposing to merge the three groups (media, telecoms and sport) suggests that staff who do similar work in each of these groups should be pooled together, provided that their roles are broadly interchangeable. So, for example, the three creative directors should be pooled together and all the creative managers should be pooled together.⁷ In principle, the fairest method would be to pool the London employees with the Manchester employees, provided that their roles are broadly interchangeable; however,

[8]It is OK to make a point which might appear contradictory to what you have said previously, as long as you acknowledge and explain that inconsistency. In law there are often alternative possibilities and this is one example of different possible arguments.

[9]Highlight any issues you can see with the criteria suggested. The fact that they might be discriminatory is the obvious criticism.

[10]Think about how criteria are measured and applied too – creativity is a useful one where relevant, but the implementation is potentially problematic.

[11]Length of service is a tricky one and you need to engage with it because it is still such a popular criterion.

[12]Suggest possible suitable criteria – but remember the focus is on reasonableness.

[13]It is always useful to finish with a summary of your advice to show you have fully answered the question.

this does rather undermine the argument that the two offices are separate establishments. If this is to be the case (and in which case no collective consultation is applicable in Manchester), employees should be pooled separately.[8]

Once the pools have been identified, clear selection criteria need to be identified and applied. The proposed criteria raise some issues. Attendance and commitment may both raise issues of disability discrimination for employees who are absent with a disability or on pregnancy-related absence. It might also amount to indirect sex discrimination of women with family commitments.[9] Creativity is quite subjective, although it may be necessary to consider the 'creativity' of the creative directors. However, this should be considered by reference to the employee's performance and appraisals, rather than a manager's perception of an employee's creativity.[10] Experience is a relevant and appropriate criteria, although care should be taken not to equate experience with length of service, as this may amount to indirect discrimination on the grounds of age and, unless it is objectively justifiable, it may be unlawful. Length of service cannot be disregarded completely, as is evident in cases concerning the 'last in, first out' approach to redundancies, which, though perhaps unfair, has shown incredible durability as a concept: in **Rolls Royce v Unite (Trade Union)** [2008] All ER (D) 174 (Oct), HC it was confirmed that length of service can indeed be taken into account.[11] Computer skills and experience should be used only if such skills are relevant and necessary for the role. Suitable criteria might include skills, knowledge and experience by reference to the requirements of the new roles and should be as objective/reasonable as possible.[12] In fact, it is the overall reasonableness of the criteria which will determine their lawfulness.

In summary, then, Max should start his consultation process immediately and work with the union or employer representatives to agree the number of redundancies and reorganisation, as well as the criteria for selection, which should be as transparent and objectively fair as possible.[13]

✓ **Make your answer stand out**

- Expand your discussion of the proposed selection criteria, saying a little bit more about the problems with using factors like attendance and commitment.
- Consider how consultation should be approached, what might be achieved in this case through consultation.
- Mention the question of alternative jobs and whether they might be reasonably refused.
- Address the answer more directly to Max to make it less abstract.

! **Don't be tempted to…**

- Presume that the two offices are one establishment – you need to justify this if that is indeed what you think.
- Provide advice on one issue based on two offices as one establishment and then advise on the next issue as if they are not. You need to flag up the different possibilities and then decide which you think is more likely.
- List the criteria and information about process without applying it to the specific situation you have here. This is about what Max should do, not about what one should do generally speaking.

Question 4

Critically examine what will be considered a fair procedure in relation to the selection of employees in a redundancy situation.

Answer plan

→ Intro: a fair selection procedure is needed to show the employer acted reasonably.
→ There is no statutory definition of a selection procedure, so the courts have wide scope.
→ Consider LIFO as a selection process.
→ Examine other factors such as attendance, performance, etc.
→ Explain discriminatory selection.
→ Consider LIFO in conjunction with other factors.
→ Conclude: fairness still seems to be linked with LIFO, although that can be questioned.

Diagram plan

| Wide scope given to ET | → | LIFO | → | Other factors | → | Discrimination | → | Is fairness achieved? |

A printable version of this diagram plan is available from www.pearsoned.co.uk/lawexpressqa

[1]If you can say in your first sentence why the selection procedure is important, you are signalling to the examiner that you know what you are talking about. This should give them confidence for the rest of the answer.

[2]There really is no need to learn the quote and certainly not which judge said it but some students remember details like this and it is a good alternative way of structuring your sentences, adding interest. Paraphrasing is OK, though.

[3]This gets the uncontroversial aspects out of the way quickly. You are still showing you know the law but are demonstrating a broader understanding by giving yourself time and scope to deal with the more difficult aspects in detail.

[4]Start building your argument logically from the start. This gives you the maximum marks for critical thinking and analysis.

[5]This section shows a good awareness of application of the law, which many examiners look for. Knowing the law is one thing; understanding how it operates shows a much deeper level of awareness.

Answer

In order to establish that the employer acted reasonably, the ET must be satisfied that the employer had a fair selection procedure.[1] Phillips J said,[2] in **Cox v Wildt Mellor Bromley Ltd** [1978] IRLR 157, EAT, that the employer must 'show how the employee came to be dismissed for redundancy, upon what basis the selection was made, and how it was applied in practice'. Criteria should be capable of being objectively checked against such matters as attendance record, job efficiency, experience and length of service. In deciding whether selection is fair, account need only be taken of employees in the same undertaking who hold similar positions. Length of service by the employee should never be ignored. Section 105 of the Employment Rights Act 1996 (ERA 1996) provides that if an employer makes an employee redundant and the situation is such that he had a choice about who to make redundant, such redundancy will be deemed to be automatically unfair if the reason the particular selection was made was an inadmissible reason (e.g. relating to trade union membership).[3]

Quite often, such selection procedures are based on the LIFO (last in, first out) rule.[4] If there is no procedure, it is generally deemed reasonable to dismiss an employee with the shortest service first, but other personal factors may be relevant. Merely having detailed criteria for selection for redundancy is not sufficient (see the decision of the **EAT in Protective Services (Contracts) Ltd v Livingstone** [1992] (Unreported)). They must be properly applied so that a potential candidate is compared with another in relation to each of the criteria used.[5]

As there is very little legal definition of the selection procedure, ETs have a great deal of scope in deciding whether a selection procedure

[6]Bumping redundancies provide a useful illustration of how selection can work and a useful case study for fairness, so are worth mentioning. This section is a little descriptive, though, and you could add more detailed comments on how this is fair or not.

has been properly carried out. If the unit of selection is wider than a department, then an employee in one department may 'bump' a less senior employee in another department.[6] In **Thomas and Betts Manufacturing Co v Harding** [1978] IRLR 213, EAT Mrs H worked originally as a packer and was subsequently transferred to make 'fittings'. A redundancy situation arose in the fittings section and Mrs H, who had been employed for two years, was made redundant, while a packer of only five weeks' service was retained. This was held to amount to unfair dismissal because, although s 105 was restricted to employees who *held positions similar to that held* by the claimant, the general test (s 98(4)) was not to be confined to a consideration only of those employees working in the same section. A more recent case also illustrates this – **Lionel Leventhal Ltd v North** [2005]. Here, the EAT confirmed that a redundancy dismissal was unfair because the employer failed to consider 'bumping' a more junior employee from his post in order to accommodate his more senior colleague.[7]

[7]Bumping redundancies can be difficult to explain in the abstract so using a couple of case examples shows the examiner that you are not confused about how this works.

It is important to note that, just because a customary arrangement is followed, this does not necessarily mean that the selection will be deemed fair under s 98(4). In **Wooding v Stoves Ltd** [1975] IRLR 198, Ind Trib the redundancy procedure agreed with the union stated that the non-union members should be treated differently from union members. W, a non-union member, was nevertheless held to have been unfairly dismissed. Other factors may sometimes supersede customary arrangements. In **Best v Taylor Woodrow** [1975] IRLR 177, Ind Trib, B had worked for the company since January 1972, whereas G had been employed from October 1973. Both did the same job and were considered for redundancy. Both were equally efficient. The normal practice was LIFO but the company also considered whether this should apply in individual cases. B had been late on 153 occasions whereas G had only been late twice. B had received two verbal and four written warnings. G had none. Absence and lateness caused considerable difficulties because of the nature of the work. It was held that B's dismissal was fair, as the initial preference was logically outweighed by G's superior timekeeping.

[8]Here you are showing that you appreciate employment practice as well as law and this should pick up extra marks. You are recognising that not all employers will have redundancy procedures in place.

If there is no procedure, then the overall reasonableness (s 98(4)) of the selection will be considered.[8] Length of service is only one factor to be considered. In **Hobson v Park Brothers** [1973]

(Unreported), H, a group manager, had 25 years' service. The other manager was very much his junior. The company decided that only one was required and made H redundant. The employer decided to keep the younger man because he was more suitable for the future task. H's seniority was considered, but this was only one factor and the dismissal was thus fair. In **Farthing v Midland House Stores** [1974] IRLR 354, Ind Trib, F was chosen for redundancy in spite of fairly equal performance with a more junior colleague. It was decided that the dismissal was unfair. It would have been different if there had been severe criticism of F but, as there had not, his seniority should have been considered.

[9]This is a useful reminder to the examiner that you do appreciate that fairness is really about showing reasonableness.

When selecting workers for redundancy, employers need to ensure that they do not infringe any of the statutory protections against discrimination in employment. If they do so the redundancy selection procedure cannot be deemed reasonable.[9] In **Whiffen v Milham Ford Girls' School** [2001] All ER (D) 256 (Mar), CA[10] a school's redundancy selection criterion was applied first to those employed on fixed-term contracts before considering any other permanent employees, which on the facts disadvantaged women. In lawfully applying LIFO as the selection procedure for redundancy, employers need to consider any potentially discriminatory aspects of the process. In **Clarke v Eley (IMI) Kynoch Ltd** [1982] IRLR 482, EAT, a part-time female munitions worker with long but intermittent service, who worked a basic 25-hour per week plus overtime, was found to be unfairly selected for redundancy. In **Brook and Others v London Borough of Haringey** [1992] IRLR 478, EAT the EAT permitted women craft employees to be disproportionately selected for redundancy by affirming length of service as a lawful selection criterion. Such inconsistencies at appellate level do not always appear to fulfil the legislative intent to protect employees against unfair selection for redundancy. LIFO is inherently discriminatory against all employees with short service, but as a procedure it is remarkably durable. For example, in **Anderson v Pringle of Scotland Ltd** [1998] IRLR 64, OH the Court of Session affirmed that an employee was entitled to an interim order prohibiting the employer from selecting employees for redundancy on any basis other than LIFO. Whether LIFO is really a fair way of assessing redundacy is questionable as it is rather too easy to ignore other factors in this process.[11] However, it seems that

[10]An example is always useful to highlight complex issues and it shows the examiner your detailed knowledge of the law.

[11]Here you are stating your conclusion and presenting your analysis in a nutshell. You will pick up marks for this but will get additional ones because your argument has led you logically to this point through a clear structure.

it is here to stay and the potentially harsh consequences for some employees is countered by the fact that there is a requirement of reasonableness and by anti-discrimination provisions.

✓ Make your answer stand out

- Consider other factors such as attendance, performance, etc, in more detail, perhaps with more examples from case law you have discussed in your lectures.
- Expand your criticism of LIFO. Might this be age discrimination? Why do you think it is so durable as a concept?
- You could discuss discrimination in selection with reference to the Equality Act 2010 and the protected characteristics in more detail to really show how these areas of law interlink.
- Offer advice as to what you think would make a fair selection procedure. Consider what sort of selection grid or score card you could use and how that might operate.
- Make clearer the difference between having an established procedure which should be followed and situations where there is no procedure, where there is just an overall requirement of reasonableness. This would show a deeper understanding of the law.

❗ Don't be tempted to…

- Outline what redundancy is or what the criteria for it are. The question is just about selection so that is where you have to focus your answer.
- Ignore LIFO (as some students do) because you think it is unfair, and focus on discussing what you think would be fairer. Given that LIFO is so often used, you really do need to engage with it fully.
- Go overboard with case examples. Some examples liven things up and illustrate your points, showing that you know the area of law well. If you give too many examples you risk running out of time and being too descriptive.

10

Transfer of undertakings

How this topic may come up in exams

Where the law on transfer of undertakings forms part of the syllabus, this topic is popular for examination questions. Both problem questions and essay questions are easily set and will test your full understanding of this area of law. Essay questions are likely to ask about the purpose of the law and whether it fulfils its purpose. Problem questions, on the other hand, usually focus on advising businesses or individuals as to their rights and duties in a transfer situation.

■ Attack the question

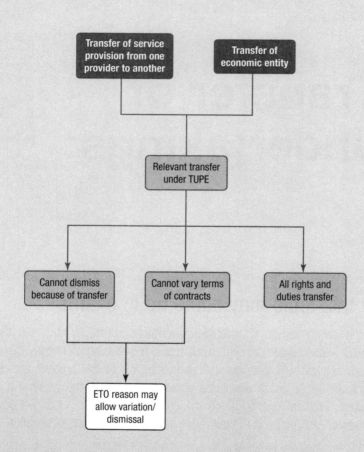

🧭 Question 1

'Although the Süzen decision has been described as involving a shift of emphasis or a clarification of the law, nothing was said in Süzen which casts doubt on the correctness of the interpretation of the directive in [earlier decisions]. The importance of Süzen [has], I think, been overstated.'

Analyse the law relating to transfers of undertakings. To what extent do you agree with the statement of Mummery LJ?

Answer plan

→ Explain the aim of TUPE and *Süzen* as a case concerning contracting out.

→ Consider the pre-*Süzen* position on contracting out.

→ Consider *Süzen* and whether it narrowed the net and limited the application of TUPE to contracting out. Was this a shift in emphasis?

→ Did it clarify the law and how was TUPE 2006 needed in this respect?

Diagram plan

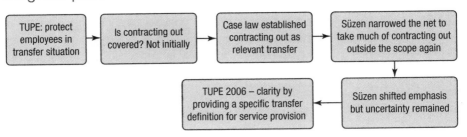

A printable version of this diagram plan is available from www.pearsoned.co.uk/lawexpressqa

Answer

At common law, a contract of employment was a personal contract between the employer and employee. The sale or transfer of any business thus resulted in the termination of any existing contract of employment. This situation changed with the passing of the Acquired Rights Directive and its implementation in 1981 through the Transfer of Undertakings (Protection of Employment) Regulations (TUPE).

[1]Introduction that briefly sets out the context and aim of the law under consideration shows you know what you're talking about from the start.

These Regulations attempt to put the transferee employer in the same position as the transferor, so that the rights and obligations contained in the contracts of employment with the first employer are transferred to the second.[1]

[2]By setting out limitations such as this early on, you keep the chronology of legal development, make your point and avoid having to go back over this ground later. It often makes sense to deal with things chronologically in essays such as this one.

TUPE has been said to represent a major limitation on both the principles of freedom of contract and the power of employers to arrange their commercial and corporate affairs in such a way as to minimise their employment liabilities (Deakin and Morris, 2009).[2] Moreover, greater uncertainty resulted from the extension of the TUPE principles in the fifteen or so years between the introduction of the Regulations and the ECJ decision in **Süzen v Zehnacker Gebäudereinigung GmbH Krankenhausservice** [1997] ECR I–1259, ECJ, which was concerned with the question of contracting out. Clarity was brought only following the implementation of the 2006 TUPE Regulations.[3]

[3]Summary of the issue to be considered and a hint at your conclusion – it provides a useful signpost for the reader, making it easy to follow your argument.

In order to determine whether TUPE covered contracting out, the court in **Dr Sophie Redmond Stichting v Bartol** [1992] ECR I–3189, ECJ applied the same test for transfers that had been formulated in the much earlier case of **Spijkers JMA v Gebroeders Benedik Abattoir** [1986] ECJ. Thus the principal test, under the Directive and hence TUPE, is whether there has been a transfer of a stable economic entity which retains its identity after the transfer has taken place. If the new owner carries out the essential business activity, it is likely that there has been a transfer within the meaning of the Regulations.[4]

[4]Now you can begin setting out the law as it was, stating the transfer definition and how it was then applied to contracting out through case law.

Traditionally, it was believed that the Directive applied to only the transfer of an identifiable economic activity and not to the transfer of a contract purely for services (i.e. cleaning maintenance, security etc). However, the ECJ dispelled this in **Rask v ISS** [1992] ECR I–5755, ECJ. In this case, a company decided to contract out the running of its works canteen. The new employer in turn agreed to employ the former canteen staff at the same rates of pay. Under the new firm, there was an administrative change to the way in which wages were paid and Rask complained that this constituted an alteration of the previous terms of employment. The court held that the variation of the contract term constituted a change in the applicant's working conditions. Moreover, it was held that the transfer of the service was within the scope of the Directive and the fact that

[5] A brief consideration of the facts helps clarify how service provision is different from transfers of businesses in the traditional sense.

[6] Here you highlight that problems remained and the next paragraph summarises the effects of the case law to that point, showing that you have identified the issue and know the relevant law.

[7] This is a really useful summary indicating that you fully understand the arguments made before and are now moving on to the next issue to be considered.

[8] Now you can start the consideration of the case in question but, as the facts are similar to those already outlined, you do not need to go into any detail.

[9] This is a useful example of using academic commentary and ideas. You are using your own words and integrating an academic's ideas into your argument and then acknowledging that in a reference.

[10] If you can remember quotes, this is great because it really shows you know your law but it's not necessary to spend ages learning quotes. Paraphrasing this would be equally good.

those activities were ancillary to the main activities of the original company was irrelevant.[5]

Irrespective of the retained economic identity issue, a further problem that has been encountered is as a result of competitive tendering, particularly in situations that have involved 'second phase' contracting out. However, **Dines v Initial Health Care Services and Pall Mall Services** [1994] IRLR 336, CA, and **Christel Schmidt** [1994] ECJ confirmed that situations where transfers took place in two phases could fall within the Directive and thus TUPE.[6]

The result of cases such as **Spijkers**, **Rask**, **Schmidt** and **Dines**, was that the presumption, by the mid-1990s, was that any transfer of services was likely to be caught by the Directive and TUPE and thus job security in the context of transfers of undertakings, was a foregone conclusion.[7] However, in 1997, in **Süzen** the ECJ held that a mere loss of a service contract to a competitor cannot by itself indicate the existence of a transfer within the meaning of the Directive. The facts of **Süzen** are similar to those in **Dines**, albeit that the applicants were not offered any employment by the new contractor.[8]

This judgment in **Süzen** in effect meant that a non-TUPE bid could, in certain circumstances, be possible when tendering for services; and thus it introduced a new uncertainty into decision making both by employers and the courts. It seemed that the idea of continuation of identity of the function alone as the paramount factor, decided by Schmidt, was no longer tenable (McMullen, 1999).[9] The ECJ held, in **Süzen**, that the transfer of a service contract is not a transfer of a part of a business within the Directive 'if there is no concomitant transfer of significant tangible or intangible assets or the taking over by the new employer of a major part of the workforce, in terms of their numbers and skills, assigned by the predecessor to the performance of the contract'.[10]

Moreover, where the business is an activity that is being trans-ferred, the effect of the judgment is to make the application of the Directive depend on the willingness and consent of the transferee to take on the transferor's workforce. If the transferee takes care not to acquire any substantial tangible assets (or intangible assets such as goodwill), he can frustrate the purpose of the Directive altogether and refuse to take any of the old employees. This

[11]Here you are telling the reader that the judgment is problematic and did indeed change the law, so this is a key part of the argument.

[12]Here you are demonstrating that the decision was not a 'one off' or esoteric ECJ decision but found application in the UK too. This highlights your detailed knowledge of the area much more than limiting your analysis to just one case.

[13]You have been leading up to this point and now state your first conclusion with direct reference to the question, even if it is a little scary to say a judge was wrong!

[14]Conclusion on the second part – this also brings your answer up to date by acknowledging the statutory change dealing with the confusion left by case law.

clearly turns the Directive on its head. The whole point of the Acquired Rights Directive was to protect workers caught up in such a transaction.[11]

A number of UK decisions have applied the **Süzen** test and ruled against a transfer where there were insufficient assets and or employees (e.g. **Superclean Support Services plc v (1) Lansana (2) Wetton Cleaning Services Ltd** [1997] Unreported 20 May EAT; see J. McMullen, 'TUPE – Sidestepping Suzen' (1999) 28 ILJ 360 for a comprehensive list). In **Betts v Brintel Helicopters Ltd** [1997] CA, the Court of Appeal said that Süzen represented 'a shift of emphasis, or at least a clarification of the law' and, on the facts, found that there had been no transfer.[12]

It is submitted that by drawing the distinction between an 'economic entity' and an 'activity', particularly in cases where the activity consists of supplying specific services, **Süzen** can be regarded as having at least narrowed the test for determining what is a relevant transfer. Lord Justice Mummery's statement, in **ECM**, that the importance of **Süzen** has been overstated, is incorrect.[13] It cannot be denied that the pre-**Süzen** position on transfers was considerably wider and more protective towards employees than post-**Süzen**. Certainly, there has been a shift in emphasis. However, clarification only came with the 2006 TUPE Regulations, which specifically dealt with the uncertainty relating to contracting out.[14] Instead of trying to make sense of the previous case law and codifying it, legislators started with a blank sheet and inserted a new transfer definition into TUPE 2006. Regulation 3(1)(b) now deals with first and second generation contracting out as well as contracting back in and ensures that TUPE protection will be the norm for employees. It ensures the aim of the Directive is met and thus achieves what nearly two decades of case law could not.

 Make your answer stand out

- You could add academic commentary: McMullen has written a lot about this topic and there are useful sections in S. Deakin and G. Morris (2009) *Labour Law*.
- If you have time, a little detail about the cases (particularly *Dines* and *Schmidt* might help highlight your points but do not go overboard on this.
- Consider whether TUPE 2006 really has solved the problem. You can highlight the remaining issues by examining the case of *OCS Group UK Ltd* v *Jones and Another* [2009] EAT.

Don't be tempted to...

- Ignore the 2006 Regulations. The question is historical in focus but you need to bring your answer right up to date.
- Ignore the case law leading up to *Süzen* – you need to establish the position pre-*Süzen* to be able to comment on the effect of the case.
- Go into lots of factual detail about the cases – it does not really add anything and will detract from the argument that you are making.

Question 2

To what extent do the Transfer of Undertakings (Protection of Employment) Regulations 2006 protect employees in transfer situations?

Answer plan

→ Outline that business transfers are common and consider where they leave the employee.

→ Consider when the Regulations apply: what is a relevant transfer (regulation 3)?

→ Address what are the key rights that need protecting:
 – terms and conditions – reg 4
 – dismissal – reg 7
 – consider ETO reasons in relation to both
 – other rights (collective, consultation, no contracting out).

Diagram plan

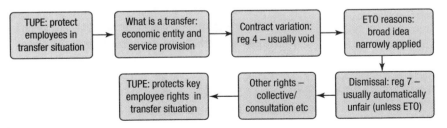

A printable version of this diagram plan is available from www.pearsoned.co.uk/lawexpressqa

Answer

It is not uncommon for a whole business or parts of a business to change hands and be transferred from one owner to another. The question then arises as to what happens to the employees in that business.[1] The European Acquired Rights Directive 2001/23 deals with exactly that question. It has been implemented in the UK in the form of the Transfer of Undertakings (Protection of Employment) Regulations 2006 (TUPE 2006) which replace similar legislation from 1981.

The 'standard' definition of a transfer is contained in reg 3(1)(a) of TUPE 2006, which applies the Regulations to: a transfer of an undertaking, business or part of a business situated immediately before the transfer in the United Kingdom to another person where there is a transfer of an economic entity which retains its identity. Regulation 3(2) defines 'economic entity' as an organised grouping of resources which has the objective of pursuing an economic activity, whether or not that activity is central or ancillary. This 'standard' definition has been interpreted (see also **Spijkers Gebroeders v Benedik Abbatoir CV and Alfred Benedik en Zonen BV** (1986) ECJ).[2]

[2]To be able to examine the extent to which TUPE offers protection, you first need to set out the scope of TUPE and what sort of transfers it applies to. The first two paragraphs do this.

Service provision changeovers are given preferential treatment under TUPE. The supplementary definition of a transfer under reg 3(1)(b) of TUPE 2006 on service provision change provides that a transfer for the purposes of TUPE takes place if service activity by Employer A is stopped; and that service provision is taken on by Employer B; and there was a group of employees whose main job it was to carry out those activities for Employer A.

[3]Now you can start looking at the protected rights and dealing with them in regulation order makes sense here because the key rights are dealt with early in the Regulations.

Regulation 4 provides that a transfer does not terminate the contracts of employment of the employees working in the grouping which is to be transferred.[3] Instead their contracts are treated as if they had been entered into by the new employer. Regulation 4(2) transfers the transferor's rights, powers, duties and liabilities under or in connection with the contract. The ability of an employer to vary employment terms before or after a TUPE transfer has always been heavily circumscribed, even where the employee consents to such change.[4] Under EU law, an employee may not waive rights granted to him or her under the Acquired Rights Directive 2001 (**Foreningen af Arbejdsledere I Danmark v Daddy's Dance Hall A/S** [1988]

[4]You need to state what the problem here is – employers might want to vary terms on takeover but that could put employees in a vulnerable position.

ECR 739, ECJ). TUPE thus provides that a purported variation will be void if the 'sole' or 'principal' reason is either the transfer itself; or a reason connected with the transfer that is not an economic, technical or organisational (ETO) reason entailing changes in the workplace (TUPE 2006, reg 4(4)). The problem with the first variation permitted is that **Daddy's Dance Hall** does not expressly allow for variations which are for an ETO reason. It appears to invalidate variations which are 'by reason' of the transfer. However, it seems illogical to permit dismissals for an ETO reason (see below), but not variations of contract.[5]

[5]If you are going to deal with a point more explicitly or detailed later on, refer the reader to it now so that the marker does not think you have missed the point. As long as you signpost clearly, your structure should be easy to follow.

An ETO reason is not defined in the Regulations[6] but, according to the DTI guidance note on the Regulations, is likely to include a reason relating to the profitability (an 'economic' reason), equipment or processes (a 'technical' reason) or management structure (an 'organisational' reason) of the transferee's business. However, the words 'entailing changes in the workforce' impose important limitations on the ETO justification for contractual change. It is only when the employer sets out to change the structure of his workforce, by reducing numbers or changing the functions which individuals perform, that the reason will entail an ETO 'change' in the workforce. Harmonisation, by definition, cannot therefore constitute an ETO reason and case law suggests that courts will interpret ETOs narrowly (see **Wheeler v Patel** [1987] IRLR 211, EAT, **Hynd v Armstrong and Others** [2007] IRLR 338, IH).[7]

[6]And neither have you dealt with it in detail above, so it is useful to explain ETO reasons in more detail before moving on.

[7]The final sentence of this paragraph sums up the key point, which is that changes cannot be made to terms and conditions simply to harmonise them with the existing workforce.

Under reg 4(9), the employee may treat the contract as being terminated by the employer on any 'substantial change of working conditions to his material detriment'.[8] This will greatly enlarge the prospect of employee initiated claims arising from changes in working conditions short of actual breach of contract. An employee can present a claim for constructive unfair dismissal. The employee also retains the right to claim constructive dismissal arising from a right arising outside the Regulations by terminating the contract without notice in acceptance of a repudiatory breach of contract by the employer under reg 4(11).

[8]Now you move on to dealing with the consequences of changes to the conditions. As this is also the beginning of potential dismissal scenarios in TUPE, you are also creating a natural link to the next section.

Under reg 7(1) of TUPE 2006, where, either before or after the transfer, an employee of the transferor or transferee is dismissed, the employee is automatically unfairly dismissed if the sole or principal reason for the dismissal is the transfer itself; or a reason

[9]You do not have to say all that much here because you have already talked about ETO reasons above.

[10]You have dealt with key rights relating to dismissal and contract variation; the others are perhaps less important but should still be mentioned.

[11]You do not need to say that much about this but it is important to mention it. If you could contract out, TUPE would be pointless.

[12]State your conclusion based on the rights outlined above and referring directly back to the question.

connected with it that is not an ETO reason entailing changes in the workforce. Where there is an ETO reason entailing changes in the workforce, reg 7(1) ceases to apply and the dismissal is not automatically unfair (see reg 7(2)). Regulation 7(3)(b) in TUPE 2006 provides that such dismissals may be regarded as having been by reason of redundancy where the appropriate test in s 98(2)(c) of the ERA 1996 is satisfied.[9]

In addition to the regulations in relation to dismissal and contract variations, TUPE protects certain other rights on transfer.[10] Regulation 5 transfers a collective agreement from a transferor to a transferee. Regulation 6 transfers trade union recognition. Under regulation 11, the transferor has to notify to the transferee the employee liability information (such as identity of employee; particulars of employment which must be given under ERA 2006, s 1; information on disciplinary or grievance procedures in relation to the employee, etc) of any person employed by him or her who is assigned to the organised grouping of resources or employees that is the subject of a relevant transfer. Regulations 13–15 deal with the duty to inform and consult appropriate employee representatives, informing them of the fact that a transfer is to take place and approximately when, as well as the implications and any measures the transferor or transferee anticipate taking in relation to the transfer. Finally, reg 18 contains restrictions on contracting out of TUPE. It prevents contracting out by incorporating s 203 of the ERA 1996, which is a general prohibition on the contracting out of employment legislation.[11]

Overall, therefore, the TUPE Regulations provide protection to employees of businesses which are being transferred. The two key areas, dismissal and contract variations, are covered in some detail and employees should find their rights are adequately protected. The key protection is strengthened by ensuring collective rights and consultation requirements are also respected. The restriction on contracting out of rights further protects the employees' position. TUPE thus goes some considerable way to protecting employees in this context.[12]

✓ Make your answer stand out

- Add academic commentary on this issue: see in particular the writings of McMullen.
- Comment on the historical development pre-2006 Regulations, where the issue of contracting out was particularly complex. See cases such as *Süzen* that seemed to allow the bypassing of the TUPE Regulations.
- Comment more on whether the protection has gone too far the employees' way – how does TUPE impact on businesses (in particular, perhaps the desire to harmonise conditions for pre- and post-transfer employees)?

! Don't be tempted to…

- Just list the legislative provisions. Although the question requires a relatively descriptive answer, you should comment on the law's effectiveness as much as possible.
- Spend too much time on defining a relevant transfer; simply set out the definition and move on to focus on the protective provisions.
- Go into lots of case detail. If you find you have time, you can add a little detail but you have a lot to get through and the case detail is less important than your overall argument.

? Question 3

Your client 'Translate' is about to take over a small rival company called LanguageCo. LanguageCo specialises in translating academic texts including lengthy and technical textbooks and this is a market into which Translate has been looking to expand. LanguageCo is being transferred as a going concern and will become the newly formed 'academic division' within Translate. Translate is happy to take on most of the LanguageCo staff but has concerns over two particular individuals. First, Angela is the sales manager at LanguageCo and she has a very aggressive sales style which does not fit well with Translate's more gentle approach. Secondly, Translate is aware that one of the translators, Mark, has a reputation for sloppy work and missing deadlines. Translate would rather LanguageCo dismissed these employees before the transfer takes place.

Translate are also a little concerned about the terms and conditions LanguageCo staff are employed under. While the pay is almost identical to that of Translate employees, LanguageCo staff currently work five hours less per week and are entitled to an additional five days' annual leave. They also receive bonuses for delivering their translations before the deadlines set. Translate would like to harmonise the working conditions and are prepared to better some of the Translate terms to meet the LanguageCo terms in the middle ground.

You are asked to advise Translate.

Answer plan

→ Consider whether the takeover of LanguageCo falls within the definition of a relevant transfer (TUPE, reg 3(1)) – yes it does.

→ Can Angela and Mark be dismissed? Consider whether the dismissal is automatically unfair because of the transfer or if it is related to transfer and not to ETO reason (reg 7).

→ Consider contract variation under reg 4. Is the variation void because of the transfer or a reason related to it and not an ETO reason?

→ Summarise your advice to Translate.

Diagram plan

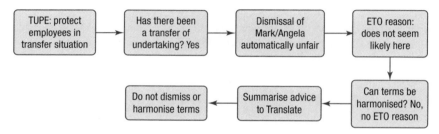

A printable version of this diagram plan is available from www.pearsoned.co.uk/lawexpressqa

Answer

This question requires an examination of the law relating to transfers of undertakings contained in the Acquired Rights Directive of 2001 and the Transfer of Undertakings (Protection of Employment) Regulations 2006 (TUPE 2006). In this answer, we will first consider whether the takeover of LanguageCo falls within the definition of relevant transfer for the purposes of TUPE and, if it does, whether Angela and Mark can be dismissed and employment conditions can be harmonised.[1]

[1] This introduction sets out the area of law under consideration, defines the legal issues and indicates the structure of the answer.

The definition of a relevant transfer can be found in reg 3(1)(a) of TUPE 2006:' a transfer of an undertaking, business or part of a business situated immediately before the transfer in the United Kingdom to another person where there is a transfer of an economic entity which retains its identity.' In **Spijkers Gebroeders v Benedik**

Abbatoir CV and Alfred Benedik en Zonen BV [1986] ECJ the basic definition of a transfer of an undertaking was coined: A transfer of an undertaking involves the transfer from one person to another of an economic entity retaining its identity and the following factors will help determine whether or not this is the case:

- consideration of the type of undertaking or business concerned;
- whether assets, tangible or intangible are transferred;
- whether employees are taken over;
- whether customers are transferred;
- the degree of similarity between activities carried on before and after the transfer and the period, if any, for which those activities are suspended.[2]

2You have set out the law clearly here and in a situation like this most examiners should be happy to accept bullet points. If in doubt, check with yours and, if needs be, write it out as prose.

3This section states your conclusion as to whether the transfer falls within the definition but you then need to justify that conclusion – demonstrate how you have applied the law and thus make your thought process explicit.

4State the law and give your conclusion – then justify it; that is a useful way to demonstrate your skills in applying the law. The justification comes next.

5Offer an alternative way of dealing with a legal issue – it shows an overall grasp of the subject and that you are prepared to think outside the box and consider non-legal solutions.

In the given scenario there seems little doubt that a relevant transfer is to take place. LanguageCo is being taken over as a going concern and will simply be slotted into Translate as a new division. Customers and employees are taken over, the work to be carried out remains the same and assets (intangible mostly) will be transferred. The Regulations thus apply to the scenario.[3]

Regulation 7 stipulates that employees cannot be dismissed because of the transfer or for a reason relating to the transfer unless the reason is an economic, technical or organisational (ETO) reason. A dismissal would be automatically unfair. In relation to the two employees Translate has concerns about, there seems to be no justification for dismissal.[4] In relation to Angela, her aggressive sales technique might not fit in with Translate but this is hardly an ETO reason (especially given that an ETO reason must entail a change in the workforce, which does not seem to be the case here) and retraining might well solve this issue. Mark can also not be dismissed. Translate's concerns seem to be based on his poor reputation and this is something which the company would have to consider once Mark has been working for them. If it indeed holds true that he misses deadlines and his work is sloppy, Translate should implement its policy procedure in relation to capability and competence issues and deal with him in that way.[5] Asking for him to be dismissed prior to transfer or dismissing immediately following the transfer is likely to be seen as a dismissal for a reason relating to the transfer and it does not fall within the ETO exception, so it would therefore be automatically unfair.

The changing of terms and conditions is covered by reg 4 and TUPE thus provides that a purported variation will be void if the 'sole' or 'principal' reason is either the transfer itself; or a reason connected with the transfer that is not an economic, technical or organisational (ETO) reason entailing changes in the workplace (TUPE 2006, reg 4(4)). On the other hand, an employer and employee may agree a variation if the sole or principal reason for the variation is a reason connected with the transfer that is an ETO reason entailing changes in the workforce; or a reason unconnected with the transfer (reg 4(5)). As confirmed in **Berriman v Delabole Slate Ltd** [1985] IRLR 305, CA, this expression means there must be a change in the numbers of the workforce or possibly their job functions which involves no overall reduction in numbers but does involve a change in the individual employees who together make up the workforce. This interpretation has been confirmed by the EAT in **London Metropolitan University v Sackur** [2006] UK EAT 0286 06 1708 (17 August 2006). The ETO reason must relate to the transferor's future conduct of the business (**Hynd v Armstrong and Other** [2007] IRLR 338, IH and **Whitehouse v Blatchford and Sons Ltd** [1999] IRLR 492, CA). [6]

[6]This paragraph simply sets out the law, which shows you have understood the provisions but you have not yet said anything about what this means for your client. You must do this next.

In this case it seems that any change would be because of the transfer or at the very least a reason connected with the transfer and, in the absence of a change in workforce, there cannot be an ETO reason which would make the changes lawful. However, in **Power v Regent Security Services Ltd** [2008] 2 All ER 977 the Court of Appeal considered the extent to which a transferee and transferring employee can agree between themselves to vary the employee's contract of employment and concluded that variations agreed prior to the transfer might be enforceable, at least if they are in the employee's interests. It might therefore be possible for Translate to negotiate new terms and conditions before the transfer.[7] However, as it seems that at least some of the terms would be less favourable, this might not be an option.

[7]This is worth mentioning as a possibility but also you must acknowledge that it is not a great option here because the terms are not going to be better than the terms the employees currently work under.

To conclude, Translate must therefore be advised that they should not insist on the dismissal of Angela and Mark and should not dismiss them following the transfer. In addition, the contract variation is also not something Translate should force through as it is likely to be unlawful under TUPE.[8]

[8]Summarise the advice at the end by telling Translate what you think they should or should not do. Do not presume that you will always be able to give the advice the client wants to hear.

Make your answer stand out

- You could give additional advice as to how the terms and conditions can be harmonised in the future – consider the usual process for contract variations for the entire workforce.
- You could comment in more detail on the management issues arising from Angela's approach and the sort of training and guidance/support she might need.
- You could also give a little more detail on the possible dismissal of Mark after a capability procedure (link to unfair dismissal).

! Don't be tempted to...

- Consider the provisions and case law relating to the transfer of service provision – the question is clearly not about that.
- Go through possible ETO reasons in lots of detail – the problem question gives you enough information to conclude that an ETO reason is very unlikely here.
- Try to find a solution you think your client wants to hear. If your conclusion is that the law prevents your client from doing what they want to do in an ideal situation, then you need to tell them that.

❓ Question 4

Sally started work for Happyclean, an industrial cleaning contractor, in 1995. Sally and 32 others of Happyclean's 40 employees cleaned the offices of AnyCo. After a tendering process, Happyclean lost the AnyCo contract to Quickclean, a rival company. Happyclean dismissed the AnyCo staff with effect from 31 January, and they were all employed by Quickclean from 1 February. Quickclean did not buy any of Happyclean's equipment. On 15 February, Quickclean announced that Sally's wages would be reduced from £200 to £175 per week. Sally objected to this and was consequently dismissed.

Advise Sally of her rights against Quickclean. If she is successful in any claim she makes, what remedy might she expect?

Answer plan

→ The scenario is concerned with TUPE 2006.

→ Examine whether there is a TUPE transfer here, given that staff are taken on but no equipment is bought.

→ Presuming there is a transfer, all rights and duties transfer, giving Sally some protection:
  - reduction in wages is unlawful
  - Sally's complaint regarding reduction leads to the dismissal, which is thus automatically unfair under ERA 1996, s 104.

→ Explain the remedies available. Reinstatement is possible but more likely to be compensation.

Diagram plan

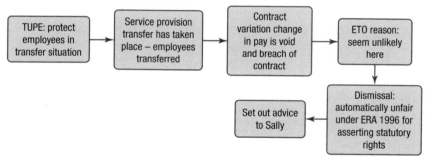

A printable version of this diagram plan is available from www.pearsoned.co.uk/lawexpressqa

[1]Setting out your answer in the form of a letter to the client can set your answer apart and make it more interesting for the reader. You are not asked to do this here but there is also nothing to suggest that you should not do so.

[2]Once you decide to (or are told to) write in letter format, you must then stick to that style all the way through and make it as authentic as possible. Think what you would write if Sally really was your client.

Answer

Dear Sally,[1]

Thank you for your enquiries made to this office. My advice is set out below but if there is anything you do not understand, please do not hesitate to get in touch.[2]

Your situation is covered under the Transfer of Undertakings (Protection of Employment) Regulations 2006 (TUPE 2006),[3] which provide some protection for employees in a situation where either an undertaking or a service provision is transferred from one owner to another. In order to help you understand the situation fully, I will first set out why I think the transfer falls within the

[3]Make sure you clearly identify the relevant law so the examiner knows that you know it.

[4]Setting out the structure clearly really helps the reader follow your points through. It also helps you because you can refer back to it as you write.

[5]You do not need to spend a long time considering the undertaking point. Service provision is clearly more appropriate, so it is fine to say that and then concentrate on the relevant provisions.

[6]This is a quote from the case but you could paraphrase just as well. Either way, you should cite the authority, though, to show off your legal knowledge.

[7]Apply the law to the scenario, as done here, to highlight your skills in applying the law. It is the application to the scenario that examiners are looking for.

[8]Setting out the law in the abstract is fine, as it shows you know the provisions; but without this application you will not pick up many marks in a problem question.

scope of the Regulations and then I will go on to explain your rights in more detail. Finally, I will set out what remedies you might be entitled to.[4]

In your case it seems that staff have transferred from Happyclean to Quickclean but there does not seem to be a transfer of any other assets. Regulation 3(1)(a) of TUPE 2006 covers the transfer of an undertaking but it seems that in your case there has not been such a transfer. Rather, it is just staff that have transferred. The more appropriate regulation for your situation is therefore reg 3(1)(b) and (3) of TUPE 2006, where the conditions required for a service provision transfer are given.[5] Under this regulation, TUPE 2006 applies to a transfer of service provision where an 'organised group of employees which has as its principal purpose the carrying out of the activities concerned on behalf of the client' transfers (**Hunt v Storm Communications Ltd and Others** [2006] Case No 2702 546/2006, 27 March 2007, Reading Tribunal 2007).[6] It seems to me that there was a group of employees at Happyclean who were employed to clean on behalf of AnyCo. It thus seems that your situation falls within TUPE 2006.[7]

According to reg 4 of TUPE 2006, all transferor's *rights, powers, duties and liabilities* transfer to the transferee. TUPE thus provide that a purported variation will be void if the 'sole' or 'principal' reason is either the transfer itself or a reason connected with the transfer that is not an economic, technical or organisational (ETO) reason entailing changes in the workplace (TUPE 2006, reg 4(4)). In other words, your contract should have transferred as it was and no variation should have been allowed unless an ETO reason is present.[8]

On the other hand, an employer and employee may agree a variation if the sole or principal reason for the variation is a reason connected with the transfer that is an ETO reason entailing changes in the workforce; or a reason unconnected with the transfer (reg 4(5)). As confirmed in **Berriman v Delabole Slate Ltd** [1985] IRLR 305, CA, this expression means there must be a change in the numbers of the workforce or possibly their job functions which involves no overall reduction in numbers but does involve a change in the individual employees who together make up the workforce. This interpretation has been confirmed by the EAT in **London Metropolitan University v Sackur** [2006] UK EAT 0286 06 1708 (17 August 2006). The ETO reason must relate

[9]You do not have the information to deal with this fully, so highlight the fact that you have recognised that, so the examiner knows.

[10]Remember, this is crucial.

[11]As you do not have all that much information, it is worth asking.

[12]Tell the client the likely outcome – that's what they want to know!

[13]Where there is more than one legal remedy possible, you should tell the client which option you think they should take. This shows real awareness of practical issues and that you understand the context in which employment law works.

[14]The question specifically asks about remedies, so you need to deal with them in a bit of detail.

to the transferor's future conduct of the business (**Hynd v Armstrong and Others** [2007] IRLR 338, IH and **Whitehouse v Blatchford and Sons Ltd** [1999] CA). There is no indication that any of this applies to your situation but do let me know if I have got that wrong.[9]

Applying this to your situation,[10] it seems to me that there is no ETO reason (but please do let me know if you have any additional information on this as you did not provide me with much in your original enquiry).[11] A change can therefore not be made to the terms and conditions of the contract you had with Happyclean. Reducing your pay can be seen as a repudiation of your contract and on that basis you could see yourself as constructively dismissed.[12] However, there is no need to make this claim as you can bring an automatically unfair dismissal claim under s 104 of the Employment Rights Act 1996 (ERA 1996). You have asserted your statutory right not to have your wages reduced (see ERA 1996, s 13) and have been dismissed as a result. This is automatically unfair and you would therefore be entitled to the remedies available for such a claim.[13]

If you wish to claim unfair dismissal in these circumstances, the remedies available to you if you are successful would be reinstatement to your old job or re-engagement by the same employer in a different role if this is appropriate.[14] However, in most cases the remedy is compensation. The basic award is calculated in accordance with s 118 of the ERA 1996 by adding up the following amounts, but only continuous employment within the last 20 years can count:

- 1½ weeks' pay for each complete year of employment between the ages of 41 and 65 inclusive;
- 1 week's pay for each complete year of employment between the ages of 22 to 40 inclusive;
- ½ week's pay for each complete year of employment below the age of 22.

The maximum number of weeks' pay that may be awarded is 30. There is also a maximum week's pay that can be used to calculate the award. This is currently set at £380 and is increased annually. You do not say how old you are, so I cannot set out the calculation for you; but please do get in touch if you need help with this. The week's pay you should use in your calculation is £200.

The compensatory award compensates you for the loss suffered as a result of the dismissal insofar as the employer is responsible for this loss. It is an amount the tribunal considers just and equitable in the circumstances, but there is a maximum compensatory award. The current figure is £65,300.

[15]Remember to sign off your letter but if you are in an exam which is being anonomously marked do not sign your name!

Yours sincerely,

A Solicitor[15]

 Make your answer stand out

- The TUPE 2006 provisions allow for changes to terms and conditions where a business is insolvent and the transferee is 'rescuing' it. Ask Sally if this is the case here.
- Provide a sample calculation to show Sally how to work out her basic award.
- Point out that one cannot contract out of TUPE (*Foreningen af Arbejdsledere I Danmark v Daddy's Dance Hall A/S* [1988] ECR 739, ECJ).
- Explain ETO reasons in more detail, especially considering the need for a change in the workplace. That way Sally is in a better position to tell you if she thinks there might be such a reason.
- To show off your broader knowledge you could mention the fact that service provision was only included explicitly in TUPE 2006 to clarify the confusion that existed in the case law previously. Do not get bogged down in this, though; think about how much an interested client would really want to know.

! **Don't be tempted to…**

- Go into detail about the transfer of undertaking definition. It is clear that the question relates to service provision here.
- Ignore the remedies. The question specifically asks you to advise on remedies, so you must do so in more detail than simply saying she is likely to get compensation.
- Set out all the rights and protection offered by TUPE; you do not need to tell the examiner everything you know. You demonstrate understanding much more effectively by focusing on the issues raised in the question.

11

Trade unions and their members

How this topic may come up in exams

Collective labour law is not covered in every employment law course and, where it is, the breadth and depth of coverage varies, so please check carefully what your syllabus requires. Where the topic is covered, essay questions tend to focus on an analysis of the effectiveness or appropriateness of the statutory provisions relating to recognition of trade unions. Problem questions often cover matters relating to the lawfulness of union activities or statutory protection for union members.

■ Attack the question

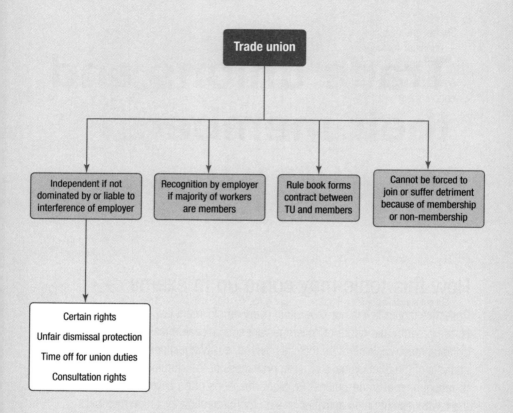

A printable version of this diagram plan is available from www.pearsoned.co.uk/lawexpressqa

 **Question 1**

Critically analyse the legislative provisions governing trade union recognition in the UK.

Answer plan

→ Discuss that voluntary recognition is preferred but that there are statutory steps in place where this is not achieved.

→ Set out the procedure:
  – consider formal requests made by an independent trade union
  – examine the formal requirements.

→ Assess why only a few applications are made and many are withdrawn – is legislation encouraging voluntary recognition?

Diagram plan

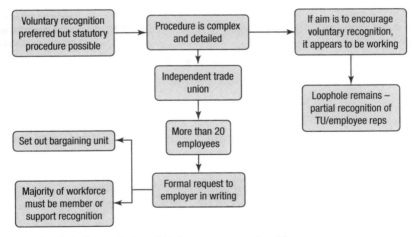

A printable version of this diagram plan is available from www.pearsoned.co.uk/lawexpressqa

Answer

This essay considers the law in relation to trade union recognition in the UK. For the most part, law leaves the relationship between employers and trade unions and the collective bargaining process to industrial relations and shies away from statutory interference.

However, the Employment Relations Act 1999 gave trade unions new legal rights to be recognised by employers where they could demonstrate majority membership or support. The current procedure of trade union recognition is contained in Schedule 1 to the Employment Relations Act 1999 and has been subject to criticisms relating to the balance between voluntary and statutory routes, the complexity of the procedures and the methods of enforcement.[1]

Recognition is important for trade unions in a number of respects. It brings with it the right to disclosure of information in relation to collective bargaining, the right to be consulted in relation to redundancy and transfers of undertakings as well as time off rights for union officials and members.[2]

The preferred government route for industrial partnership is the voluntary recognition of a trade union by the employer (if substantially supported by employees) and, wherever possible, a voluntary agreement should be signed. It is worth noting, though, that a signed agreement is not necessary when the union is in practice recognised by the employer: for example, by negotiating with the union on terms and conditions of employment, the union is classed as being recognised. Where recognition cannot be achieved on a voluntary basis, the law will step in to assist.[3]

The trade union may in certain circumstances apply to the Central Arbitrations Committee (CAC) for a declaration that it should be recognised for collective bargaining in a specific bargaining unit. Paragraph 4 of the relevant Schedule requires a union or unions seeking recognition to make a request for recognition to the employer. Only independent trade unions can do this and they must be listed as such by the Certification Officer.[4] An independent union is one which is not under the domination or control of an employer and is not 'liable to interference' tending towards such control (Trade Union and Labour Relations (Consolidation) Act 1992, s 5). In **Blue Circle Staff Association v CO** [1977] 2 All ER 145 the EAT approved criteria for independence developed by the Certification Officer (CO). These criteria for independence include the financing of the union, any other material support such as use of premises, the history of the union, the union's rules, etc. Direct financing from the employer is said to be potentially fatal to the independence of a trade union. Furthermore, in **Squibb UK Staff Association v CO** [1979]

[1] This introduction sets out clearly what the essay is about and what the key considerations are going to be. There should now be no surprises.

[2] A useful starting point in any discussion is identifying why the issue under discussion is important or relevant. It shows you know your subject.

[3] You are setting the scene here. The fact that voluntary is preferred is important because it says something about the aims of the legislation, which you have to identify in order to assess the provisions.

[4] Set out the eligibility requirements and then explain them. To fully evaluate something you must first understand it and this is what you are showing here.

2 All ER 452, CA it was held that a risk of interference is sufficient – interference does not have to be likely.

In addition to the 'independence' requirements and the need to have at least 20 employees in the affected business, a request must comply with the following if it is to be considered 'valid':[5] the request must be in writing, identify the union and state that it is made under Schedule A1. It must also be received by the employer. It should be noted that while a request may be made by more than one union, acting jointly, it may relate only to a bargaining unit comprising workers of a single employer. Allowing multi-union claims was justified by the need to respect workers' freedom to join the union of their choice. This was, however, qualified by the requirement imposed on unions making joint requests to satisfy the CAC that they will co-operate over collective bargaining, even to the extent of committing themselves to joint bargaining, should the employer require this.

[6]This sentence functions as quite a useful reminder of where we are in the process and just helps the reader keep track of the argument.

The employer can at this point accept the request, refuse it or accept it in principle but take issue with the bargaining unit.[6] Where there is disagreement over details, it is usually expected and the union and employer will negotiate and reach a voluntary agreement, with the help of ACAS if necessary. Where the bargaining unit is at issue, the CAC can be asked to make a decision and it will do so taking into account the need for effective management, existing agreements and the need to avoid fragmented bargaining. The bargaining unit must therefore be a relatively large proportion of the workforce and it must be coherent. A useful example is **TGWU v Gala Casinos Ltd t/a Maxims Casino Club** [2001] 1 November[7] where the bargaining unit was held to be the workforce across a number of casinos rather than just one. Where the request for recognition is refused, an application is made to the CAC for a decision. Recognition should be granted where 50% or more members of the bargaining unit are union members unless a ballot is required in the interest of good industrial relations, union members write to confirm they do not want the union to bargain for them or there is other evidence leading to a similar conclusion. The CAC can then organise a secret ballot to determine whether recognition should be granted.

[7]Case examples not only show that you do really know the law but also make your argument less abstract.

Where membership is below 50% of the bargaining unit, the union can try to persuade the CAC that the majority of the workforce would support collective bargaining. Compelling evidence such as a signed petition from over 50% of the workforce is required. In **ISTC v MFI – formerly Hygena (Scunthorpe)** [2001] 2 February this was not achieved because the union could not show that it had sufficient support from the workforce. Where recognition is granted, the employer has 30 days to commence collective bargaining, which must cover pay, hours and holidays as a minimum.

Overall, relatively few claims have been made to the CAC[8] and, even where such claims are made, they often are withdrawn because voluntary agreement is reached; but research evidence also suggests that a great deal more voluntary agreements have been reached since the introduction of the procedure. From the government's perspective, it can thus be argued that the law is working relatively well and is encouraging voluntary agreement.[9] However, criticisms remain.[10] In particular, the 20-worker limit excludes small businesses from ever having to enter into collective bargaining, even where the entire workforce is comprised of union members. Secondly, the law provides a loophole which prevents formal applications where there is part recognition of a union in some areas (for example, discipline) or recognition of a staff association which a company could itself have set up. Clearly this provides an easy get-out clause for any company not wishing to be subject to full union recognition and collective bargaining.[11] An illustration of how this operates can be seen in the CAC decision on the admissibility of a recognition application by the National Union of Journalists (NUJ).[12] In that case, around half of the journalists in the proposed bargaining unit were NUJ members and at most one worker in the bargaining unit was a member of a rival independent non-TUC affiliated union, the British Association of Journalists (BAJ). Despite this, the employer, MGN Limited, recognised the BAJ and its recognition, the panel found, sufficed to block the NUJ's application. In addition, the law remains complex and the procedure must follow the formalities, making it difficult, in particular, for smaller unions. However, overall the law seems to be encouraging union recognition, which must be seen as a positive step towards ensuring workers' rights.[13]

[8]Here you are directly addressing the effectiveness and the obvious starting point is the number of CAC decisions. This also shows that you have some wider knowledge of the area of law.

[9]Remember you identified the government's preference for voluntary recognition earlier, so you are coming full circle in your argument here, which is great.

[10]Just because it is encouraging voluntary recognition does not mean it is uncontroversial, and you demonstrate that here.

[11]This is a major issue which you need to flag up. It is useful to explain this in relatively simple terms – there is no point in overcomplicating matters.

[12]Then use an example to illustrate this and show it is not just a theoretical loophole but one that can and is being used quite cynically. It shows you are aware of the law and its application and problems.

[13]Finish with your overall assessment, which should relate back directly to the question to make sure you have really answered it.

✓ **Make your answer stand out**

- Say a little more about the role of the CAC and CO.
- Add in academic commentary such as R. Dukes, 'The Statutory Recognition Procedure 1999: No Bias in Favour of Recognition' (2008) 37 ILJ 236.
- Expand on why recognition is important. This is relevant as it sets the context in which you are evaluating the procedure for recognition.

❗ **Don't be tempted to…**

- Explain the procedure without reference to what it is trying to achieve – that would make it impossible to judge its effectiveness.
- Conclude that, because there have been few cases brought and even fewer decisions made by the CAC, the provision isn't working – that depends on what the purpose is.

 Question 2

To what extent do collective agreements form a binding agreement between the employer and employee?

Answer plan

→ Briefly discuss collective agreements as gentlemen's agreements.
→ Consider the possibility of incorporating into the contract:
  – custom and practice
  – reference
  – agency.
→ Identify the problems regarding which agreement and which terms are incorporated.
→ Conclude by assessing whether binding agreements are possible only where the terms have been incorporated into contract.

Diagram plan

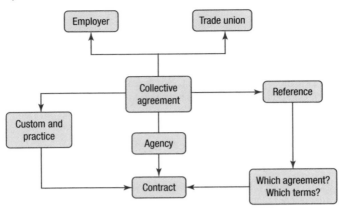

A printable version of this diagram plan is available from www.pearsoned.co.uk/lawexpressqa

Answer

Collective agreements can be negotiated nationally or locally and in some cases a national agreement is supplemented by a local agreement.[1] These agreements will include some terms that affect the individual employee directly,[2] but will also cover matters related to the relationship between the employer and the union rather than that between the employer and the employee. In general, these agreements between unions and employers are not intended to be legally enforceable and are not legally binding unless the parties explicitly agree that they should be. There is a statutory presumption against enforceability in s 179 of the Trade Union and Labour Relations (Consolidation) Act 1992: this acts to prevent an employer from suing the union on the agreement.[3]

Even though these agreements are not binding between the employer and the union, they can have legal effects on the individual contracts of employment.[4] One possibility is that they are incorporated into individual contracts by custom and practice. In **Young v Canadian Northern Pacific Railway** [1931] AC 83, PC the employee argued this before the Privy Council (PC). The PC held that it had not happened in the instant case but left open the possibility of a collective agreement being incorporated into individual contracts by custom and practice.

[1] An opening statement that shows you have an appreciation of the sort of agreements the question is asking about gets you off to a good start.

[2] You should not waste time in an exam. There is nothing wrong with getting straight to the point as you do here and stating that there will be some elements of the agreements directly impacting on employees.

[3] This may seem like you are going off track given that the question asks about employees but this is important context so include it, albeit briefly.

[4] This sentence does two things: first, it goes some way to answering the question set; and, secondly, it justifies your previous paragraph by explaining why even non-binding agreement can have a legal effect on individual employees here.

A more usual way of incorporating the terms is by reference, creating what is really a species of express term. This occurs where reference is made to the collective agreement or some other document as a source of terms (**National Coal Board v Galley** [1958] 1 All ER 91, CA). **Robertson and Jackson v British Gas Corp** [1983] CA provides a useful example.[5] Robertson was a meter reader for the gas board and the trade union had negotiated a bonus scheme for these employees. Reference to the bonus scheme was made in his letter of appointment. Later the employer wished to abandon the scheme, so it stopped making bonus payments. However, the bonus scheme had been incorporated into the individual contracts and could be abandoned only by agreement with the TU or with Mr Robertson himself.

[6]Even if you are not convinced by a particular legal solution, you should still mention the possibility, otherwise the examiner will not know why you discounted it. It is better to mention it but explain why it is unsatisfactory.

A third possible way in which the collective agreement can find its way into individual contracts is through agency. Generally this is not a satisfactory analysis, as unions do not act as the agents of their members but as principals acting in their own right.[6] However, it is not impossible for the union to act as agent of its members in negotiating terms and conditions and if, on the facts, this can be shown then the terms can be incorporated in this way. **Edwards v Skyways** [1964] 2 All ER 494, HC is an interesting example of the use of this analysis. However, if the agency method of incorporation applies, then those who are not members cannot automatically benefit from any negotiated enhancement of terms. **Singh v British Steel Corp** [1974] IRLR 131, Ind Trib illustrates this argument.[7] Singh resigned from the union and informed his employer expressly that he no longer regarded the union as acting on his behalf. He then used this as the basis of an argument that he was not bound by a negotiated change in working practices. In **Harris v Richard Lawson Autologistics Ltd** [2002] EWCA Civ 442, CA, a shop steward represented that he had been given members' authority to negotiate over disputed conditions with their employer. As the members in question had represented that the shop steward had this authority, he had acted as their agent and they were bound by the variation that he had negotiated on their behalf.

[7]Using case examples, as done here, helps clarify your argument and make it less abstract. Generally speaking, the more we can relate to something, the easier we understand it, so examples are a good way of showing you understand and convincing the reader of your argument.

This is not the end of difficulties with collective agreements. Even if it is accepted that collective agreements can be incorporated into individual contracts, it must then be decided which collective agreement terms should be taken from and which terms are in fact contractual ones. Strictly speaking, the bargain closest to the individual ought to take precedence. However, the courts have consistently refused to accept this understanding of the way in which collective bargaining takes place. In **Gascol Conversions Ltd v Mercer** [1974] IRLR 155, CA the national agreement provided for a 40-hour working week, whereas a local agreement provided for a longer one. If the longer one had been incorporated, Mercer would have been entitled to a higher redundancy payment. The court preferred to accept that it was the national agreement and took the view that the local agreement was only a 'gentleman's agreement'.

When deciding which terms are incorporated, a distinction must be made between terms about matters such as rate of pay, hours of work and holiday entitlement and terms relating to matters such as a disputes procedure, negotiating machinery or shop stewards' facilities. In **British Leyland (UK) Ltd v McQuilken** [1978] IRLR 245, EAT, the term related to the redundancy procedure. In **Tadd v Eastwood and Daily Telegraph Ltd** [1983] IRLR 320 it related to a dispute procedure, and in both of these cases it was held that these were intended to be binding in honour only between the employer and the union. In **Ali v Christian Salvesen Food Services Ltd** [1997] 1 All ER 721, CA the collective agreement contained a complex procedure for averaging wages out in seasonal employment. When Mr Ali was made redundant he had been working in excess of the standard hours and he argued that he should receive payment based on hours actually worked. The Court of Appeal held that, since the agreement was wholly silent on the consequences of premature termination, any implication would have to be drawn from the surrounding circumstances; the court considered the agreement to be intended as a clear and binding agreement, so the payment should be based on standard hours, not hours actually worked.[8]

[8]Setting out the facts here helps clarify your argument. Do not do this for all the cases – you will not have time – but go into a little more detail for one or two cases. That will suffice to make your point.

It can be seen, then, that collective agreements can and do influence the individual employment contract. While, on the whole, collective agreements are binding in honour only and do not form a legally enforceable contract between the employer and the union, individual terms of collective agreements can be incorporated into the employment contract and thus create legally binding contractual rights and duties between the employer and the employee.[9] The difficulties in relation to this are that it is not always clear whether a collective agreement has been incorporated and, if so, which

[9]This is your answer to the question set. Make sure it appears somewhere in the conclusion – it doesn't have to be right at the end.

[10]You do not have a clear solution for the problem but you can speculate as to what might happen and, chances are, cases will continue to come up.

agreement and which terms from the agreement. Cases seeking to resolve these issues are thus likely to continue.[10]

Make your answer stand out

- Set your answer in context by saying a little bit about the purpose of collective bargaining.
- Consider briefly other ways of making employers honour collective agreements such as industrial action.
- Link your conclusion more explicitly back to the question by using the same language used in the question and answering it directly.

Don't be tempted to...

- Just provide a list of cases relating to the incorporation of terms into contracts; your argument must come first and then you can illustrate that with cases.
- Ignore the difficulties of which agreement and which terms to incorporate – just because there are technical legal ways of making incorporation possible does not mean the problems are solved.
- Ignore the possibility of custom and practice and agency just because they are not as common as incorporation by reference.

? Question 3

The Union of the Elite Workers has just received recognition from Elite Ltd. Svetlana started working for Elite Ltd three months ago and yesterday was told by her human resources manager that she will have to join the Union of Elite Workers or be dismissed. Anisa, one of the members, is unhappy, because she has found out that the union is giving money to the local Labour party to help its candidates in a forthcoming election. Anisa votes Liberal Democrat and does not want to support the Labour party. Steve, another member, who is a member of the Conservative party, is also unhappy because the union is contributing to a campaign that supports abortion. He holds strong anti-abortion views. However, the union secretary, Jimmy, is very happy because Elite Ltd has agreed to give the union £3,000 to help finance their activities.

Discuss.

Answer plan

→ Identify that the problem relates to trade unions and their members.

→ Discuss the right to join and not to join a union (TULR(C)A 1992, s 152). Can Svetlana be forced to join?

→ Address the fact that political activities must be expressly allowed in rule book and funded separately. Anisa should check if this is the case.

→ What other activities are limited by rule book? Is pro-abortion work lawful?

→ Examine whether the money from the employer given to the union calls into question its independence (TULR(C)A 1992, s 5).

Diagram plan

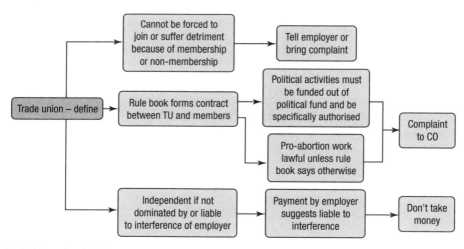

A printable version of this diagram plan is available from www.pearsoned.co.uk/lawexpressqa

Answer

[1]Clear identification of the area of law to be covered and structure of what is to follow. This makes marking easy because you know what comes next.

This question requires the consideration of a number of issues relating to trade unions and their relationship with their members and employers. This essay will therefore discuss rights and responsibilities in relation to trade unions in the order they are presented in the scenario given.[1]

As well as the well-established right to join trade unions, there is now also a right to dissociate. Following the case of **Young, James and Webster v UK** [1981] IRLR 408, EctHR, in which UK rules on closed shop agreements in force at the time were held to be in violation of Article 11 of the European Convention on Human Rights and Fundamental Freedoms (ECHR), no one can be forced to join a trade union. Section 152 of the Trade Union and Labour Relations (Consolidation) Act 1992 (TULR(C)A 1992) now deals with dismissal in relation to trade union activities and membership and subs (1)(c) states that a dismissal is automatically unfair under the Employment Rights Act 1996 where the dismissal is because the employee 'was not a member of any trade union, or of a particular trade union, or of one of a number of particular trade unions, or had refused, or proposed to refuse, to become or remain a member'.[2] This section clearly applies to the scenario given.[3] Svetlana cannot be forced to join the Union of Elite Workers. She should therefore point out to her employer that she has the right not to join the trade union under TULR(C)A 1992.[4] If the employer still insists on dismissing her, that dismissal would be automatically unfair and Svetlana should be advised to apply to her local employment tribunal. It is also worth noting that under TULR(C)A 1992, s 146(1)(c) discriminatory action short of dismissal is also unlawful and Svetlana, should she experience such detrimental treatment, could bring a case on that basis.[5]

The issues raised by Anisa and Steven both relate to the union's activities and how membership fees can be spent. Section 72 of TULR(C)A 1992 specifies that funds should not be used for 'the furtherance of the political objects [specified in the Act]' unless the union has made a political resolution approving the furtherance of such objectives and provisions are made for the political activities to be funded from a separate political fund from which members may be exempt if they so wish. Political objects are further defined in s 72 of TULR(C)A 1992 and include financial contributions in connection with the candidature of any person in connection with any election to a political office.[6] Clearly the actions of the Union of Elite Workers come within the scope of this definition.

If the union has complied with the formalities relating to the use of a political fund, i.e. they have made the relevant resolution and have set up a separate fund and allow members like Anisa not to contribute to that particular fund, it would appear that backing

[2] Clear explanation of what the law says, highlighting your legal knowledge.

[3] Say it applies and then explain what that actually means. That way you are demonstrating the skills required to apply the law fully.

[4] Remember that heading straight for a tribunal is not usually the best course of action. Many disputes can be resolved much more informally and including that here shows you have engaged with the subject fully and not just learnt the legal provisions.

[5] You are not asked about this point directly but it is relevant because the employer may agree not to dismiss her but then subject her to detriment in other ways, so she needs to know her rights.

[6] Set out the law first and then say how it applies to the scenario.

a Labour party candidate financially is lawful. However, if those requirements are not met, union funds cannot be used for the purposes. Anisa should therefore check whether a resolution is in place and whether there is a separate membership contribution in relation to the political fund.[7] If there is, it is likely that she will want to stop paying the political fund part of her membership fee.[8] She is, of course, also free to leave the union altogether. If no separate fund exists, Anisa should draw the unlawfulness of the financial contribution to the Labour party candidate's campaign to the union's attention and point out that it is breaching union rules. A complaint could also be made to the Certification Officer.[9] Steven's situation is legally straightforward. The funds are not being used for political purposes or to fund political activities as defined in s 72 of TULR(C)A 1992 and therefore do not fall within s 71 of TULR(C)A 1992.[10] Supporting a pro-abortion campaign is thus lawful providing there is nothing in the Union of Elite Workers' rule book to say otherwise.[11] A complaint in relation to a breach of union rules (which would include a complaint relating to the improper use of funds for political activity) is generally made to the Certification Officer under TULR(C)A 1992, ss 108A–108C rather than the High Court.

The final issue relates to Elite Ltd paying £3,000 to the union. The payment raises the question of whether the Union of Elite Workers is an independent union under s 5 of TULR(C)A 1992.[12] An independent union is one which is not under the domination or control of an employer and is not 'liable to interference' tending towards such control. In **Blue Circle Staff Association v CO** [1977] 2 All ER 145 the EAT approved criteria for independence developed by the Certification Officer (CO). These criteria for independence include the financing of the union, any other material support such as use of premises, the history of the union, the union's rules, etc. Direct financing from the employer is said to be potentially fatal to the independence of a trade union. Furthermore, in Squibb UK Staff Association **v** CO [1979] 2 All ER 452, CA it was held that a risk of interference is sufficient; interference does not have to be likely.[13] In this case it therefore seems that the Union of Elite Workers is indeed liable to interference.[14] Having received £3,000 from the employer suggests that the union is at risk of interference from the company even if in practice interference may be unlikely. Were the Union of Elite workers to apply for a certificate of independence

8Solutions do not have to be legal solutions – pragmatic ones are fine too!

9If there is more than one course of action, state them in order of formality with the least formal first.

10Stating the law like this focused on the question keeps this relatively uncontroversial issue short and saves you time.

11This is worth just noting because the rule book could, of course, say something about this.

12This sentence succinctly identifies what the legal issue is.

13After identifying the issue, you then need to state what the law is.

14State your conclusion but remember to justify it – that comes next.

they would be unlikely to be successful in these circumstances. However, independence is important because independent trade unions have various statutory rights, such as consultation rights in relation to redundancies and transfers of undertakings, rights to collective bargaining, the right not to suffer detriment for taking part in legitimate union activities and time off with pay for their lay officials, which others do not have.[15]

[15]Clarifying why independence is important shows that you understand this area of law and that it is more than just a theoretical exercise.

In conclusion, therefore, the Union of Elite Workers, if seeking a certificate of independence, should avoid taking money from Elite Ltd and must also clarify its rules in relation to activities – in particular its political activities, which must be financed from a separate political fund if they are to be lawful. It should further be stressed that Elite Ltd cannot force its employees to become members of the union and cannot subject them to detriment if they choose not to join.[16]

[16]As usual in problem questions, finish with a summary of your advice specific to the scenario.

✓ Make your answer stand out

- You could comment on the fact that, if the union has been recognised through the statutory recognition procedure, it must have been an independent union and thus the £3,000 is less of an issue.
- You could provide a little more information regarding the possibility of Svetlana suffering detriment short of dismissal.
- When discussing the pro-abortion support you could consider the role of union rule books in a little more detail to consider how the rule book might constrain the union's activities.

! Don't be tempted to...

- Assume that the union does not have a political fund – you do not know that, so your advice should be that Anisa needs to check this out.
- Jump to the conclusion that abortion campaigns are political activity because abortion is a politically controversial topic – it must fit the statutory definition.

❓ Question 4

Sidra is a member of the union All for One, along with most of her fellow workers at Long Hours Ltd. She has asked the company to recognise All for One but it refuses. She would like to attend a course organised by All for One on how to be a better branch secretary. She is secretary of her local branch, which has in membership employees from Long Hours Ltd and 15 other companies.

Advise Sidra.

Answer plan

→ Briefly outline that the question is about recognition of trade unions and the rights of officials.

→ Discuss recognition and the fact that it is usually voluntary but there is a statutory procedure.

→ Set out the procedure and evaluate whether the request should be granted.

→ Consider what rights recognition brings:
  – time off for activities within the scope of the legislation
  – if the activities are within its scope, then time off is paid for officials – is this the case here?
  – whether unpaid time off is a right.

Diagram plan

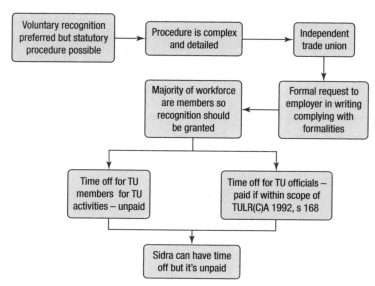

A printable version of this diagram plan is available from www.pearsoned.co.uk/lawexpressqa

Answer

[1]A useful intro which sets out
the issues to be considered
and signposts the reader
as to how you are going to
answer the question.

This question relates to the recognition of trade unions and the rights of union officials. In order to advise Sidra we first need to consider the right of trade unions to recognition by employers. Secondly, we must consider her right to attend the course mentioned.[1]

[2]Here you are saying you
understand the law and the
context in which it operates.

Although the government policy is to favour voluntary recognition of trade unions, there is now a statutory recognition procedure under the Trade Union and Labour Relations (Consolidation) Act 1992 (TULR(C)A 1992).[2] Sidra should first make a formal request for recognition of All for One to Long Hours Ltd. In order for that formal request to be valid, Long Hours Ltd must employ more than 20 workers and Sidra must identify the bargaining unit that the union represents. In order for a valid request to be made, All for One must also be listed as an independent trade union by the Certification Officer.[3] If the union has not yet received such a certificate of independence, it should apply now. Section 5 of TULR(C)A 1992 states that an independent union is one which is not under the domination or control of an employer and is not 'liable to interference' tending towards such control. In **Blue Circle Staff Association v CO** [1977] 2 All ER 145 the EAT approved criteria for independence developed by the Certification Officer (CO). These criteria for independence include the financing of the union, any other material support such as use of premises, the history of the union, the union's rules, etc. Direct financing from the employer is said to be potentially fatal to the independence of a trade union. Furthermore, in **Squibb UK Staff Association v CO** [1979] 2 All ER 452, CA it was held that a risk of interference is sufficient; interference does not have to be likely.

[3]Clearly identify the
requirements but write
directly in relation to the
problem, not in the abstract.

[4]Given that you do not have
a lot of information, the point
here seems rather abstract.
The same can be said for the
discussion on independence
above. They are important
points which you cannot
ignore but you also do not
have enough information to
apply them specifically, so this
will have to do.

Following the request, Long Hours Ltd may decide to recognise the union after all or it may agree in principle but take issue with details such as the bargaining unit identified. If this is the case, application can be made to the Central Arbitration Committee for a decision relating to the bargaining unit. It will reach its decision on the basis that there is a need for effective management and to avoid fragmented bargaining within the workforce.[4] If All for One is still not recognised by Long Hours Ltd, the CAC can be asked to make a decision on recognition. Where there is clear evidence that the majority of the workforce are members of the union, no ballot needs to be held and the CAC will grant recognition as long as there is no evidence which suggests that members do not want the union to bargain on their behalf. The scenario suggests that the majority of workers are members and this is therefore the most likely course of action.[5]

[5]The scenario tells you that the majority are members, so you do not need to discuss what would happen if this wasn't the case.

Very little information is given in the scenario but, providing All for One meets the eligibility requirements and Long Hours Ltd does not already (part) recognise another union or staff association for the purposes of collective bargaining, it seems likely that a claim for recognition would be successful.[6]

[6]Summarise your advice before moving on to the second part. This helps the reader because it obviously concludes one point before moving on.

Once recognition has been achieved, the union and its officials and members have certain rights including the right to time off for union activities. As a union official, Sidra would have the right to take reasonable time off, which is paid, to carry out her role as union official. While paid time off for training is permitted, it will be reasonable only if it relates directly to union activities, and reasonableness will be assessed with reference to the relevance of the training, the amount of time taken off, the amount of notice given to the employer and the employer's ability to cover during absence. The course Sidra wishes to attend seems unconnected with s 178(2) TULR(C)A 1992 matters, which include matters that can be subject to collective bargaining, such as terms and conditions of employment, termination of employment and discipline. As such, the course does not fall within the scope of TULR(C)A 1992, s 168 and Sidra is not entitled to paid time off. However, the course does fall under s 170, which deals with time off for union activities, and she has a right to time off but not with pay.[7] These rights are only available to Sidra once recognition has been achieved and Sidra will therefore not be entitled to the time off if the union has yet to achieve recognition.[8]

[7]If you can summarise the law while applying it to the scenario you can save considerable time in an exam. Some might, however, prefer to set out the legal provisions here in more detail and then apply them because that aids structure and logical argument.

[8]Your concluding sentence serves as a useful way to come full circle and conclude your answer to the problem question as a whole.

✓ **Make your answer stand out**

- Provide a quote or summary of the various sections such as ss 168 and 170 to clarify your point.
- You could consider in a little more detail why recognition is important (collective bargaining, etc).
- Set out in more detail the different time off rights for officials and members before applying the law directly to Sidra.

! Don't be tempted to...

- Deal with the time off issue in isolation – it follows on from the importance of recognition.
- Assume that because Sidra is an official and the course is union organised she is entitled to time off with pay – you need to apply the law meticulously here.
- Assume that recognition will be automatic – you do not know if the Union is independent.

Industrial action

12

How this topic may come up in exams

In courses where collective labour law is on the syllabus, industrial action is a popular topic for examination because it lends itself well to problem questions and also because essay questions can test your knowledge of policy and political contexts as well as just the legal provisions. Essays tend to concentrate on whether the correct balance has been struck between employer and employee/union rights whereas problem questions often focus on the extent to which individuals taking part in strike action are protected from sanctions.

■ Attack the question

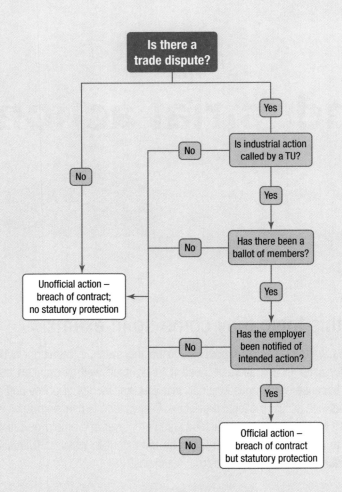

A printable version of this diagram plan is available from www.pearsoned.co.uk/lawexpressqa

❓ Question 1

Salaried employees in local government are taking industrial action for improved pay. They are going on strike one day each week. Some local councils are deducting a day's pay each week; some are refusing to pay any salary at all to those who will not work normally. A lot of work contracted out by councils is delayed because of an administrative backlog and Allan, a private contractor, is without work because of this. Nasty Borough Council dismisses those of its employees who are taking strike action but re-engage everyone except the union officials when the strike is over. The strikes had the official support of the union but it turns out that the ballot was not carried out in accordance with the statutory requirements.

Discuss.

Answer plan

→ Outline that common law takes a strict approach and does not recognise the right to strike.

→ Discuss whether reducing pay is lawful by applying the relevant cases.

→ Consider the implication of *Ticehurst* on whether full performance can be required.

→ Is the strike official and protected?

→ If it is, the union has statutory immunity which has been lost here because of the lack of a valid ballot.

Diagram plan

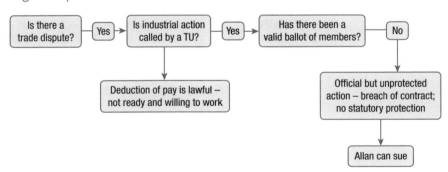

A printable version of this diagram plan is available from www.pearsoned.co.uk/lawexpressqa

Answer

This scenario requires consideration of the law relating to industrial action and in particular the extent to which employees taking part in such action are protected. The common law takes a strict approach and sees strike action as a repudiatory breach of contract. Under the common law it is therefore not only lawful to not pay employees when they are not ready and willing to work, the employees taking part would in fact be in breach of their contracts and the breach is so fundamental that the employers could terminate the employment relationship immediately. Statutory protection is required to protect employees' interests in this area.[1]

Dealing with pay first, it is lawful to deduct pay pro rata for imperfect performance. In **Royle v Trafford BC** [1984] IRLR 184, QBD where a teacher was trying to further union policy on maximum class size: his class already had 31 pupils and he refused to accept a further five. His employers paid him 31/36ths of his salary and this was upheld. In **Miles v Wakefield MDC** [1987] 1 All ER 1089, HL a Registrar of Births, Deaths and Marriages refused to work three hours on a Saturday morning, this being the busiest time of the week.[2] The employer's decision to deduct 3/37ths of salary was upheld. Following this line of reasoning, the councils can lawfully deduct one day's pay per week because of the employees' incomplete performance.[3]

Alternatively, the councils can require full performance, in the absence of which no pay at all is given. **Ticehurst v British Telecommunications Ltd** [1992] IRLR 219, CA confirms this position although it concerned industrial action short of a strike. The employees withdrew goodwill; they performed their duties, but did what they could to cause administrative overload. Eventually the employer insisted that the employees work normally or be sent home without pay. Ms Ticehurst was sent home and later claimed her unpaid wages. It was held that the obligation to serve the employer faithfully was breached by choosing to carry out duties in the manner most likely to cause disruption, even though the course of action might quite properly be chosen in the honest exercise of her duties.[4] Following the reasoning in **Ticehurst** it might therefore be suggested that, where the councils make clear that they require

5State what the case might mean for the scenario to make sure you really are applying the law, not just stating it.

6Explain why *Ticehurst* might be different in an actual strike situation rather than action short of a strike. It shows engagement with the question and critical thinking.

7This is the legal problem which you then need to go on and apply to the scenario.

8Again, this statement of the common law position shows that you have understood this area rather than just learnt the relevant statutory provisions.

full performance in the absence of which no pay at all will be paid, they can lawfully withhold the salaries of those workers on strike.[5] However, **Ticehurst** was a rather extreme example and it could be argued that, where employees are willing to work normally for the rest of the week and simply take part in strike action one day per week, withholding the entire salary breaches the general duty to pay wages.[6]

The fact that the ballot has not been conducted properly will not change the fact that the strike action was official but it does mean it is not protected because, as we shall see below, the union has lost its immunity in tort. Therefore, employees taking part will not be protected under unfair dismissal legislation unless dismissals are selective and targeted at ringleaders, for example. In that case, dismissal is potentially fair and must be reasonable to be lawful.[7] In the given scenario, therefore, the union officials may have unfair dismissal claims which the council can defend only if it can show that the dismissal was in fact reasonable.

Furthermore, since **Taff Vale Railway v Amalgamated Society of Railway Servants** [1901] AC 426, HL it is clear that trade unions can be sued and, as industrial action by definition includes the commission of a number of civil wrongs, strike action would become a very risky business because unions would open themselves up to civil actions every time.[8] As a result, statute law created a set of legal immunities enjoyed by trade unions and their officials where they are engaged in official strike action. One of the immunities still in place covers inducing a breach of contract, which is the claim that Allan could bring against the union. Immunity is achieved where there is a trade dispute as defined in s 218 of the Trade Union and Labour Relations (Consolidation) Act 1992 (TULR(C)A 1992). A dispute about pay clearly falls within this definition. However, the union has not conducted the ballot lawfully, so immunity in law is lost (TULR(C)A 1992, s 226). Allan may therefore succeed in an action in tort against the union for damages for inducing breach of contract. To be successful, Allan would need to show that the union induced the employees to a contract to break it without justification. One of the first cases was **Lumley v Gye** [1853] 2 E&B 216 QBD in which G, a theatre owner, persuaded an opera singer to break her contract with a rival theatre in order to sing for him. The court held that the defendant was liable for inducement of the breach of contract. The

231

elements of the tort are as follows: the conduct must be intentional; there must be clear evidence that there was an inducement – for example, pressure or persuasion; and the defendant must have known of (or could have discovered) the existence of the particular contract which was broken.

There has been some uncertainty shown as to the requirement of intention. In **Falconer v ASLEF and NUR** [1986] IRLR 331, Cty Ct, Falconer was unable to travel by train (despite having bought a ticket) because of an industrial dispute. The union claimed that it had intended to injure British Rail, not Falconer. However, the court said that this was 'naive and divorced from reality' and Falconer was awarded damages. It thus seems likely that a similar argument could be applied in Allan's case, allowing him to succeed in the action.

✓ Make your answer stand out

- Explain statutory immunity in more detail, focusing on the relevant action of inducing breach of contract
- Give more detail on the elements of the tort of inducing a breach of contract and how this is a unified tort as a result of the HL decision in *OBG* v *Allan*.
- Consider the possible factors to assess whether dismissal of the union officials is reasonable.

! Don't be tempted to...

- Set out in more detail the provisions protecting employees in official and protected action; you only need enough for the point you are making to make sense.
- Waste time considering if there is a trade dispute here – it's obvious, so move on quickly.
- Ignore the possible claim Allan has; you need to explain the tort of inducing breach of contract.

? Question 2

Various unions, including all the transport unions, combine to call a one-day strike to protest against the government's refusal to increase state pensions. Sinead, a consultant, is unable to travel to London and loses a day's fee as a result. Oana is a member of the Together Union whose rules state that 'any member not supporting a constitutionally determined decision of the union will be subject to a fine'. Together Union holds a ballot and a very large majority votes in favour of taking industrial action. Oana is concerned about the possible damage to her career if she goes on strike and so decides to work normally. After the strike, she is told by the union's secretary that the union is fining her a week's pay.

Advise Sinead and Oana.

Answer plan

→ State that trade unions have certain immunities if they fulfil the conditions laid down in statute.

→ Evaluate whether there is a trade dispute.

→ Consider whether the action is unprotected and if immunity is lost.

→ Address whether Oana's concerns are unfounded and what protection exists in relation to lawful industrial action.

→ Discuss statutory provisions that address whether or not members can be subjected to discipline for not taking part in strike action.

Diagram plan

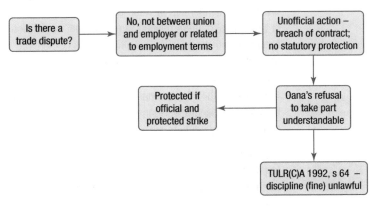

A printable version of this diagram plan is available from www.pearsoned.co.uk/lawexpressqa

Answer

This problem question requires a consideration of the law relating to industrial action and in particular the immunity from legal action afforded to trade unions in certain circumstances, as well as the powers of trade unions to discipline and fine their members.

Following the case of **Taff Vale Railway v Amalgamated Society of Railway Servants** [1901] AC 426, HL there is a clearly established principle that trade unions can be sued for breaching civil law. Claims for inducing breach of contract, for example, are thus possible in common law. However, in certain circumstances trade unions are immune from such action and industrial action effectively becomes lawful. In order to make use of that immunity a number of conditions must be met. First, there must be a genuine trade dispute. Once that is established, further requirements include the need for a lawful ballot, proper notice, no unlawful picketing and no dispute concerning a prohibited reason such as enforcing closed shop agreements.[1]

[1]This paragraph helpfully sets out what the legal issue is and what conditions need to be fulfilled for the legal solution to apply. It's a useful summary which then guides the reader through the answer.

In order to meet the definition of a trade dispute in the legislation, the so-called golden formula is applied. Section 218 of the Trade Union and Labour Relations (Consolidation) Act 1992 (TULR(C)A 1992) defines a trade dispute and includes disputes which are wholly or mainly about the terms and conditions of employment, recruitment, dismissal and suspension of workers, allocation of work, matters of discipline, membership of trade unions, facilities for union officials or procedural matters relating to recognition, negotiation or consultations of/with trade unions. Political protests therefore fall outside the definition of trade disputes. **BBC v Hearn** [1977] *The Times*, 20 May is a clear example, where the refusal of BBC technicians to broadcast the FA cup final to South Africa was a political rather than a trade dispute. Furthermore, the dispute must be between the employees and workers and their own employer.[2]

[2]There is no need here to quote the statutory provision or set out all of it. Just give a clear idea of what is included within the definition and then apply that – see the next paragraph.

Applying this to the scenario given, it seems that the dispute fails to satisfy the definition of trade dispute on two accounts.[3] First, it is not concerned with the matters listed in the relevant section of TULR(C)A 1992 as it relates to the increase of state pensions rather than contractual terms and conditions. The protest thus appears political in nature and is designed to damage the government rather than the employers. Secondly, the dispute is not between the workers and their own employer but between the government and the workers. The union has therefore lost its immunity in this case, allowing Sinead the possibility of suing the union for inducing breach of contract.[4]

[3]That's your conclusion. Don't stop there, though, explain how you got to it.

[4]Finish off with an explanation of what your conclusion with regard to the legal position actually means for the scenario.

To be successful Sinead would need to show that the union induced the employees to a contract to break it without justification. The elements of the tort are as follows: the conduct must be intentional; there must be clear evidence that there was an inducement – for example, pressure or persuasion; and the defendant must have known of (or could have discovered) the existence of the particular contract which was broken.

There has been some uncertainty shown as to the requirement of intention. In **Falconer v ASLEF and NUR** [1986] IRLR 331, Cty Ct, Falconer was unable to travel by train (despite having bought a ticket) because of an industrial dispute. The union claimed that it had intended to injure British Rail, not Falconer. However, the court said that this was 'naive and divorced from reality' and Falconer was awarded damages. It thus seems likely that a similar argument could be applied in Sinead's case, allowing her to succeed in the action.[5]

Oana would have some protection as a result of taking part in official industrial action as long as that industrial action is also protected. She would be able to claim automatic unfair dismissal, for example. However, there is no right not to suffer detriment short of dismissal in relation to strike action and, as we have seen above, the strike does not seem to be protected because it fails to satisfy the definition of a trade dispute; so Oana's fears are not unfounded.[6] It is possible that she could be dismissed as a result of taking part in strike action and she might also suffer other detriment such as a cut in pay or the withdrawing of goodwill from the employer.

The union rule book does state that fines can be imposed where union members do not take part and, for the most part, the law interferes very little in the running of the union and its rule book. However, TULR(C)A 1992, s 64 gives members the right not to have unjustifiable disciplinary action taken against them for certain types of specified conduct. If a member fails to support or participate in industrial action then he may have a remedy, if disciplined as a result (s 64(2)(b)). Discipline which subjects a member to any detriment will be relevant discipline for this purpose; and s 64(1) and (2)(b) of TULR(C)A 1992 clearly state that subjecting members to a fine comes within the scope of the provisions. Section 288 of TULR(C)A 1992 confirms that it is not possible to contract out of the provisions and the rule book is therefore void where it conflicts with the statute.[7] Oana therefore does not need to pay the fine and, if forced to do so, she can make a claim against the union.

Make your answer stand out

■ Include a discussion that details the golden formula in more detail and refers to relevant case law.

■ Explain a little more why there is no trade dispute here – not with employer and not within the scope of the provisions – you can clarify this further.

■ Write to Oana direct. It shows you are confident in giving your advice and it also shows a bit of creativity.

 Don't be tempted to...

■ Go through the other requirements for immunity – once there is no trade dispute, there can be no immunity.

■ Consider the rule book over and above the statute – contracting out is not possible here.

■ Ignore Oana's concerns; you need to deal with every aspect of the scenario, so comment on whether her fears are unfounded or not.

Question 3

In early 2010, the RMT balloted its members in relation to proposed industrial action. Ballots were conducted through five different groups of workers but it was unclear whether or not one key group comprising signalmen had actually voted in favour of the action. Critically analyse the balloting provision RMT must comply with and consider the remedies Network Rail would have had against the RMT if the ballot was indeed invalid and industrial action had commenced.

Answer plan

→ Outline that there is protection for unions in law if certain conditions are fulfilled.

→ Consider whether there is a trade dispute.

→ Was the ballot carried out properly?

→ Discuss the conditions and evaluate whether the signallers were balloted correctly.

→ Discuss the remedies available to the individuals and to the union.

Diagram plan

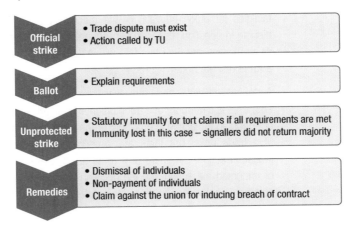

Official strike
- Trade dispute must exist
- Action called by TU

Ballot
- Explain requirements

Unprotected strike
- Statutory immunity for tort claims if all requirements are met
- Immunity lost in this case – signallers did not return majority

Remedies
- Dismissal of individuals
- Non-payment of individuals
- Claim against the union for inducing breach of contract

A printable version of this diagram plan is available from www.pearsoned.co.uk/lawexpressqa

Answer

This essay deals with the trade dispute between RMT and Network Rail concerning the proposed revisions to the existing pension schemes. In the United Kingdom, the trade union as a quasi-corporate body will be protected from tort liability in such a situation, providing it is acting 'in furtherance of a trade dispute' and is complying with statutory balloting provisions before the commencement of such industrial action. This essay will consider the legality of the proposed strike and consider the remedies available to Network Rail if an unlawful strike had in fact gone ahead.[1]

[1]This is a clear statement of what the issues are and shows you understand the area of law and its context.

Certain forms and types of industrial action make the employees who participate in them immune from any action against them by their employer. Section 219 of the Trade Union and Labour Relations (Consolidation) Act 1992 (TULR(C)A 1992) establishes the 'immunities'. It says that the act done 'in contemplation or furtherance of a trade dispute' is not actionable in the courts just because it makes someone breach a contract of employment or it interferes with a contract of employment.

The first test is to establish whether or not there is a 'trade dispute'. This is defined in s 244 of TULR(C)A 1992 as a dispute that relates 'wholly or mainly to' one of the following: terms and conditions; recruitment, suspension or dismissal; work allocation; discipline; facilities for union officials; or the machinery of negotiation. The dispute in question relates to pension provisions by Network Rail for its employees and therefore falls within the scope of the definition of a trade dispute under TULR(C)A 1992.[2]

[2]It is not enough to just set out the law – you need to say what that means in relation to the question set.

A strike is 'official' – and employees therefore protected – where the employee is a member of a trade union and the union has authorised or endorsed the action in question; or the employee is not a member of a trade union but there are, among those taking part in the industrial action, members of a trade union, which has authorised or endorsed the action and the decision was taken by a person or committee authorised to do so by statute.

It would appear that all of these requirements have been fulfilled as RMT is the union empowered to endorse such actions, and therefore the strike is an official strike. Individuals taking part in the action are thus protected by statute. TULR(C)A 1992 protects individuals from dismissal by declaring a dismissal made within the first 12 weeks of official and protected industrial action as automatically unfair. Dismissals made after that time are potentially fair but must be shown to be reasonable.[3] Official but unprotected strike actions are more complex and employees will lose the right to protection where the union has lost its statutory immunity. This point must therefore be considered next.

[3]It may feel like you are going off topic here but you need to set up your argument logically.

In order for the union to retain its immunity it must also have carried out a balloting procedure prior to commencing the industrial action. The ballot does not have to define every single issue of the dispute but there must be a dispute in existence (**London Underground v NUR** [1989] IRLR 341, QBD. Sections 226–235 of TULR(C)A 1992 set out in some detail the conditions a ballot has to comply with.[4] They detail time limits for notice requirements and the return of ballots. They also make provision for the information that must be contained on the ballot form, such as who is authorised to call the industrial action, a warning that taking part in industrial action may be a breach of contract and a notification relating to the right not to be unfairly dismissed. The Act further stipulates that the ballot must be secret and conducted by post (TULR(C)A 1992, ss 227–230) and that it must cover all those reasonably believed to be called upon to take part in the proposed industrial action. In addition, where there

[4]That does not mean you have to, though. It is fine to summarise them.

are more than 50 employees or workers who are likely to be called upon to strike, an independent scrutineer should be appointed in order to oversee the ballot. Importantly, s 228 requires separate ballots for separate workplaces unless only common terms are at issue and, where separate workplaces are balloted, each workplace must return a majority for the industrial action to go ahead. Members of the union should be informed of the result, including the number of votes cast, as soon as possible and industrial action should begin within four weeks of the last day of voting (**RJB Mining v NUM** [1997] IRLR 621, QBD), although this period can be extended (s 234).

[5]By adding a comment on the procedure here, you are avoiding a purely descriptive answer.

The balloting procedure is comprehensive and complex and it is unsurprising that many unions struggle to follow it to the letter.[5] However, TULR(C)A 1992 states that the union can lose its immunity if the balloting procedure is carried out incorrectly. A relatively minor mistake can therefore have serious consequences. This harsh effect was mitigated a little in **RJB Mining v NUM** [1997] IRLR 621, QBD, where the High Court indicated that a union is not expected to achieve 100% perfection but should have in place the structures that enable it properly to ballot all the relevant workers. In addition, accidental failure to comply with the requirement relating to those that are entitled to be included in the ballot which is on a scale unlikely to affect the ballot result, can be disregarded.

[6]This is a slightly odd paragraph because it reads like an answer to a problem question. This is fine because here you have an essay question that is essentially based on a real industrial action, so there will be problem question elements to your answer.

In the case of RMT's ballot, it seems unlikely that a failure to include signalmen correctly would fall within the category that could be disregarded. In addition, statute clearly states that where separate workplaces are balloted a majority is required in each. If no such separate majority was obtained for the signalmen, this will be a procedural irregularity. It may be possible for RMT to argue that there were no separate workplaces and that it reasonably believed this to be the case. If a court could be persuaded that this was a genuinely held and reasonable belief at the time of the ballot, it would remain valid. However, this seems unlikely based on the factual situation in this case.[6]

From the information available it is difficult to say conclusively whether there were procedural irregularities, although we know from reports on this issue that the High Court did in fact grant an injunction preventing strike action and that the RMT did agree to hold a re-ballot. Therefore, it seems likely that, if the industrial action had gone ahead, Network Rail would have had a number of remedies at its disposal.

Injunctions are the most popular legal remedy sought by employers. They may be granted where there is an allegation of unlawful action which will result in harm greater than that suffered by the employee in calling off the action and the damages that could be awarded at a later trial would not be a suitable remedy (**American Cyanamid Co v Ethicon Ltd** [1975] 1 All ER 504, HL). Where an injunction is now sought or granted, however, Network Rail may be able to seek a remedy against either the union or individual employees.

[7] You therefore do not need to go over it again!

The possibility of dismissing employees has been discussed above.[7] In addition, employers can deduct pay as the right to be paid is dependent upon the employee being ready and willing to work. Employees are not, therefore, entitled to be paid for any period during which they are on strike.

Employers who anticipate a dispute may lock out their workers under the Employment Rights Act 1996, s 235(4) (see **Webb and Others v Sandaw Products Ltd and Hall Foundries Ltd** [1979] EAT 477/79).

[8] As this relates to a real and widely reported industrial dispute, if you know what happened, include that.

Network Rail could also consider suing the union in tort for damages for inducing breach of contract. In actual fact, an injunction was obtained, preventing the strike in the first place.[8]

Make your answer stand out

■ Add a little more context about the actual events. This is based on a real dispute – and the more context you can add, the more you show you have really engaged with the issues.

■ You could include a consideration of additional recent cases such as the **British Airways plc v Unite the Union** [2009] EWHC 3541 (QB) litigation and, possibly, **Metrobus Ltd v Unite the Union** [2009] EWCA Civ 829.

■ Explain lockouts in more depth.

! Don't be tempted to...

■ List the balloting procedure and remedies without reference to the context; although this is an essay question, it is set in the context of a real scenario and you need to acknowledge that.

■ Speculate about issues you are not sure on; as this is a real case scenario, if you do not know something, say so and move on rather than guessing or making it up.

Question 4

'The courts have generally assumed that a strike, as a total cessation of work, will always constitute a breach of the contract of employment, regardless of the circumstances which provoked it.' How far is this a reflection of the legal situation today and to what extent does the law protect all the parties involved in an industrial dispute?

Answer plan

→ Identify that common law does not recognise the right to strike.

→ Discuss how statute steps in where there is protected official industrial action, regarding trade dispute, balloting procedure and notification.

→ Examine how protection is afforded and the relationship with unfair dismissal.

Diagram plan

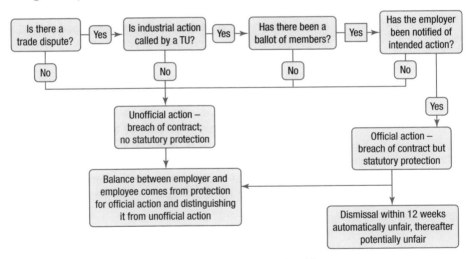

A printable version of this diagram plan is available from www.pearsoned.co.uk/lawexpressqa

Answer

The right to collectively withdraw labour as the ultimate choice available to a trade union in a dispute with an employer has long been recognised in international law. However, the common law does

[1]In an essay such as this one, it is really useful if you can clearly show at the beginning that you understand what the problem is. It shows the examiner that you are confident about the answer and are on the right track.

[2]If you can clearly set out what the law intends to do, then it is much easier to assess whether it meets that aim later, so this statement neatly sets up your later argument.

[3]Stating how the law seeks to balance interests here shows that you have really thought about this and understand how the law is supposed to work.

[4]A practical example such as this one further highlights your understanding because it shows that you appreciate what the legal provisions might mean in practice.

[5]Quickly stating the law like this is absolutely fine even if it contains a potentially problematic concept. You are going on to set out the definition of trade dispute next.

not recognise a right to strike. The implied duty on the employee to be ready and willing to work suggests that taking part in industrial action is in fact a repudiatory breach of contract allowing the employer to dismiss the employee without further notice (**Simmons v Hoover Ltd** [1976] 3 WLR 901, EAT).[1]

In order to redress the balance between employer and employee, and in order to uphold international law concerning the freedom of association and to take industrial action, legislation was required which would provide some protection for employees and trade unions engaged in industrial action. The Trade Union and Labour Relations (Consolidation) Act 1992 seeks to achieve a balance between the interest of the employers not to be held to ransom by workers making (unreasonable) demands and trying to enforce them by walking out on strike and the interest of employees to protest against unfair working practices or unwelcome changes in terms and conditions, for example.[2]

The Act does so by distinguishing between official and unofficial strike action and by providing statutory immunity to trade unions in certain circumstances.[3] Strike action is official where the employee is a member of a trade union and the union has authorised or endorsed the action in question; or the employee is not a member of a trade union but there are, among those taking part in the industrial action, members of a trade union, which has authorised or endorsed the action and the decision was taken by a person or committee authorised to do so by statute. Where unofficial action takes place, TULR(C)A 1992, s 237 stipulates that there is no right to an unfair dismissal claim and employers are free to dismiss employees as they see fit. They could, for example, lawfully dismiss just the ringleaders.[4]

However, where employees are to receive the full protection of the law the industrial action must also be protected. This means that the union must fulfil the conditions to retain its statutory immunity. The industrial action must therefore be in furtherance of a trade dispute.[5] This is defined in s 244 of TULR(C)A 1992 as a dispute that relates 'wholly or mainly to' one of the following: terms and conditions; recruitment, suspension or dismissal; work allocation; discipline; facilities for union officials; or the machinery of negotiation. The union must have gone through a clearly set out balloting procedure as well as having complied with notice requirements. The balloting procedure is complex and causes problems, as can be seen in cases such as the proposed RMT strike action in relation to a dispute with Network Rail, where signallers were not balloted correctly and Network Rail successfully applied for an injunction preventing industrial action. Sections 226–235 of TULR(C)A 1992 set out in some detail the conditions a ballot has to comply with.[6] TULR(C)A 1992 states that the union can lose its immunity if the balloting procedure is carried out incorrectly. A relatively minor mistake can therefore have serious consequences. This harsh effect was mitigated a little in **RJB Mining v NUM** [1997] IRLR 621, QBD, where the High Court indicated that a union is not expected to achieve 100% perfection but should have in place the structures that enable it properly to ballot all the relevant workers.

Where strike action is official and protected in this way, employees taking part will be protected from unfair dismissal as dismissal will be deemed automatically unfair within the first 12 weeks of industrial action.[7] Thereafter, dismissal is potentially fair but must in the circumstances be reasonable. This reasonableness requirement includes the need for the employer to have taken all reasonable steps to bring the dispute to an end.[8]

However, it is worth remembering that there is no right not to suffer detriment in relation to strike action as there is in relation to trade union activities more generally, and employers can therefore impose sanctions on striking employees.[9] In addition, case law confirms that employers are under no duty to pay employees during strike action, and cases such as **British Telecommunications v Ticehurst** [1992] IRLR 219, CA suggest that they can insist on proper performance or withhold pay entirely, where this is made clear to the employee. However, **Ticehurst** did concern industrial action short of a strike and not full strike action, leaving some doubt as to whether not paying a striking employee at all if they are, for example, working four out of five days per week is compatible with the general duty to pay wages.[10]

Overall, it seems that the law has tried to get the balance right but this area of law is incredibly liable to political interference and changes; and the future of the trade unions and the protection they and their members receive can change with every new government.[11] The

[12]Do not try to sit on the fence or justify different arguments. Say what you think. You have built up a sufficiently strong argument throughout to justify this conclusion, so have confidence in it.

[13]If possible, your last sentence should refer directly back to the question using the same language used there. This can also help you check that you have really answered the question and that your argument flows logically.

distinction between official and unofficial action makes some sense, as does the protection afforded to unions through the statutory immunity. The requirements and procedures to ensure that immunity is not lost are still complex and many unions do fall foul of them. While it might be reasonable to conclude that unions should ensure they follow correct processes and where they do not should be subject to sanctions such as losing immunity, it seems particularly harsh that employees also lose protection as a result. Ordinary trade union members should not be penalised for the union getting things wrong where the members believed they were taking part in properly organised industrial action.[12] It is therefore suggested that the unfair dismissal protection should extend to official but unprotected industrial action to achieve a more appropriate balance between the interests of trade unions, employers and employees.[13]

 Make your answer stand out

- Add a comment about detriment short of dismissal.
- Add commentary such as Hendy, 'Article 11 and the Right to Strike' (2000).
- Consider in more detail any changes that would bring about a more appropriate balance: for example, protecting individuals who thought they were taking part in official and protected action even where the action was actually not protected.

! **Don't be tempted to...**

- Go through the requirement for official and protected industrial action in too much detail.
- Sit on the fence; you should tell the examiner whether or not you think the balance is appropriate, and why.

Bibliography

Brodie, D. (2004) 'Reflecting the Dynamics of Employment Relations: Terms Implied from Custom or Practice and the Albion Case', 33 ILJ 159

Brodie, D. (2008) 'Mutual Trust and Confidence: Catalysts, Constraints and Commonality', 37 ILJ 329

Cabrelli, D. (2007) 'Discretion, Power and the Rationalisation of Implied Terms', 36 ILJ 194

Davies, P. and Freedland, M. (1993) *Labour Legislation and Public Policy* (Oxford: OUP)

Deakin, S. and Morris, G. (2009) *Labour Law*, 5th edn (Oxford: Hart Publishing)

Department of Trade and Industry (1998) *Fairness at Work* (Cm 3968)

Dex, S. and Sheibl, F. (1998) 'Should We Have More Family Friendly Policies?' 16(5) *European Management Journal* 586

Dukes, R. (2008) 'The Statutory Recognition Procedure 1999: No Bias in Favour of Recognition', 37 ILJ 236

Fitzpatrick, B. (1997) 'Straining the Definition of Health and Safety' *Industrial Law Journal*, 26, No. 1, pp. 115–135

Gatrell, C. (2007) A fractional Commitment? 'Part time work and the maternal body'. *International Journal of Human Resource Management* 18(3) 462–475

Hall, M. and Edwards, P. (1999) 'Reforming the Statutory Redundancy Procedure', 28 ILJ 299

Hayward, B., Fong, B. and Thornton, A. (2007) *The Third Work-Life Balance Employer Survey: Main Findings* Employment Relations Research Series No. 86, London: BERR available at http://www.berr.gov.uk/files/file42645.pdf

Hendy, J. (2000) 'Article 11 and the Right to Strike' in *Human Rights at Work* (K.D. Ewing, ed.), Institute of Employment Rights, 81 6.

James, G. (2006) 'The Work and Families Act 2006: Legislation to Improve Choice and Flexibility', 35 ILJ 272

Kodz, J. *et al* (2002) *Work–Life Balance: Beyond Rhetoric* (Report 384, Brighton: Institute for Employment Studies)

Lewis, D. (2001) 'Whistleblowing at Work: On what principles should legislation be based?' 30 ILJ 169

Linsday, J. (2001) 'The Implied Term of Trust and Confidence', 30 ILJ 1

McColgan, A. (2000) 'Family friendly frolics? The maternity and parental leave etc. Regulations 1999', Ind Law J 2000 29: 125–144

McMullen, J. (1982) 'A Synthesis of the Mode of Termination of Employment', *Cambridge Law Journal*, pp.110–141

McMullen, J. (1999) 'TUPE – Sidestepping Suzen' 28 ILJ 360

McMullen, J, (2005) 'International Outsourcing and Transnational Transfers of Undertakings – United Kingdom Perspective', *The Company Lawyer*, p. 296

McMullen J, (2006) 'An analysis of the Transfer of Undertakings (Protection of Employment) Regulations 2006', *Industrial Law Journal*, pp.113–139

Morrell, J., Boyland, M., Munns, G. and Astbury, L. (2001) Gender Equality in Pay Practices, Research Discussion Series (Manchester: Equal Opportunities Commission)

Smeaton, D. and Marsh, A. (2006) Maternity and paternity rights and benefits: survey of parents 2005. Employment relations research series. London: Department of Trade and Industry. Available at http://www.berr.gov.uk/files/file27446.pdf

Smith, I. and Thomas, G. (2009) *Smith and Wood's Employment Law* (Oxford: OUP)

Sprack, J. (2006) *Guide to the Age Discrimination Regulations* (West Sussex: Tottel Publishing)

Szyszczak, E. (1985) 'Pay Inequalities and Equal Value Claims', 48 MLR 139

Thane, P. (2010) *Unequal Britain: Equalities in Britain Since 1945* (London: Continuum International Publishing Group Ltd)

TUC (2008) *The return of the long hours culture* (London: TUC)

TUC (2009) *Slaying the Working Time Myths* (London: TUC)

Whitehouse, G., Haynes, M., MacDonald, F. and Arts, D. (2007) *Reassessing the Family Friendly Workplace*. Trends and influences in Britain 1998–2004. Employment relations Research Series no 76. (London: BERR)

Wintermute, R. (1997) 'Recognising New Kinds of Direct Discrimination: Transsexualism, Sex Orientation and Dress Code', 60 MLR 343

Index

advertisements for jobs 86
affirmative action 108
age discrimination 103, 105–8, 105–9, 159
   redundancy 170, 181
agency
   collective agreements 215
agency workers 14, 15, 16, 26, 28, 30
   equal pay 127
alcoholism 99
annual leave 67, 68, 72–3
   pay in lieu of notice and 76
   self-employed 19
associated employers 118
association, discrimination by 64, 102–3
atypical workers 13–17, 28, 30

ballots
   industrial action 231, 234, 236–40, 242–3
   trade union recognition 211, 223
bonus scheme/payments
   collective agreement and individual contracts
      215
   wrongful dismissal 138–9
breach of contract
   dismissal *see* wrongful dismissal
   by employer: constructive dismissal 44, 144,
      151, 195, 204
   employment tribunals 4, 5–6
   garden leave 47
   inducing 231–2, 234–5, 240
   industrial action 230–2, 242

   limitation period 158
   pay in lieu of notice 76
   repudiatory 35, 44, 195, 204, 230, 242
breaks, rest 67, 71, 72, 73
burden of proof
   race discrimination 94

capability and competence issues 149, 162
   transfer of undertakings 199–200
carers *see* family friendly rights; flexible
   working
casual workers 14, 15, 16, 30
Central Arbitration Committee (CAC) 210, 211,
   212, 223–4
closed shop agreements 234
collective agreements
   extent to which binding 213–17
   national and local 216
   transfer of undertakings 196
collective bargaining 221, 224
   trade union recognition 209–13, 222–5
commission 4–5
   receipt of personal 39
compensation *see* damages
competition 35–6, 40, 46
   see also restrictive covenants
confidential information 36, 40, 45–8, 78–82
constructive dismissal 44, 144, 151, 195, 204
consultation
   redundancy 171–2, 179–81, 210, 221
   transfer of undertakings 196, 210, 221

continuity of service 25
  maternity leave 62–3
contract of employment 31–48
  breach of *see* breach of contract
  collective agreements and 214–16
  deductions from pay 76–7
  dismissal for gross misconduct 153, 162
  duties 19, 34–6, 38–40, 43–4, 45, 46, 48,
    66–7, 242
  express terms 33–4, 35, 39, 46–7, 67, 153
  flexible working 54, 58–9
  good faith 37–41
  implied terms *see separate entry*
  maternity leave and pay 68
  staff handbook 135
  variation 34, 41–3, 64, 215
  variation and transfer of undertaking 194–5,
    200, 203–4
contract of service 19
control test
  employment status 28
costs
  employment tribunals 5, 6, 9
courts
  employment tribunals and 4–6, 157–8
custom and practice
  collective agreements and individual contracts
    214
  implied terms 34

damages/compensation
  adjusted for unreasonableness 8
  aggravated damages 99
  breach of statutory rights 73, 107
  discrimination 92, 94, 99, 104
  inducing breach of contract 232, 235, 240
  injury to feelings 81, 94, 99
  mitigation of losses 136, 139–40
  pay in lieu of notice 4, 76
  unfair dismissal 145, 146, 150, 155, 158–9,
    164, 204–5
  whistleblowers 81
  wrongful dismissal 135–6, 138–40, 159

declarations
  discrimination 92, 99, 104
deductions from pay 4, 5, 74–7
dependants
  definition 64
  time off to care for 53, 54, 57–8, 63–4, 68
deposits
  employment tribunals 9
detriment
  strike action 235, 243
  trade union activities 221, 243
  trade union non-membership 219, 221
  whistleblowers 81
direct effect: EU principle 117
disability discrimination 38, 95–9
  by association 64, 103
  redundancy 181
disciplinary action by TUs, unjustifiable 235
disciplinary and dismissal procedure (DDP) 8
disclosure
  whistleblowers 36, 46, 78–82
discrimination 44
  age 103, 105–8, 105–9, 159, 170, 181
  by association 64, 102–3
  combined (previously 'dual') 88
  consolidation of law on 88
  disability 38, 64, 95–9, 103, 181
  gender reassignment 87, 91–2, 103
  positive action 108, 109
  post-employment 86
  pre-employment 86, 100, 103–4
  race 86, 87–9, 92–4
  religious 88
  sex 86–7, 88–9, 103–4, 181, 185
  sexual orientation 89, 101–2
  trade union non-membership 219
dismissal
  industrial action 231, 235, 238, 242, 243,
    244
  unfair *see* unfair dismissal
  wrongful *see* wrongful dismissal
dissociate, right to 219
duty of care 67

economic reality
  employment status 28
employees
  duties 19, 34–6, 39–40, 43, 45, 46, 48, 242
  good faith 37–8, 39–40
  identifying *see* employment status
  reputation 35, 38
  transfer of undertakings *see separate entry*
  unfair dismissal law favouring employers or
    143–7
  working knowledge 46
employers 157
  disciplinary and dismissal procedure (DDP) 8
  duties 19, 34–5, 36, 38–9, 40, 43–4, 46, 66–7
  good faith 37–9, 40–1
  unfair dismissal law favouring employees or
    143–7
employment status 27–30
  atypical workers 13–17, 28, 30
  cattery workers, question on 22–6
  definition of employee 27–8
  nanny, question on 17–22
employment tribunals
  breach of statutory rights 73, 76
  discrimination 87, 92, 98–9
  equal pay 115, 124–5, 128
  jurisdiction 3–6, 157
  legal aid 5, 6
  no hearing 9–10
  procedure 6–10
  time limits 5, 73, 76, 92
  unfair dismissal 157
  wrongful dismissal 157–8
equal pay 111–29
  associated employers 118
  effectiveness of legislation 117–21
  equal value, work of 114, 115, 117, 119,
    124–5, 127, 128
  equivalent, work rated as 114–15, 119, 124
  EU law, importance of 113–17
  experts 115, 120, 124, 128
  genuine material factors 116, 117, 119–20,
    123, 125, 128

job evaluation scheme 114–15, 119, 120,
    124, 125, 128
  like work 114, 119, 123
  night shift premium 123
  part-time workers 116
  pay gap 120
  pensions 116, 127
  qualifications 124
  single source responsible for pay 116,
    118–19, 127
  time limits 116
  token man/woman defence 115, 128
equality *see* discrimination; equal pay
Equality and Human Rights Commission (EHRC)
    87
European Convention on Human Rights
  Art 11: freedom of association 219
European Union
  direct effect 117
  equal pay law in UK and 113–17
  freedom of movement 88
  retirement age 107
  sex and race discrimination law in UK and
    85–9
  supremacy doctrine 87
ex-employees
  sensitive information 45–8
express terms 33–4, 35, 39, 46–7, 67, 153

family friendly rights 51–5
  work–life balance 55–60, 68
fidelity, or loyalty and honesty, duty of 34, 39–40,
    45
  confidential information 45, 46, 48
  dismissal 162
fines
  non-participation in industrial action 235
fixed-term contracts
  redundancy 170, 185
  unfair dismissal 164
flexible working 53–4, 58–9, 69
  carers of adults 63–4
freedom of movement 88

garden leave 45, 47, 48
gender reassignment 39, 87, 91–2, 103
golden formula 234
good faith 37–41
  whistleblowers 80, 81
goodwill 66
gross misconduct 153, 162, 164
  duty to disclose misconduct 39–40

harassment 44, 92, 93, 94, 97, 157
  conduct covered by 102, 103
  sexual 89
health and safety 19, 36, 66–7
  safe system of work 67
holidays
  annual 67, 68, 72–3, 76
  maternity leave and 62
  self-employed 19
hours of work *see* working time
human rights
  trade unions: right to dissociate 219

immunities
  trade unions 231, 233–4, 237–8, 239, 242–3,
    244
implied terms 19, 33–6, 242
  bonus payments 139
  custom and practice 34
  of fact 34, 36
  fidelity 34, 39–40, 45, 46, 48, 162
  good faith 37–41
  mutual trust and confidence 34–5, 36, 38–9,
    40, 43–4, 66–7
indirect discrimination 88, 92
  age 106, 181
  gender reassignment 92
  race 93
  redundancy 170
  sex 86, 89, 103–4, 181, 185
  sexual orientation 101
inducing breach of contract 231–2, 234–5, 240
industrial action 227–44
  ballots 231, 234, 236–40, 242–3

common law 230, 241–2
disciplinary action, unjustifiable 235
dismissal 231, 235, 238, 242, 243, 244
fines for non-participation in 235
golden formula 234
immunities 231, 233–4, 237–8, 239, 242–3,
  244
inducing breach of contract 231–2, 234–5,
  240
lockouts 240
notice 234
official strikes 238, 242, 244
pay for imperfect performance, pro rata
  230–1, 240, 243
political protests 234
prohibited reason 234
trade dispute 234, 237–8, 242
unfair dismissal 231, 235, 238, 242, 243, 244
unlawful picketing 234
information
  ballot forms 238
  confidential 36, 40, 45–8, 78–82
  trade unions 210
  transfer of undertakings 196
injunctions 239, 240, 243
insolvency
  transfer of undertakings 205
integration test
  employment status 28
intellectual property 5, 6

job evaluation scheme 114–15, 119, 120, 124,
  125, 128
judicial discretion 146, 151
jurisdiction
  employment tribunals 3–6

'keeping in touch' (KIT) days 63

last in, first out
  redundancy 170, 175–6, 181, 183, 184, 185
legal aid
  employment tribunals 5, 6

legal representation
    employment tribunals 5, 6, 9
limitation period 158
lockouts 240

maternity rights 52–3, 54–5, 57, 58, 59, 63
    contractual rights other than pay 62–3
    'keeping in touch' (KIT) days 63
    self-employed 19
    unpaid leave 53, 54, 57, 59, 68
media
    public interest disclosure 81
misconduct
    duty to disclose 39–40
    gross 153, 162, 164
mitigation of losses 136, 139–40
multi-factor test
    employment status 14–16, 19–21, 24–5,
      28–30
mutual trust and confidence 34–5, 36, 38–9, 40,
    43–4, 66–7
mutuality of obligation
    employment status 14–16, 20, 24–5, 26, 29,
      30

National Insurance (NI) 19
nationality 88, 89
negligence 67
night shift premium 123
notice
    annual leave 73
    insufficient or lack of 134, 137–8, 164
    pay in lieu of 4, 75–6
    of retirement 107

officious bystander test 34
offshore fisherpersons 162

parental leave 53, 55, 57, 58, 59
    Scandinavian systems 60
Parliament 146, 151
part-time workers
    pensions 116

redundancy 170
paternity leave 53, 54–5, 57, 58, 59
pay
    deductions from 4, 5, 74–7
    definition of wages 76
    equal *see* equal pay
    imperfect performance: pro rata 230–1, 240,
      243
    in lieu of notice 4, 75–6
    maternity 19, 52–3
    night shift premium 123
    pension benefits 116
    sick pay 19
    union officials: time off with 221, 224
pensions
    equal pay 116, 127
    part-time workers 116
personal injury claims 5, 6
political objects
    trade unions: use of funds for 219–20, 221
political protests
    definition of trade disputes 234
positive action 108, 109
pre-hearing reviews
    employment tribunals 8–9
precedent 146, 151
pregnancy
    discrimination 89
    maternity rights *see separate entry*
    redundancy 181
public duties
    time off 68
public interest disclosure
    whistleblowers 36, 46, 78–82
public policy 46–7, 48

race discrimination 86, 87–9, 92–4
    ethnic group 93, 94
re-engagement
    redundancy 171
    unfair dismissal 150, 155, 159, 164, 204
recommendations
    discrimination 92, 94, 99, 104

redundancy 108, 167–86
 absence and lateness 184
 alternative employment 171, 176
 basic award 176–7
 bumping 171, 184
 compensatory award 176, 177
 consultation 171–2, 179–81, 210, 221
 customary arrangements 184
 definition 170, 174–5
 diminution in needs and dismissal 175
 discrimination 170, 181, 185
 inability to adapt 176
 last in, first out 170, 175–6, 181, 183, 184, 185
 notification to DWP 172, 179
 obligations of employers 169–73
 reasonableness 171, 176, 181, 184–5
 selection procedure 170–1, 172, 175–6, 180–1, 182–6
 self-employed 19
 staff handbook: enhanced 135
 time limits 5, 171, 172, 179
 transfer of undertakings 196
 unfair dismissal 183, 184, 185
reinstatement
 unfair dismissal 145–6, 150, 155, 159, 164, 204
religion
 discrimination 88
remedies 82
 damages/compensation see separate entry
 declarations 92, 99, 104
 injunctions 239, 240, 243
 re-engagement 150, 155, 159, 164, 171, 204
 recommendations 92, 94, 99, 104
 reinstatement 145–6, 150, 155, 159, 164, 204
repudiation of contract 35, 44, 195, 204, 230, 242
rest breaks 67, 71, 72, 73
restrictive covenants 45, 46–7, 48
retail workers 77
retirement age 106–8, 109

secret profits 39
self-employment
 advantages and disadvantages 19
 identifying 13–30
sex discrimination 86–7, 88–9
 by association 103
 indirect 86, 89, 103–4, 181, 185
sexual harassment 89
sexual orientation
 discrimination 89, 101–2
sick pay 19
small businesses 69
 collective bargaining 212
smoking 99
statutory regulation of hours see working time
strikes see industrial action

tax 19
temporary workers 28, 30
till shortages
 deduction from pay for 76–7
time limits
 age discrimination 106–7
 collective bargaining 212
 discrimination claims 92, 98, 104
 employment tribunals 5, 73, 76, 92
 equal pay claims 116
 flexible working 54, 63, 64
 industrial action 238, 239, 243
 maternity rights 52–3, 57
 parental leave 53, 57
 paternity leave 53, 57
 redundancy claims 5
 redundancy process 171, 172, 179
 retirement, notice of 107
 unfair dismissal 162
 unfair dismissal claims 5, 25, 26, 148, 151, 153, 157, 158, 162
 wrongful dismissal 158
tort 19, 91, 94, 157, 237
 inducing breach of contract 231–2, 234–5, 240

trade unions 207–25
  ballots 211, 223
  bargaining unit 211, 223
  Certification Officer 210, 220, 223
  dissociate, right to 219
  independent 210–11, 220–1, 223
  industrial action *see separate entry*
  political objects, use of funds for 219–20, 221
  recognition 209–13, 222–5
  redundancies 171–2, 179–81, 210, 221
  right to dissociate 219
  time off 68, 210, 221, 224
  transfer of undertakings 196, 210, 221
  unfair dismissal 162, 164, 219, 231
training
  time off 68, 224
transfer of undertakings 187–205
  aim of law 189–90
  capability and competence issues 199–200
  collective agreements 196
  constructive dismissal 195, 204
  consultation 196, 210, 221
  contracting out of TUPE 196
  economic entity 190–2, 194, 198–9
  employee information to transferee 196
  ETO reason 195–6, 199, 200, 203–4
  extent of protection for employees on 193–7
  insolvency 205
  service provision change 190–2, 194, 202–5
  Süzen case 189–93
  trade union recognition 196, 210
  unfair dismissal 195–6, 199–200, 204–5
  variation of contract 194–5, 200, 203–4
  waivers not permitted 194
transsexuals 39, 87, 91–2, 103

unfair dismissal 6, 19, 108, 141–65
  age 159
  automatic *see* unfair dismissal, automatic
  basic award 150, 155, 164, 204
  compensatory award 150, 155, 164, 205
  conduct 153, 162, 164

constructive 44, 144, 151, 195, 204
differences between wrongful and 156–60
direct or actual 148–9, 153, 162
disciplinary and dismissal procedure (DDP) 8
eligibility to claim 148, 152–3, 161–2
favouring employer or employee 143–7
fixed-term contracts, non-renewal of 164
gross misconduct 153, 162, 164
incapability 149, 162
industrial action 231, 235, 238, 242, 243, 244
maternity rights 62
principal or motivating cause for dismissal
  151
procedural fairness 145, 146, 149–50, 154,
  155, 158–9, 163–4
reasonableness 144, 149–50, 153–4, 163–4,
  231, 238, 243
redundancy 183, 184, 185
remedies 145–6, 150, 155, 158–9, 164,
  204–5
retrospective justification 159
time limits 5, 25, 26, 148, 151, 153, 157, 158,
  162
trade union membership or non-membership
  162, 163, 164, 219
trade union officials and industrial action 231
transfer of undertakings 195–6, 199–200,
  204–5
unfair dismissal, automatic
  continuous employment 148, 153, 157, 162
  industrial action 235, 238, 243
  maternity: return to work 62
  trade union membership 162, 163, 164
  trade union non-membership 219
  transfer of undertakings 195–6, 199–200, 204
  whistleblowers 81
unions *see* trade unions

variation of contract 34, 41–3
  flexible working 64
  shop steward acting as agent 215
  transfer of undertakings 194–5, 200, 203–4

vicarious liability 19, 92, 94, 99
victimisation 92, 93, 97
  whistleblowers 81

wages *see* pay
waivers 194
whistleblowers 36, 46, 78–82
work–life balance 55–60, 65–9
workers
  whistleblowers 81
  Working Time Regs applicable to 71
working time 67–74
  maximum hours per week 67, 71, 72

wrongful dismissal 131–40
  breach of contract 134, 137–8, 157
  contractual procedure for dismissal 135
  damages 135–6, 138–40, 159
  differences between unfair and 156–60
  gross misconduct 134–5, 138
  justification for breach 134–5, 138, 159
  notice, lack of or insufficient 134, 137–8
  retrospective justification 159
  time limits 158

young workers
  maximum hours per week 72